Law, Governance and Technology Series

Volume 44

Series Editors

Pompeu Casanovas, UAB, Institute of Law and Technology, Barcelona, Spain

Giovanni Sartor, University of Bologna and European University Institute of Florence, Florence, Italy

The *Law-Governance and Technology Series* is intended to attract manuscripts arising from an interdisciplinary approach in law, artificial intelligence and information technologies. The idea is to bridge the gap between research in IT law and IT-applications for lawyers developing a unifying techno-legal perspective. The series will welcome proposals that have a fairly specific focus on problems or projects that will lead to innovative research charting the course for new interdisciplinary developments in law, legal theory, and law and society research as well as in computer technologies, artificial intelligence and cognitive sciences. In broad strokes, manuscripts for this series may be mainly located in the fields of the Internet law (data protection, intellectual property, Internet rights, etc.), Computational models of the legal contents and legal reasoning, Legal Information Retrieval, Electronic Data Discovery, Collaborative Tools (e.g. Online Dispute Resolution platforms), Metadata and XML Technologies (for Semantic Web Services), Technologies in Courtrooms and Judicial Offices (E-Court), Technologies for Governments and Administrations (E-Government), Legal Multimedia, and Legal Electronic Institutions (Multi-Agent Systems and Artificial Societies).

More information about this series at http://www.springer.com/series/8808

Stanley Shanapinda

Advance Metadata Fair

The Retention and Disclosure of 4G, 5G
and Social Media Location Information,
for Law Enforcement and National Security,
and the Impact on Privacy in Australia

 Springer

Stanley Shanapinda
Optus La Trobe Cyber Security Research Hub
La Trobe University
Melbourne, Australia

ISSN 2352-1902   ISSN 2352-1910   (electronic)
Law, Governance and Technology Series
ISBN 978-3-030-50254-6   ISBN 978-3-030-50255-3   (eBook)
https://doi.org/10.1007/978-3-030-50255-3

This Springer imprint is published by the registered company Springer Nature Switzerland AG.
The registered company address is: Gewerbestrasse 11, 6330 Cham, Switzerland

This book is dedicated to the patience, love, trust, hope and courage of the Shanapinda family. To my mum, Meriam, you always wanted to be a medical doctor—but you put your family first instead. I dedicate this once in a lifetime achievement to the sacrifices you made so I can have the bright future that life unfairly denied you—this is your dream realised, albeit through me. I am only the vessel, a symbol of what our family can start to achieve. Mum, your love and prayers have worked.

Preface

Laws are social constructs. They give public authorities the power to act. Laws also prescribe limits to these powers. Another aim of the law is to ensure that power is exercised in an accountable manner. Accountability is of particular interest if the given institution is a law enforcement authority, or one tasked with safeguarding the national interest. The powers may be granted on the justification that targets of investigations use sophisticated technological means, such as encryption to evade the long arm of the law. For this reason, it is appropriate that these authorities are granted powers that can outperform techniques that are meant to evade the law. The law allows the authorities access to these technological means to enforce the laws and prevent criminal activity. This activity was originally called terrorism. It was however expanded to online hate, fake news, civil disobedience or protests against inaction on climate change and preventing animal cruelty.

Before these issues received popular attention, the retention and disclosure of telecommunications data or metadata have been met with worldwide criticism and invalidated by courts in the EU and the USA, requiring revisions. The broad range of the investigatory powers are not regarded as being consistent with the protection of privacy under human rights charters and the constitution. Australia is a country that does not protect privacy under a bill of rights in its constitution, unlike its Western peers. This book is an Australian case study about the retention and disclosure of location information for law enforcement and national security purposes, within the context of non-serious offenses such as climate change protests by digital natives and protecting journalists and whistle-blowers. It critically analyses the powers granted to the Australian Security Intelligence Organisation (ASIO) and the Australian Federal Police (AFP), the Agencies, to access and use location information that has been stored by the Australian telecommunications companies (the Telco), Internet service providers (ISPs) and multinational social media platform (SMP) companies such as Google and Facebook, with subscribers in Australia.

Melbourne, VIC, Australia   Stanley Shanapinda

Acknowledgements

Thanks to Prof. Jill Slay AM, Prof. Alana Maurushat and Prof. Clinton Fernandes for your patience, guidance and advice on this project, without which this project would not have seen the light of day! Thanks to Prof. Slay that took a chance on me, and by doing that made my childhood dream come true. It was a definite *black swan* lifetime opportunity, for which I was willing to make huge sacrifices. I am so happy I did—I have learnt and grown, as a scholar, but more so as a person. Thank you, David Vaille, for your valuable comments and edits to the original research material.

A special and hearty thank you to my mum Meriam, the Shanapinda family, Cecilia and the girls, Ricardo, Toni, Emma, Tracy, Alynsia, Louisa, Simon, Robert, Nick, Daniel and all my other dear friends, housemates and family in Katutura (Windhoek and in the whole of Namibia), Lagos, Sydney, Melbourne, York (UK), New York and *São Gonçalo* (Rio de Janeiro) who supported me on this journey! You all played an integral part in more ways than you would ever know. It takes a village to raise an aspiring scholar, and you are that global village.

I would like to thank the University of New South Wales' (UNSW) School of Engineering and IT (SEIT); the UNSW's Australian Centre for Cyber Security (ACCS); UNSW Law and the Data to Decisions Cooperative Research Centre (D2D CRC), for their financial and logistical support throughout the research period of this project.

Contents

Chapter 1
Generating 4G, 5G and Social Media Location Information

1.1 Introduction: The Balance of Power Is Off-kilter

The Snowden's revelation of America's mass surveillance programs of its own citizens, was a poignant time in history where the powers of law enforcement and national security Agencies, aided and enhanced by the most modern communications technologies, sparked curiosity about how these two aspects interacted and what impact it had on the individual. This curiosity gave raise to this book project. I find the inquiry into the dynamic relationship between how modern communications technologies are designed, structured, operated and used by the general populace and the statutory powers and their oversight limits instructive. This is because it reveals an imbalance between these powers and the privacy question. The risks become too high if the powers of the authorities and the functioning of modern communications technologies are not properly aligned. The technologies in question include the Internet-based 4G and 5G mobile communications, using satellite-based location estimates, that are shared with social media messaging applications, that are collected and processed by artificial intelligence algorithms, to reveal sensitive information about an individual, that is not necessarily suspected on reasonable grounds of a crime, and with no judicial involvement. The scales may be tipped in favour of one or the other, and this may have an impact on how the powers are exercised. The powers of the Agencies and the way the technology operates appear to be aligned for a major purpose—to reveal the best estimated location of the individual using a mobile device and is of interest to the Agencies. The dependence of the user on mobile communications technologies that are powered by big data algorithmic artificial intelligence, and its design and operational features is of great benefit to the investigations of the Agencies. And so, these powers are themselves designed and implemented to capture that which the technology reveals about the user, with great impact, because the intelligence gathered is about personal habits and traits. Managing this impact requires a fine balance of conflicting interests. The aim is to ensure laws with the least impact are in place that can ensure the accountable

© Springer Nature Switzerland AG 2020
S. Shanapinda, *Advance Metadata Fair*, Law, Governance and Technology Series
44, https://doi.org/10.1007/978-3-030-50255-3_1

exercise of power. The Agencies possess broad investigatory powers. The nature of investigations is that they reveal and encroach upon personal information. The Australian Parliament introduced measures to better protect privacy in 2015. The question is how effective these safeguards are. The nature of the Agencies investigations is that they are confidential. Apart from reports that are made public, it is difficult to measure the effectiveness of the privacy safeguards. Given this challenge, it is of great public interest that continued assessments are made, as reasonably and practically as possible, to try and understand the work of the Agencies in relation to privacy, with a view to finding out whether the safeguards in place require continuous improvement. This book is important in offering the public an analysis of the available information to assess whether they can trust that the location information retention and disclosure framework operates in a manner that is acceptable. This book tries to dissect the complex components of the framework in a manner that is digestible and can potentially be used to re-consider public policy options. The options include legal measures to limit the discretionary powers of the Agencies, as well as the discretions of the telecommunications companies. All this necessitated this project about how the various pieces of the metadata retention and disclosure framework are put together, interact and how it impacts on individual privacy, location privacy and information privacy. In the end the book argues that access to location information should be implemented in manner that is fairly balanced in relation to privacy interests—with an iterative judicial location information warrant (Shanapinda, S.: Advance metadata fair: The retention and disclosure of location information as metadata for law enforcement and national security, and the impact on privacy—An Australian story. Dissertation, UNSW Sydney (2018).

Before coming to the aforementioned conclusion, this chapter therefore describes how this location information of the user's mobile device is created by the 4G and 5G telecommunications network and shared with the social media application. This chapter starts off by describing how location information is generated by the Inter-based telecommunications network. Social media apps such as WhatsApp and Facebook messenger use the location information generated by satellite systems and the telecommunications network. Internet and satellite-based location information technologies are explained in detail against the backdrop of the legal and political frameworks for data retention, disclosure and use, showing that location information continues to be classified as metadata and therefore continues to be granted less privacy protection than the contents of a communication. Location information is however becoming more precise and revealing of personal and sensitive information. The location estimates are more precise, generating estimates in metres, and nearing centimetres in the near future with 5G. When the metadata retention laws were originally requested, the justification was that the Agencies would only get access to gross data—and that was imprecise. Given 4G and 5G mobile communications technologies, integrated with GPS functionality, original motivations and justifications no longer hold water. Given how valuable location information is, revealing the time and place with greater precision, as technology evolves, Chap. 2 describes in detail, the legal obligations of the Australian mobile telecommunications companies and the multi-national social media platforms, to store location information. The disclosures of the retained location information are then handed over to law enforcement and national security Agencies in accordance with the processes described in Chap. 3. One such process is that the companies may disclose location information voluntarily to the Agencies, but when doing so, the companies are not required to ensure that the disclosure is reasonable, necessary, justifiable or proportional. This situation does not protect privacy to the fullest possible extent but allows for differential treatment. If the Agencies request the information then the Agencies must apply these standards of proportionality, but the companies may simply disclose the location information, without applying any such standard and the Agencies are not required to apply such standards to information disclosed voluntarily. The obligations of these companies to retain and hand over location information and the powers of the Agencies to collect the location information are two sides of the same coin. As such, Chap. 4 describes the powers of the Agencies to collect and to use the location information as part of their investigations. This is done without informing the individual about the collection, and as such preventing the individual from exercising their right to complain about any potential misuse of the data. This right is simply rendered theoretical. The result is that the individual may not even know that their data was misused, and this may create a lack of accountability. Such secrecy may not be warranted in a democratic society, that is built on openness and accountability. A key part of the exercise of these powers is that the Agencies my issue their own requests for location information, as opposed to requesting prior-approval from a judge in a court of law, as is done for the contents of communication. This is allowed despite how sensitive location information is and despite how precise location estimates have become. But this state of affairs is allowed because it helps the Agencies to fill out warrant applications, without which they may face significant challenges when having to apply for a warrant under oath. To track any person in real-time using a GPS based tracker, a court warrant would be required, but to track a person in near real-time with a mobile device that is GPS-enabled, no judicial warrant is required. When seen in this light, the latter powers of the Agencies clearly do not pass the reasonableness test. This state of affairs is allowed because location information is legally described as 'subscriber data' and when classified as such, location information is granted less privacy protection than the contents of a communication. So, even though the contents of a communication may be less sensitive than the habits of a person visiting venues that may be frowned upon, such sensitive information is treated less favourably.

There are however other limits placed on the powers of the Agencies, these are critically described in Chap. 5. The Agencies are only restricted to use their powers to perform their functions, but this however goes without saying, and so does not really amount to an effective limit, especially given how broad the investigative powers of the Agencies are. The Agencies may collect and use location information to develop big data and artificial intelligence algorithmic technologies, even if the person is not suspected of having committed an offense. This applies equally to instances whether the person poses a national security threat or not. These powers can be used for minor offenses, too, such as trespassing when protesting climate change or the cruel treatment of animals. The data may be analysed for predictive policing, and this falls well within the legal rights of the Agencies. As a result, the Agencies pass their oversight inspections with flying colours. Even when the Agencies breached limits, such as not obtaining a warrant to access the metadata of a journalists, thereby negatively impacting media freedom and public interest whistleblowing, the responsible officers are not held responsible and such breaches are excused as human errors. In other instances, the legal wording is so broad that it can be interpreted in ways that grant the Agencies greater power, defeating the intentions of protecting media freedoms.

Even if location information is de-anonymised, the information reveals sensitive information about a person, who is not suspected of a crime, and just by aggregating the location information data points. This is illustrated in Chap. 6. Given the sensitive nature of location information, Chap. 7 argues that the oversight exercised over the powers of the Agencies, after they have already collected and used the location information, is misplaced. Access to location information should be restricted when it matters the most—at the time of collection and safeguards should be built into such collection in advance, such as obtaining a judicial warrant, based on a detailed affidavit sworn to under oath. Currently that is not the case.

Chapter 8 proposes the judicial location information warrant, as way to better protect privacy. Unlike countries such as the United States where the privacy is protected under the constitution, in Australia, where there is no such constitutional protection, the powers of the Agencies are not able to be tested, leaving individuals with lower privacy protections than what citizens in the US would be afforded when their location information is accessed and used. This is so despite Australia's ratification of international human rights treaties. Chapter 9 concludes, emphasising that the power balance be restored between the citizens and its government.

However, first things first, let's start at the beginning—the creation of location information and the creation of the legal duties to retain said location information.

1.2   Faster and Integrated 4G and 5G Mobile Communications

The Australian mobile telecommunications company (Telco) provides voice calls, Short Message Service (SMS) and web browsing communications services using the modern telecommunications network—the Internet Protocol (IP)-mediated 4th Generation (4G) long-term evolution (LTE) telecommunications network combined with the 5th Generation (5G) International Mobile Telecommunications (IMT)-2020 telecommunications network. These networks route most of their communications and related information via the global Internet, using packets. They are therefore be said to be IP-mediated.

Since its introduction in 2012, 4G cellular mobile communications delivered high broadband Internet-enabled mobile communications (ITU 2019). 4G enabled the use of over-the-top social media applications such as WhatsApp, Signal, Instagram and Telegram on the mobile device. The latest generation of mobile communications already introduced after only 7 years is 5G, with a mass roll out expected, as new business cases emerge. 5G promises near real-time connectivity—broadband speeds that are ten times faster and with download speeds in seconds, as opposed to in minutes with 4G (Shanapinda 2019). 5G is expected to be the revolutionary standard that will not only enhance 4G but that will replace it in the future and remain with us for longer than any previous generation of mobile communications, given its promises for an internet connection to all types of devices, from vehicles to medical sensing devices referred to as the Internet of Things (IoT). To achieve these speeds, existing 4G networks are being integrated with 5G networks. Telstra started rolling out Australia's first 5G mobile cellular communications in May 2019 (Ericsson 2019).

1.3   The Popularity of Mobile Devices and Mobile Communications

4G enabled mobile phones remain the most popular form of communication used to access social media applications for chats and voice calls in Australia. It is a major data point. With the roll out of 5G, 5G enabled mobile phones, possessing the broadband speeds referred to above, are likely to dominate the market in coming years. Generally speaking, the use of mobile phones increased from 93% in May 2014 to 96% in May 2018. An ever-increasing number of Australians rely solely on their mobile phone for voice communications. Eighty-three per cent of Australians only used their smartphones to go online. Seventy-nine per cent (approximately 15.2 million) accessed the internet via a mobile phone. Previously only 75% (approximately 14.4 million) accessed the internet via a mobile phone, in the six months to June 2017 (ACMA 2018).

It is estimated that approximately 19.2 million Australians use Google Search, 17.3 million access Facebook, 17.6 million watch YouTube and 11.2 million access Instagram every month (ACCC 2019, p. 6).

Given this, widespread use, it is no surprise that the majority (76%) of Australians are equally concerned about the retention and collection of every person's metadata by the Telco and Internet Service Provider (ISP) (Digital Rights Watch 2019).

1.4   4G and 5G Location Information

4G and 5G networks will be integrated and interconnected, to work as one system. Location information is shared between the two networks. Mobile phones will be able to change from one standard to the next, depending on the coverage available in a given geographic area.

Location information that is generated, collected and stored may include the following:

a. the identity of the mobile device that is connected to the network represented by relevant numbers;
b. the identity of the entity, thing or device that interacts with the network with the purpose of obtaining the location information, such as the identity of the cell tower or the base station transceiver (BTS). This entity may reside in or be installed on the mobile device itself;
c. the current, deferred and last known estimated location;
d. the speed at which the device is moving;
e. change of area, motion or periodic location;
f. an indication of when the device enters, leaves or is within a geographic area, which area is covered by the radius of the BTS or cell tower;
g. the time intervals between the various reports. For example, the time it takes for the device to move between areas, from one to the next;
h. the start time, stop time of the location requests, or the time stamp of the location estimate;
i. the accuracy of the location information;
j. the dialling international country codes for geographic areas;
k. the local geographic coordinates;
l. aggregate the power consumption or battery life of the mobile device;
m. geopolitical name of the area (e.g. Sydney, Surrey Hills); and
n. The International Mobile Subscriber Identity (IMSI), International Mobile Equipment Identity (IMEI) and the Subscriber Permanent Identifier (SUPI) of the mobile device, and similar Universal Integrated Circuit Cards (UICC) mobile device identifiers, for both 4G and 5G, that may be in use.

(3GPP 2019: [5.5] Pg. 27–30; Michalevsky et al. 2015; Shanapinda 2016; Shanapinda, S.: Advance metadata fair: The retention and disclosure of location information as metadata for law enforcement and national security, and the impact on privacy – An Australian story. Dissertation, UNSW Sydney (2018).

The location information listed above is information about the following types of services:

o. The location information used to deliver a Short Message Services (SMS) or a voice communication to the mobile device;
p. The location information not used to deliver the SMS or voice communication to the mobile device;

q. The location information generated prior to, during and after a voice or SMS communication has been delivered to the mobile device;

r. The location information generated when the individual is not using the mobile device, also referred to as pings or background updates and regular connections that mobile devices make to cell towers;

s. The location information stored by the Telco, ISP or Social Media Platform (SMP) for any period, for commercial purposes and for purposes to maintain the 4G and 5G networks, provided they have the location information in their possession and can access same.

(Shanapinda 2016; Shanapinda, S.: Advance metadata fair: The retention and disclosure of location information as metadata for law enforcement and national security, and the impact on privacy – An Australian story. Dissertation, UNSW Sydney (2018); *TIA Act 1979* s 187AA (1) item 6; Revised Explanatory Memorandum 2015: 44 [246.]; GSA 2019: 5; *TA 1997* ss 275A, 276, 280, 313(3), 313(4), 313 (7); *TIA Act 1979* ss 175–184).

1.5   Inferring the Location from the Mobile Phone's Battery

Social media applications using mobile platforms like Android are able to read and aggregate the power consumption of the mobile phone. The battery acts as a sensor that leaks location data. By using machine learning algorithms, the application estimates the devices location. This can be done without accessing the Global Positioning System (GPS) or other coarse location indicators. The known route and the new route can be identified and tracked in real-time (Michalevsky et al. 2015). It is for this purpose that the aggregate power consumption of the mobile device is useful.

1.6   Busting the Myth of Coarse Versus Precise Location Information

The Agencies refer to the location information that is not used to deliver a communication as 'non-communication network connections'. The Agencies also do not appear to recognise that the Global Positioning System (GPS) is used by the IP-mediated 4G and 5G network. They claim that the Telco is not required to retain GPS location information:

> The bill will not require providers to retain all location information – for example, *GPS information* **and** *the non-communication network connections that mobiles make to cell towers* are not required to be retained (emphasis added) (ASIO 2015, p. 9).

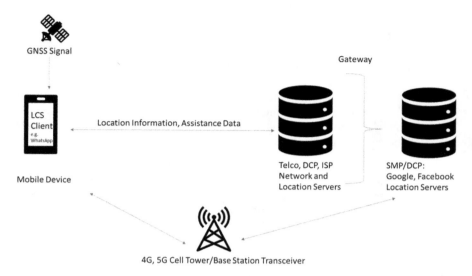

Fig. 1.1 How the mobile device is connected to the global navigational system (reproduced from ETSI 2017c: 14 [4.1.1-1]; Shanapinda 2016)

ASIO seems to assume the Telco does not use the Global Positioning System (GPS). The IP-mediated 4G and 5G network uses Global Navigation Satellite System (GNSS), which includes GPS based positioning methods to locate the position of the mobile device. This is illustrated in Fig. 1.1.

The GPS is used to locate the mobile device, whether the device is used for sending an SMS or not—whether the device is active or passive. The Telco is simply required to disclose the location information as generated by the network (AGD 2015b: 15 [1.11]). However, the precision may be between hundreds of meters and a few meters, given the area. The integration of satellite-based technology into 4G and 5G networks, and social media applications such as Google Maps, gives greater precision such as 3–5 m, and thereby potentially revealing more personal information, with greater accuracy and more reliability than before. 5G uses technology that focusses in on the mobile device so that it has direct line of sight. This gives it greater precision in single digits in meters, and potentially down to centimetres. Given the use of satellite location tracking in 4G and 5G networks, neither the Telco nor the Agencies are therefore required to triangulate the precise location, as may have been the case before (Shanapinda 2016; ETSI 2017a: 12 [4.1], 40 [8.1.2.1]).

The Telco does not have to process nor structure the location information it submits to the Agencies: 'Providers will not be required to conduct additional processing or triangulation to more precisely determine a device's location, beyond what their network does for the purposes of providing the service' (AGD 2015a). Although not a Federal law enforcement agency, the New South Wales (NSW) State Police received location information that was not precise:

With cell site location that we would normally get with metadata, we would talk about an area, for example if I am in Canberra I might be in Deakin or I might be somewhere—it does not specify. There is not the amount of specificity to say that I am in a particular place. We are talking about more gross data (Evidence to PJCIS (Lanyon) 2015, 48 cited in PJCIS and Security 95 [3.86]).

The cell tower locations that will be required to be retained by the data retention bill will only ever provide Agencies with the vicinity of the mobile phone (Evidence to PJCIS (Hartland) 2014: 5). The location estimate might itself be gross or coarse in that it is not precise, but an educated guess. However, the IP-mediated 4G and 5G networks supports more precise and enhanced location estimates than previous technologies. The location of the UE is estimated by using the known geographical coordinates of the base station that the mobile phone is connected to (ETSI 2017b: 20 [6.2.1], 49 [8.3.1]). This means location information is evolving and becoming more precise in locating the individual, especially given the use of small cells. The location estimates are not as raw and unprocessed as claimed by law enforcement agencies when the metadata retention scheme was introduced.

Given that the 4G and 5G radio networks are new radio access technologies, and is not reliant on older technologies, this enables the mobile device to be located with greater accuracy. The radio technology is planned to be technology neutral and robust for the future in providing more precise geographic locations:

... the E-UTRAN [Evolved-UMTS Terrestrial Radio Access Network] positioning capabilities are intended to be forward compatible to other access types and other position methods, in an effort to reduce the amount of additional positioning support needed in the future (ETSI 2017b:12 [4.1]).

This is the same for 5G, that will have a new radio network. The Agencies are granted access to coarse location information, but the coarse location information from a modern IP-mediated network generates and reveals more precise locations than earlier networks (Nohrborg 2017). The coarse location information are the radio measurements or positioning measurements. The radio measurements or positioning measurements are the location estimates of the mobile device as generated by the IP-mediated 4G and 5G networks, without the Telco analysing the location estimate to for example narrow down the location estimate from 100 m from the cell tower to 50 m, by triangulation. The Telco is not required to analyse the location estimate to narrow the location of the mobile device from 100 m to 50 m, for example. The Telco is simply required to disclose the 100 m location estimate to the Agencies.

The femtocell used in the IP-mediated 4G and 5G networks is also more revealing of the location of the device and of the individual compared to a traditional cell tower. The Privacy Commissioner indicated that the range of the location information may be down to several meters, making the location estimate more precise if the signal strength of various cell towers is used:

However, it is not clear whether service providers may or will be required to retain information about signal strength or whether devices are within range of multiple cell towers; this information could be used to determine location to within several metres using signal triangulation techniques (OAIC 2015: 42 Appendix B [7]).

The Telco is just required to disclose the location information of the cell that handled the voice or SMS communication. If the voice or SMS communication is made via a femtocell, the location estimate of the base station selected by the network to handle the communication, can be just as precise, as if signal strengths from various towers were used. If the femtocell's signal is the strongest, the cell phone will connect to the femtocell. The Telco is practically made to retain location information that was selected by the femtocells deployed inside and outside homes, to boost the cell phone coverage (Battersby 2012; Germano 2010; *TIA Act 1979* s 187AA).

1.6.1 Location Precision Powered by Small Cells

Similar to 4G, 5G also uses small cells. These cells are generally located within distances of 100–500 m (GSMA 2018, p. 34). This creates a dense network of cells, as indicated in Figs. 1.2 and 1.3. The difference with 5G is that 5G also uses higher frequencies in the 24 GHz to 300 GHz range whereas 4G uses frequencies below 6 GHz. The radio waves therefore travel shorter distances. This requires the base stations to be nearer to each other and at the same time, it requires more base stations. This creates a dense network of small cells, as illustrated by the letter B in Fig. 1.3 (Loughran 2019).

This increase in the number of cells to track the location of the mobile device leads to greater location precision—the network uses the GPS and other global satellite tracking technologies, referred to as Global Navigation Satellite System (GNSS). The location of the mobile phone and indirectly the location of the user

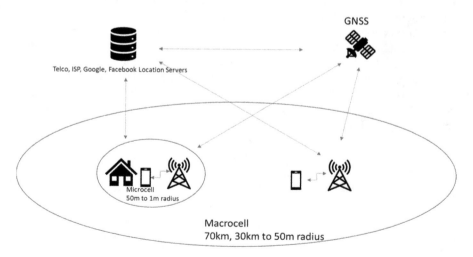

Fig. 1.2 Small cells used in the 4G and 5G Internet-based mobile network (reproduced from Nohrborg 2017)

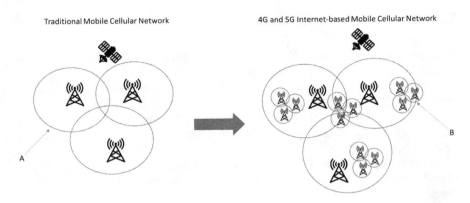

Traditional Mobile Cellular Network   4G and 5G Internet-based Mobile Cellular Network

Fig. 1.3 4G and 5G Network Densification (reproduced from Morley 2018)

within a 100 m sized cell is more precise than a 30 km macrocell tower that is generally used by 4G, as illustrated by the letter A in Fig. 1.3.

4G mobile cellular services use femtocells or small cells to connect the mobile phone for Voice, SMS, email, chat, forum, social media communications. The small cell is contained inside the bigger macrocell of the tower. Small cells are located inside homes and near buildings, similar to Wi-Fi hotspots. This is illustrated in Figs. 1.2 and 1.3.

The aim of the small cell is to boost the signal of the bigger macrocell.

Location precision is enabled using smart antenna's that focusses in on the device to deliver the radio signal, creating a line of sight position. The 5G network becomes more device-centric as a result. With 5G, estimating the location becomes even more precise—this is one of the improvements ushered in by 5G. Location precision may be reduced to 1 m or in centimetres. This is a significant improvement to what current 4G location estimates provide. Current GNSS capability only has an accuracy of 5 m. Wireless Local Area Networks (WLAN) have an accuracy of 3–4 m. The improvement to 1 m or centimetre precision only makes 5G very attractive for use in tracking vehicular traffic. Vehicular applications are being researched and may be adapted for use in mobile cell phone applications as well, as Location Services (LCS) clients. Social media applications like Google Maps, WhatsApp and Facebook use location estimates provided by the 4G and 5G networks to provide locations to their users. These social media applications are therefore referred to as LCS clients. The location estimate is requested by the SMPs social media application such as Facebook and delivered to it by the Telco's network via a gateway, as illustrated in Fig. 1.1. The SMPs collect and use the users location information (Shanapinda 2016; Koivisto et al. 2017; NGMN 2015; 5G PPP undated; 3GPP 2017; Shanapinda 2019; La Trobe University 2019; Shanapinda, S.: Advance metadata fair: The retention and disclosure of location information as metadata for law enforcement and national security, and the impact on privacy – An Australian story. Dissertation, UNSW Sydney (2018).

1.7 Conclusion

Mobile phones embedded with social media applications, that constantly track the location of the device, and indirectly the movements of the individual have become normal. The trend is to predict the exact location, to ensure that communications services are delivered with greater efficiency. At the same time location information is legally designated as subscriber data, which is the class of data that is easily accessed by the Agencies. This classification disregards the technological fact that modern communications technologies, such as 4G and 5G leak more precise location information about the user. By using satellite technology and creating a line of sight with the mobile device, the estimated location is also becoming more precise in metres.

References

3GPP (2017) 5G; Study on Scenarios and Requirements for Next Generation Access Technologies (3GPP TR 38.913 version 14.2.0 Release 14) 2017-05

3GPP (2019) TS 23.273 V1.0.0 (2019-05). Release 16. 3rd Generation Partnership Project; Technical Specification Group Services and System Aspects; 5G System Location Services (LCS). [5.5] Pg. 27–30

5G PPP (undated) 5G Vision. https://5g-ppp.eu/wp-content/uploads/2015/02/5G-Vision-Brochure-v1.pdf. Accessed 27 Aug 2019

ACMA (2018) Communications report 2017–18

AGD (2015a) Submission No 27 to the Parliamentary Joint Committee on Intelligence and Security, Inquiry into the Telecommunications (Interception and Access) Amendment (Data Retention) Bill 2014, 16 January 2015

AGD (2015b) Data Retention Frequently Asked Questions for Industry. (July 2015)

Australia Security Intelligence Organisation (ASIO) Submission No 12.1 to the Parliamentary Joint Committee on Intelligence and Security, Parliament of Australia, Inquiry into the Telecommunications (Interception and Access) Amendment (Data Retention) Bill 2014, January 2015

Battersby L (2012, July 6) Telstra offers signal boost – at a price. The Sydney Morning Herald. http://www.smh.com.au/business/telstra-offers-signal-boost%2D%2Dat-a-price-20120706-21l5f.html. Accessed 29 Aug 2019

Commonwealth of Australia (ACCC) (2019) Digital Platforms Inquiry. June 2019. https://www.accc.gov.au/system/files/Digital%20platforms%20inquiry%20-%20final%20report.pdf. Accessed 27 Aug 2019

Commonwealth, Parliamentary Debates, Senate, 25 March 2016, 2294, (George Brandis MP)

Department of Parliamentary Services (Cth), Bills Digest, No 10 of 2007-08, 3 August 2007

Digital Rights Watch (2019) Australians are increasingly concerned about expansion of surveillance powers. https://digitalrightswatch.org.au/2019/07/25/australians-are-increasingly-concerned-about-expansion-of-surveillance-powers/. Accessed 27 Aug 2019

Ericsson (2019) Australia's first 5G service goes live. 22 May 2019. https://www.ericsson.com/en/news/2019/6/5g-live-in-australia-with-telstra. Accessed 27 Aug 2019

European Telecommunications Standards Institute (ETSI) (2017a) LTE; Evolved Universal Terrestrial Radio Access Network (E-UTRAN); Stage 2 functional specification of User Equipment (UE) positioning in E-UTRAN, (3GPP TS 36.305 version 14.2.0 Release 14)

European Telecommunications Standards Institute (ETSI) (2017b) Universal Mobile Telecommunications System (UMTS); LTE; Evolved Packet System (EPS); Mobility Management Entity

(MME) and Serving GPRS Support Node (SGSN) related interfaces based on Diameter protocol'

European Telecommunications Standards Institute (ETSI) (2017c) LTE; Evolved Universal Terrestrial Radio Access (E-UTRA); LTE Positioning Protocol (LPP)

Evidence to Legal and Constitutional Affairs References Committee (LCARC), Parliament of Australia, Canberra, 2 February 2015, 49, 1.97 (Roger Clarke, Immediate Past Chair, Australian Privacy Foundation, 2015)

Evidence to Parliamentary Joint Committee on Intelligence and Security, Parliament of Australia, Canberra, 30 January 2015, 48 (Assistant Commissioner Malcolm Lanyon, Commander, Special Services Group, New South Wales Police Force), cited in Parliamentary Joint Committee on Intelligence and Security, Parliament of Australia, Advisory Report on the Telecommunications (Interception and Access) Amendment (Data Retention) Bill 2014, (27 February 2015)

Explanatory Memorandum, Telecommunications (Interception and Access) Amendment (Data Retention) Bill 2015 (Cth)

Germano A (2010) The Impact of Femtocells on Next Generation LTE Mobile Networks. ftp://www.3gpp.org/Information/presentations/presentations_2010/2010_05_Moscow/Femto_Forum_Germano.pdf. Accessed 27 Aug 2019

Global Mobile Suppliers Association (GSA) (2019) 5G Security Primer: A GSA White Paper. https://www.communicationstoday.co.in/wp-content/uploads/2019/03/190228-GSA-5G-Security-Primer-A-GSA-White-Paper.pdf. Accessed 27 Aug 2019

GSM Association (GSMA) (2018). Road to 5G: Introduction and Migration. https://www.gsma.com/futurenetworks/wp-content/uploads/2018/04/Road-to-5G-Introduction-and-Migration_FINAL.pdf. Accessed 27 Aug 2019

International Organization for Standardization and the International Electrotechnical Commission (ISO/IEC) (2005) Information technology. Metadata registries (MDR). Part 1 Framework

International Telecommunication Union (ITU) (2019) International Telecommunication Union – Radiocommunication Sector ITU-R FAQ On International Mobile Telecommunications (IMT). https://www.itu.int/en/ITU-R/Documents/ITU-R-FAQ-IMT.pdf. Accessed 27 Aug 2019

Koivisto A, Hakkarainen M, Costa M, Kela P, Leppanen K, Valkama M (2017) High-efficiency device positioning and location-aware communications in dense 5G networks. IEEE Commun Mag 55(8):188–195. https://doi.org/10.1109/MCOM.2017.1600655

La Trobe University (2019) Submission 10 to the PJCIS, Review of the mandatory data retention regime, July 2019

LCARC, Parliament of Australia, Comprehensive revision of the Telecommunications (Interception and Access) Act 1979, (2015)

Legal and Constitutional Affairs References Committee (LCARC) (2015) Parliament of Australia, Comprehensive revision of the Telecommunications (Interception and Access) Act 1979, 2015:77 [71.182]

Loughran S (2019, August 2) There's no evidence 5G is going to harm our health, so let's stop worrying about it. The Conversation. https://theconversation.com/theres-no-evidence-5g-is-going-to-harm-our-health-so-lets-stop-worrying-about-it-120501. Accessed 27 Aug 2019

Michalevsky Y, Schulman A, Veerapandian GA, Nakibly DBG (2015) PowerSpy: Location Tracking using Mobile Device Power Analysis. 4th USENIX Security Symposium [USENIX Security '15]. https://crypto.stanford.edu/powerspy/files/powerspy.pdf. Accessed 27 Aug 2019

Morley D (2018) 5G Small Cells and Cable Realizing the Opportunity. https://www.nctatechnicalpapers.com/Paper/2018/2018-5g-small-cells-and-cable-realizing-the-opportunity/download. Accessed 27 Aug 2019

Next Generation Mobile Networks Ltd (NGMN) (2015) 5G white paper. https://www.ngmn.org/uploads/media/NGMN5GWhitePaperV10.pdf. Accessed 27 Aug 2019

Nohrborg M (2017) LTE 3GPP. http://www.3gpp.org/technologies/keywords-acronyms/98-lte. Accessed 27 Aug 2019

Office of Australian Information Commissioner (OAIC) (2015) Submission No 92 to the Parliamentary Joint Committee on Intelligence and Security, to Inquiry into the Telecommunications (Interception and Access) Amendment (Data Retention) Bill 2014, January 2015

Parliamentary Joint Committee on Intelligence and Security (PJCIS) (2015) Parliament of Australia, Advisory Report on the Telecommunications (Interception and Access) Amendment (Data Retention) Bill 2014, (27 February 2015)

Revised Explanatory Memorandum, Telecommunications (Interception and Access) Amendment (Data Retention) Bill 2015 (Cth), 2015

Shanapinda S (2016) The types of telecommunications device identification and location approximation metadata: under Australia's warrantless mandatory metadata retention and disclosure laws. Commun Law Bull 35(3):17–19. http://www.camla.org.au/communications-law-bulletin/. Accessed 23 July 2017

Shanapinda S (2019, 23 May) Blocking Huawei from Australia means slower and delayed 5G – and for what? The Conversation. https://theconversation.com/blocking-huawei-from-australia-means-slower-and-delayed-5g-and-for-what-117507. Accessed 27 Aug 2019

Telecommunications (Interception and Access) Act 1979 (Cth) (TIA Act 1979)

Telecommunications Act 1997 (Cth) (TA 1997)

Chapter 2
The Legal Scheme for Mobile Telecommunications Companies and Social Media Platforms to Retain Location Information

2.1 Legally Defining Location Information

Location information includes radio measurements, positioning measurements, assistance data, and location estimates. Location information is legally classified as information that relates to the affairs of a customer. This categorisation is in line with how the 4G and 5G networks operate (ETSI 2017a: 28 [7.1.2.3]; *TA 1997* ss 275A, 276; ETSI 2017b: 79 [7.3.1]). Legally, location information is considered as information about a customer, and as 'telecommunications data' (*TIA Act 1979* s 276, Chapter 4). This is evident from the legal phrase: '. . . the affairs or personal particulars (including any unlisted telephone number or any address) of another person . . .' (*TIA Act 1979* s 276). This legal phrase refers to:

(a) 'information of a kind specified in or under section 187AA; or . . . documents containing information of that kind; relating to any communication carried by means of the service' (*TIA Act 1979* Chapter 5, Part 5-1A s 187A (1)), to
(b) 'the kinds of information that a service provider must keep, or cause to be kept, under subsection 187A(1)' (*TIA Act 1979* s 187AA) and
(c) to '. . . any information or document that . . . relates to . . . the contents or substance of a communication' (*TIA Act 1979* s 276).

Prospective location information is referred to as 'near real-time location and other subscriber information . . . .' (IGIS 2015: 24). Other terms used to refer to the metadata include: 'telecommunications data', 'communications data', 'non content data', 'subscriber data', 'retained data' and 'traffic'. These terms are used to interchangeably refer to the various types of metadata (Explanatory Memorandum 2015: 20 [20], 7, 192 [32]; *TIA Act 1979* Chapter 4; AGD 2015a Submission No 27, 11 [1.1.]—[1.2.], 59 [2.1.]; LCARC 2015: 26-27 [1.10]; *TIA Act 1979* 5(1) (definition of 'retained data').

© Springer Nature Switzerland AG 2020
S. Shanapinda, *Advance Metadata Fair*, Law, Governance and Technology Series 44, https://doi.org/10.1007/978-3-030-50255-3_2

2.2   Location Information As Metadata

Metadata means different things in different contexts. Metadata is a loosely described term and is not defined but is usually used to refer to data that provides information about other data. Metadata includes the longitude and latitude positions of the mobile phone, and the cell tower information. Data is defined as a 'reinterpretable representation of information in a formalised manner suitable for communication, interpretation or processing' (ISO/IEC 2005: 2 [3.2.6]). Metadata is itself data, so it can be in a format that humans can read and understand. The location information the Telco is required to keep was referred to as metadata. Metadata was also defined as communications data. Telecommunications data is also defined as communications data. In turn communications data is defined as information that is about a communication event, and not the content or substance of the communication. For mobile phones, it also includes the location of the communication event. Metadata is also defined as the data that defines and describes other data. With the introduction of the of the *Assistance and Access Act 2018* the type of metadata the Telco and the Social Media Platform companies (SMP) are required to disclose to the Agencies is referred to as 'technical information' (Commonwealth 2016; LCARC 2015: 77 [71.182]; Evidence (Clarke) 2015: 49, 1.97; *Privacy Commissioner court case* 2 [5]; ISO/IEC 2005: 2 [3.2.6], 4 [3.2.16], 10, 18 [42]; Telstra court case 3 [2]; Explanatory Memorandum 2015: 38 [213], xxxvi; *TIA Act 1979* Chapter 4; ETSI 2017a: 28 [7.1.2.3]; *AAA 2018* s 317E).

As can be seen, names matter and it matters what phrasing a legal term is given, either to avoid controversy or much like a re-branding exercise. At the end of the day, at the minimum, 'technical information' is materially metadata, is location information, is information related to the contents or substance of a social media application chat. The key difference is that 'technical information' is so broad that it covers the types of metadata the Telco is required to retain, plus all the metadata the Telco would retain voluntarily for its commercial and network maintenance and cybersecurity purposes.

2.3   The General Legal Requirement to Retain Location Information

The very legal description of location information as metadata, as subscriber data, authorises the retention of location information under the scheme. The Telco is required to create and retain the types of information specified in or under section 187AA; or the documents containing information of that kind. The information must relate to any communication carried by means of the telecommunication service. The kinds of information referred to are the '. . . information or document that . . . relates to . . . the contents or substance of a communication'. The 'information or document' is not the contents of a communication, but the non-contents of a communication.

The contents of a communication requires a preservation notice, followed by a judicial warrant, to retain (Explanatory Memorandum 2015: 3 [7]; *TA 1997* ss 276; *TIA Act 1979* ss 107J(2), 174(1), 175(1), 176(1), 177(2), 178(1), 179(1), 180 (1), Chapter 5, Part 5-1A s 187A (1)).

The metadata retention policy framework was originally introduced as a policy in May 2012, when 4G was new to the market. It was retracted but then re-introduced on the 30th of October 2014, 5 years before 5G was commercially introduced (PJCIS 2013; *TIA Act 1979* Chapter 5, Part 5-1A ss 187A (1), 187AA).

As a general rule, the Telco is required to retain location information in respect of every type of communication. Long-term Evolution (LTE) is identified as a service whose location information must be retained. LTE refers to the 4G standard. The voice and SMS services provided via the IP-mediated 4G and 5G networks include Voice over Long-Term Evolution (VoLTE). LTE is listed as a relevant service to which the retention obligations apply (*TIA Act 1979* s 187AA (1) items 5–6). The same legal requirement does apply to the 5G standard.

The retained location information is referred to as 'retained data'. Retained data means information, or documents, that a service provider is or has been required to keep under Part 5-1A (*TIA Act 1979* s. 5(1) (definition of 'communication'). Retained data must be distinguished from location information the Telco retains voluntarily. Different rules apply to each category and this has different impacts on privacy.[1]

2.3.1   The 2-Year Minimum Retention Period

The Telco is required to store location information for a minimum period of 2 years (*TIA Act 1979* s 187C). The 2-year retention period could lead to the collection of 100 locations in a single day, amounting to a large volume over 2 years (OAIC 2015).

Location information may even be retained for a longer period, at the discretion of the Telco (*TIA Act 1979* s 187C). Telstra, was interested in retaining telecommunications data for longer than 2 years:

> Finally, we also operate under a requirement in the *Privacy Act* to destroy or de-identify data once no longer required for purposes for which they were collected. This could be interpreted as meaning we are legally required to immediately destroy or make amendments to the data retained under the Act as soon as the two-year retention period has ended, thereby creating a further rolling obligation and additional cost on industry unrelated to commercial purposes that we have not yet factored into our assessment of the Act. To help limit this impact, we believe that if there were to be different data retention periods across technologies as part of this scheme, we would recommend that telecommunication service providers be given the option of retaining data for the longest permitted period without breaching the law (Telstra Submission No 112 2015: 5[8]).

---

[1]See Sect. 2.4 of this Chapter.

During this period, the location information remains available to the Agencies. Effectively, without a specific legal obligation to destroy location information after the 2 years, the continued storage of the location information by the Telco can extend the retention period indefinitely. The acceptance of this proposal appeared to be a cost saving measure, in the interest of the Telco and not in the interest of the privacy of the individual customer. The Telco is only required to retain location information generated at the start and at the end of a communication.

The privacy interests of the customer are subjected to the commercial interests, the need for maintenance of the telecommunications network by the Telco, and the law enforcement and security interests, in an unbalanced manner. Despite the evidence that most location information is collected within 6 months after its generation, the commercial and financial interests of the Telco may have led to the mandated 2-year retention period and the option to retain the location information indefinitely thereafter.

2.3.2 The Exclusions Not to Retain Certain Categories of Location Information

Not all categories of location information are required to be retained. The law excludes location information to be retained under two instances. These are the two exclusions to the obligation to retain location information:

(a) The Telco is only required to retain location information that is used to provide the communications service to the mobile device; and
(b) The Telco is only required to retain the location information at the start and at the end of a communication (*TIA Act 1979* ss 187A (1), 187A(4)(e),187AA (1) item 6).

These exceptions may be referred to as 'the Exclusions'.

2.3.2.1 The Obligation NOT to Retain Location Information That Is NOT Used to Provide the Communication Service

A mobile device constantly communicates with the cell tower and the small cells in the 4G and 5G networks. The location of the device needs to be constantly tracked to be able to deliver the communications to the phone and for the Telco to bill the customer for the services. Even when the metadata is not used for billing the location information is still tracked and stored in the network of the Telco (Shanapinda, S.: Advance metadata fair: The retention and disclosure of location information as metadata for law enforcement and national security, and the impact on privacy—An Australian story. Dissertation, UNSW Sydney (2018)). The Telco is only required to retain location information 'used in connection with a communication' (*TIA Act 1979* ss 187A (1), 187AA (1) item 6). The location information that is not required to be retained includes:

> ... information about the location of a telecommunications device that is not information used by the service provider in relation to the relevant service to which the device is connected. This could include, for example, a record of which cell tower, base station or other network access point a device was connected to (*TIA Act 1979* s 187A (4)(e); Explanatory Memorandum 2015, 44 [246]).

The Telco is not required to retain every location information record that has been generated. The AG's Department (AGD) informed the Telco not to retain location information about a poll or background update. In the event the communications service does not use a type of location information to operate, the Telco is not required to create and retain that type of location information (Explanatory Memorandum 2015: 15-16 [1.15.]). The Telco is not required to retain location information when the device is not communicating voice, SMS, email, chat, forum, social media communication and when software applications are updating in the background. (*TIA Act 1979* s 187AA (1) item 5; Explanatory Memorandum 2015: 12, 14–15 [1.11]). ASIO informed the Parliamentary Joint Committee on Intelligence and Security (PJCIS) that the regular connections mobile phones make to cell towers are not related to calls, are not related to communications and are therefore not required to be retained:

> The bill will not require providers to retain all the location information—*the regular connections mobiles make to cell towers*, for example. What the bill does require is for providers to retain the location information when communications occur. For example, what cell tower did the mobile connect to when they made a call? This does not amount to tracking as some people have suggested. If ASIO has a requir[e]ment to monitor individuals, other capabilities can be deployed—for example, tracking devices under warrant (emphasis added) (Evidence to PJCIS 2014: 5 (Hartland).

The Telco is only required to retain the exact records generated by the communication service the Telco provides. Telstra indicated it disclosed location information used for billing to the Agencies, but only the location information of the cell tower the mobile device communicated with at the time the communication started:

> (d) The mobile cell location provided "... only concerns the location of the mobile cell with which a mobile device communicates when a call is first connected and/or an SMS message is sent or received (in relation to the A Party and/or the B Party, but only where the party is a Telstra customer), and the location of the mobile cells to which a mobile device periodically connects for billing purposes during a data session (emphasis in original)." (*Telstra court case* [61(2)(d)]).

The Telco is not required to:

(a) generate and keep location records that are more detailed than or different to the location records used in relation to the relevant service, or
(b) keep location records on a continuous basis (PJCIS 2015: 81 [3.33]).

If a person does not make a call and location information is nevertheless generated, the Telco is not required to retain the location information generated. The Telco is only required to retain those types of location information that has been generated by 4G and 5G networks, based on the functionality of the IP-mediated 4G and 5G network.

The Telco is not required to create other types of location information to retain. For example, if the precision range of the mobile device is calculated by the network to be 10 m, the Telco is not required to manually calculate the positioning to, say 5 m justifying triangulation. The precision record of 10 m that has been obtained based on the configuration of the IP-mediated 4G and 5G network is good enough to be retained, as is.

The Telco is also not required to retain the Cell-ID of a neighbouring cell that was not used to deliver the voice or SMS communication to the mobile device (*TIA Act 1979* s 187A(4)(e)). Cell-ID is defined as the: 'identity of the cell from which a mobile telephony call originated or in which it terminated' (ETSI 2017b: 5 [3.1]). A method referred to as the Enhanced Cell-ID positioning method (E-Cell-ID) gives greater location accuracy. The E-Cell-ID uses the location information about the neighbouring cell, to calculate the location estimate of the mobile phone. E-Cell-ID is not restricted to only use the cell-ID that the mobile phone is connected to that actually delivered the voice or SMS communication—the location estimates from the neighbouring cell and the serving cell are both used to help calculate a more precise final location of the mobile device (ETSI 2017c: 44 [8.1.3.2.2]). As such, stating that the Telco is not required to retain the location information of the neighbouring cell is not a useful restriction to limit the privacy exposure of the individual user—it amounts to a distraction.

2.3.2.2   Retain the Location Information at the Start and at the End of a Communication

The Telco is required to retain the location identifier of the cell tower that provided the voice, SMS or email communication to the mobile phone, and only at the start and at the end of the voice, SMS or email communication. This cell-ID is referred to as the serving cell-ID. The serving cell-ID is the cell that the mobile phone is connected to and is used to deliver the communication and not the neighbouring cell, that does not perform this function. With this restriction of limiting the location information to be retained to the serving cell-ID, the data retention and disclosure scheme is aimed at protecting the privacy and personal information of the individual. The legal limit is that location information that relates to a voice, SMS, email, chat, forum, social media communication, should only be collected at the start and at the end of the voice, SMS, email, chat, forum, social media communication (Explanatory Memorandum 2015: 14–15 [1.11]). There is therefore a restriction to the volume of location information and other metadata that may be collected, stored and therefore handed however to the law enforcement and national security Agencies. The law states:

[Section] 187AA Information to be kept
(1) The following table sets out the kinds of information that a service provider must
    keep, or cause to be kept, under subsection 187A(1):

4	The date, time and duration of a communication, or of its connection to a relevant service	The date and time (including the time zone) of the following relating to the communication (with sufficient accuracy to identify the communication): (a) the **start** of the communication; (b) the **end** of the communication; (c) the **connection** to the relevant service; (d) the **disconnection** from the relevant service
5	The type of a communication or of a relevant service used in connection with a communication	The following: (a) the type of communication; Examples: **Voice, SMS, email, chat, forum, social media**
6	The location of equipment, or a line, used in connection with a communication	The following in relation to the equipment or line used to send or receive the communication: (a) the **location of the equipment** or line at the start of the communication; (b) the **location of the equipment** or line at the end of the communication. Examples: **Cell towers**, Wi-Fi hotspots

(emphasis added) *(Data Retention Act 2015)*

The Telco is not required to retain location information prior to, during and after the communication (PJCIS 2015: 81, fn 31). The Telco is not required to retain the location information at the times and at the places the individual is not using the communications service:

Obligations do not extend to metadata that is not customer information and is not related to a particular communication or session. For example, a mobile network operator is not required to keep the location of a handset when the customer is not using the handset (Revised Explanatory Memorandum 2015: 8).

The limits to only retain location information at the start and at the end of the communication and the restriction not to retain the location information that did not play a role in delivering the voice, internet browsing or SMS communication, may be referred to as the Exclusions. The Exclusions aim to exclude the retention of location information generated at any other time than at the start and end of the social media communication or voice call. The effect of this Exclusion is that the location information is not stored while the individual is communicating. This Exclusion serves to prevent the real-time storage of the location of the user. So, no historic location record while the communication was ongoing would exist. If the individual started the communication at point A and ended the communication at point D, there would be no record of location B, or any other location. The Cell-IDs of the towers at points A, B, C and D may hand over the connection to each other, but not recording the data at points B and C significantly reduces the location information that is stored and collected. The question is how effective the Exclusions are in protecting privacy, given that the Telco is not prohibited from retaining data about locations B and C, and may do so voluntarily for commercial or maintenance purposes, and the record may be available to the Agencies to collect as long as the Telco possesses the record.[2]

2.4   Voluntary Retention and Use of Location Information

The restriction not to retain location information prior to, during or after a communication does not prohibit the Telco from retaining location information prior to, during and after the communication. Given there is no clear prohibition, the Telco may retain location information at any time and may retain it indefinitely. The Telco may voluntarily retain for any period, for commercial or for network maintenance and cyber security purposes, the location information generated prior to, during and after the communication concluded, and the Cell-ID of the neighbouring cell. This latter location information may then remain available in the network elements of the Telco. Despite the Exclusions, the Telco has the discretion to retain location information that did not provide the SMS or voice call. In fact, the Telco is advised to voluntarily retain location information during a communication, to see how the mobile device has moved while using the voice call or the SMS service:

> NOTE 4:
>
> It is advised to retain samples of cell-ids at regular time intervals during cellular telephony communication. The sampling interval is to be set to a value that is large enough to avoid massive storage of location data, but short enough to allow tracing of how the handset has moved during a communication session. A suitable value might for instance be GSM/GPRS idle mode location HLR/VLR update timers (ETSI 2017b: 9–10 [4.6]).

The European Telecommunications Standards Institute Technical Specification (ETSI 2008 TS) 102 656 outlines the 'Requirements of Law Enforcement Agencies for handling Retained Data and Lawful Interception'. The international lawful interception standards are relevant and applicable to Australia. According to the AGD, the data set listed in section 187AA (1) items 1–6 of the *TIA Act 1979* is said to be:

---

[2]See Sect. 3.2.1 in Chap. 3 and Sect. 6.3.4 in Chap. 6.

[B]roadly consistent with the categories of data set out in Article 5 of the former Directive 2006/24/EC; and ETSI Standards TS 102 656 (V1.2.1) Retained Data: Requirements of Law Enforcement Agencies for handling Retained Data, and TS 102 657 (V1.15.1) Retained Data Handling: Handover interface for the request and delivery of retained data (emphasis added) (AGD 2014: 4).

The ETSI TS 102 657 was made in 2014. The quote above reflects that this standard was eventually directly linked by the AGD to the *Data Retention Act* and therefore the metadata retention scheme. The Exclusions safeguard is therefore ineffective. The Telco may need to store more information for maintenance and other commercial purposes.

2.4.1   The Use of Location Information by the Telco

The Telco may use both the information it is legally required to retain and the location information it voluntarily chose to retain for its commercial and maintenance purposes, but subject to the Australian Privacy Principles (APPs). Telecommunications data can be used to improve the network and to increase revenue (He et al. 2016). The interest to use the 'retained data' was demonstrated by the Telco asking the AGD whether the retained data may be used for other business purposes, in addition to maintenance purposes, such as network trouble shooting. The AGD advised the Telco to the consult the APPs (AGD 2015b: 16–17 [2.3]). APP 6 outlines in general terms whether covered organisations (including the Telco) may use or disclose personal information if this is intended to be done for a 'secondary purpose' rather than the 'primary purpose' for which it was collected, taking into account an extensive series of factors (AGD 2015b: 16–17 [2.3]).

In its privacy policy, Vodafone indicated how it collects personal information. Vodafone collects location information from the mobile device of the individual. The Telco can collect and use location information if the location information is reasonably necessary for their functions and activities. The Telco may collect the location information if the person is notified and is informed of the purpose of the collection. The individual is generally informed that the location information is collected and used for commercial interests, and that the location information is disclosed to the Agencies. Under their privacy policies the individual is taken to have consented to the retention of the location information that the Telco retains voluntarily to use for its network maintenance, commercial interests and disclosure to the Agencies.

The policy states:

How do we collect personal information?
We collect your personal information if you do any of the below:
. . .
Visit external websites and perform online searches using your device.
. . .
Use your device.

> Use your device and this results in contact between your device and our network. This contact might tell us about you, your device, your use of our services and your location (Vodafone 2019).

The location information is used for the following commercial and maintenance purposes:

> . . .
> Carrying out market analysis and research.
> Development of our products and services.
> Understanding how customers use our network, products and services anonymously and personally.
> Analysing the things that interest you as well as where you use your device. We use those details to provide you with services, products and information suited to your needs, interests and location.
> Contacting you about our products and services and those offered under other brands that our group owns. This may include marketing these products to you.
> Identifying your location so we can send you emergency alerts.
> Protecting our network and managing the data use, volume of calls, TXTs and other uses of our network. . .
> Conducting internal investigations in relation to crime and fraud prevention, detection, recovery or prosecution (Vodafone 2019).

Vodafone uses the SAS® Customer Intelligence and SAS® Master Data Management modules, to predict customer behaviour, using that information to make investment decisions (Sarkar 2015). The SAS® Customer Intelligence 360 allows the Telco to upload the customer and location data. Location data includes geofence (Dmitry 2013: 30; SAS Institute Inc., 2015). Geofence data can be described as:

> Cell-Loc [3] provides location-based notification services known as GeoFence™ and GeoLasso™. GeoFence™ is a virtual geographic boundary such as one surrounding a factory. GeoFence events are generated whenever one of a specified list of devices is detected entering and/or exiting the area. GeoLasso™ is a one-time specification of an emergency notification area. Once an area has been defined, a list of cell phone users who are active in the area, or have recently been active, will be generated (Munson and Gupta 2002: 41 [2]).

The Vodafone privacy policy indicates location information is collected when the individual 'Uses' the mobile device and when there is an exchange of signal messages between the mobile device and the IP-mediated network. It is important that Vodafone does not rule out collecting location information when the device is not used, to access Vodafone's services but is instead in passive mode. It is not clear whether Vodafone would retain the location information generated prior to, during, and after a communication, even if the location information is generated by another cell tower than the cell tower with the best signal strength.

2.4.2   The Use of Location Information by the Social Media Platforms

The SMP is not legally obliged to retain technical information, which technical information may include location information—the SMP is required to hand over the information it has available but must not deal with the available information in any way that prevents it from complying with a request to disclose the technical information (*AAA 2018* Division 5). SMPs such as Google and Facebook opt to collect, store and use location information for their maintenance and commercial purposes. For example, SMPs collect and share the IP addresses, location information, international mobile subscriber identity (IMSI), and International Mobile Equipment Identity (IMEI) (Shanapinda 2016, 2019a, b).

2.5   Surveillance Policies

Privacy policies are not altruistically aimed at protecting the privacy of the individual user. These policies are aimed at entrenching and protecting the existing business goals of the SMP. The user does not give consent, in the true legal and practical sense of the word, to the collection and use of metadata that reveals personal and sensitive information about them. This works to the benefit of SMP by safeguarding existing business practices that best suit the SMP. Zuboff refers to the privacy policies as surveillance policies, playing its role in surveillance capitalism (Shanapinda 2019a, b; Zuboff 2019). These policies work for the benefit of both the Agencies, the Telco and the SMPs—they do not work for the individual users' privacy.[3]

2.6   Unfair Limits to Civil and Property Rights

To the AGD, the notion that the Telco is not required to retain location information when the individual is not making a call, reduces the level of detail because the Telco is not required to retain the regular continuous records about the location information:

> [T]he nature and volume of location information that service providers will be required to keep has been strictly limited to ensure that service providers are not required to keep continuous records about the location of a device, or anything approaching that level of detail (AGD Submission No 27, cited in PJCIS, 2015: 93 [3.79]).

---

[3]See Chap. 3, where the Telco and SMP is required to disclose any of the information it has available, whether retained voluntarily or mandatorily.

The detail of location information to be retained is therefore dependent on how actively the person uses the mobile device to make calls or send an SMS. This policy position sends the message that if a person wants less location information about their communications to be retained and want less personal information about them retained and disclosed, then the person should reduce their level of communication with their friends, families and other associates. Mobile devices are popular, and people are dependent on these devices (ACMA 2017, 2018). Not using the device or reducing its use would be a form of self-censorship and could create a chilling effect on the right to communicate and freedom of expression. This negatively impacts the affected person's privacy and free speech, to communicate at will, when and how they like, and not to be concerned that if they speak too often the Telco would retain more location information than they would be comfortable to disclose to the Agencies.

It even goes further—the person seeking to protect their privacy may limit their movements or choose not to carry their mobile device with them all the time. The freedom of movement of the person is curtailed. The person would also be unfairly restricted from enjoying and exercising full ownership over his or her private property.

2.7   Conclusion

The individual is caught between a rock and a hard place—on the one end the Telco and the big tech social media corporation is looking to collect and use their location information for their commercial purposes. On the other end, law enforcement agencies are looking for the same location information to enforce laws. This creates the perfect harvesting season for the individual's data, closing all the gaps. This is further enabled by giving the private companies the discretion to retain more metadata and for longer periods. The potentially indefinite retention period keeps the location information at the disposal of the Agencies to request and use the location information. This negatively impacts the individual's freedom of movement, to exercise their property rights and their civil rights, despite the exclusions to only retain location information at the start and at the end of the voice or social media communication.

References

ACMA (2017) Communications report 2016–17
ACMA (2018) Communications report 2017–18
AGD (2015a) Submission No 27 to the Parliamentary Joint Committee on Intelligence and Security, Inquiry into the Telecommunications (Interception and Access) Amendment (Data Retention) Bill 2014, 16 January 2015
AGD (2015b) Data Retention Frequently Asked Questions for Industry (July 2015)

Attorney-General's Department (AGD) (2014) Confidential industry consultation paper. Telecommunications data retention—Statement of requirements. http://www.rogerclarke.com/DV/Data_retention_consultation_1.pdf. Accessed 29 Aug 2019

Australia Intelligence Security Organisation (ASIO) Submission No 12.1 to the Parliamentary Joint Committee on Intelligence and Security, Parliament of Australia, Inquiry into the Telecommunications (Interception and Access) Amendment (Data Retention) Bill 2014, January 2015

Commonwealth, Parliamentary Debates, Senate, 25 March 2016, 2294 (George Brandis MP)

Dmitry N (2013) GeoFence services'. Int J Open Inf Technol 1(9):30–33

European Telecommunications Standards Institute (ETSI) (2008) Lawful Interception (LI); Retained Data; Requirements of Law Enforcement Agencies for handling Retained Data, ETSI TS 102 656 V1.2.1 (2008-12)

ETSI (2014) Lawful Interception (LI); Retained data handling; Handover interface for the request and delivery of retained data', ETSI TS 102 657 V1.15.1 (2014-08)

ETSI (2017a) Universal Mobile Telecommunications System (UMTS); LTE; Evolved Packet System (EPS); Mobility Management Entity (MME) and Serving GPRS Support Node (SGSN) related interfaces based on Diameter protocol

ETSI (2017b) Lawful Interception (LI); Retained data; requirements of law enforcement agencies for handling retained data'

ETSI (2017c) LTE; Evolved Universal Terrestrial Radio Access Network (E-UTRAN); Stage 2 functional specification of User Equipment (UE) positioning in E-UTRAN (3GPP TS 36.305 version 14.2.0 Release 14)

Evidence to Parliamentary Joint Committee on Intelligence and Security (PJCIS), Parliament of Australia, Canberra, 17 December 2014, 17 (Kerri Hartland, Acting Director-General, ASIO)

Evidence to Legal and Constitutional Affairs References Committee, Parliament of Australia, Canberra, 2 February 2015, 49, 1.97 (Roger Clarke, Immediate Past Chair, Australian Privacy Foundation, 2015)

Explanatory Memorandum, Telecommunications (Interception and Access) Amendment (Data Retention) Bill 2015 (Cth). https://www.sas.com/content/dam/SAS/en_us/doc/factsheet/sas-master-data-management-105360.pdf. Accessed 2 June 2019

He Y, Fei Richard Y, Zhao N, Yin H, Yao H, Qi RC (2016) Big data analytics in mobile cellular networks. IEEE Access 4:1985–1996

Inspector-General of Intelligence and Security (IGIS) (2015) Annual Report 2014–2015

International Organization for Standardization and the International Electrotechnical Commission (ISO/IEC) (2005) Information technology. Metadata registries (MDR). Part 1 Framework

Legal and Constitutional Affairs References Committee (LCARC) (2015) Parliament of Australia, 475 Comprehensive revision of the Telecommunications (Interception and Access) Act 1979, 476 2015:77 [71.182]

Munson J, Gupta V (2002) Location-based notification as a general-purpose service (Paper presented at the Proceedings of the 2nd international workshop on Mobile commerce, Atlanta, Georgia, USA, 28 September 2002)

Office of Australian Information Commissioner (OAIC), Submission No 92 to the Parliamentary Joint Committee on Intelligence and Security, to Inquiry into the Telecommunications (Interception and Access) Amendment (Data Retention) Bill 2014, January 2015

Parliamentary Joint Committee on Intelligence and Security, Parliament of Australia. Report of the Inquiry into Potential Reforms of Australia's National Security Legislation (May 2013)

Parliamentary Joint Committee on Intelligence and Security, Parliament of Australia, Advisory Report on the Telecommunications (Interception and Access) Amendment (Data Retention) Bill 2014 (27 February 2015)

Privacy Act 1988 (Cth)

Privacy Commissioner v Telstra Corporation Limited [2017] FCAFC 4, 2017, 2 [5] (Privacy Commissioner case)

Revised Explanatory Memorandum, Telecommunications (Interception and Access) Amendment (Data Retention) Bill 2015 (Cth), 2015

Sarkar N (2015) Using analytics and automation to create personalised customer journeys. Presentation at the SAS Forum, Sydney, Australia, 7 May

SAS Institute Inc. (2015) SAS master data management

Shanapinda S (2016) The types of telecommunications device identification and location approximation metadata: under Australia's warrantless mandatory metadata retention and disclosure laws. Commun Law Bull 35(3):17–19. http://www.camla.org.au/communications-law-bulletin/. Accessed 23 July 2017

Shanapinda S (2019a) 'Habilitando a Localização de Dados para Cidades Inteligentes: Explorando os Regimes de Proteção e Retenção de Metadados no Brasil'. In: Jhessica Reia, Pedro Augusto P. Francisco, Marina Barros and Eduardo Magrani (eds) 'Horizonte presente: Debates de tecnologia e sociedade'. Letramento, 2019 [trans of: Enabling Data Location for Smart Cities: Exploring the Metadata Protection and Retention Regime in Brazil, Present Horizons: Debates on Technology and Society] ISBN: 978-85-9530-081-1. http://bibliotecadigital.fgv.br/dspace/bitstream/handle/10438/27448/Horizonte%20presente%20-%20tecnologia%20e%20sociedade%20em%20debate.pdf?sequence=1&isAllowed=y. Accessed 27 Aug 2019

Shanapinda S (2019b) Asymmetry in South Africa's regulation of customer data protection: unequal treatment between Mobile Network Operators (MNOs) and Over-the-Top (OTT) Service Providers. Afr J Inf Communication (AJIC):1–20. https://doi.org/10.17159/2077-7213/2019/n23a1. (20 pages) Article number 1 28 Jun 2019. URI: https://hdl.handle.net/10539/27536. 24 July 2019

Telecommunications (Interception and Access) Act 1979 (Cth) (*TIA Act 1979*)

Telecommunications (Interception and Access) Amendment (Data Retention) Act 2015 (Cth) (*Data Retention Act 2015*) (*DRA 2015*)

Telecommunications Act 1997 (Cth) (*TA 1997*)

Telecommunications and Other Legislation Amendment (Assistance and Access) Act 2018 (AAA 2018)

Telstra (2015) Submission No 112 to the Parliamentary Joint Committee on Intelligence and Security (PJCIS), Inquiry into the Telecommunications (Interception and Access) Amendment (Data Retention) Bill 2014, January 2015

Telstra Corporation Limited and Privacy Commissioner [2015] AATA 991 (18 December 2015) (the *Telstra court case*)

Vodafone Hutchinson Australia (2019) Privacy. https://www.vodafone.com.au/about/legal/privacy. 27 August 2019

Zuboff S (2019) The age of surveillance capitalism: the fight for the future at the new frontier of power hardcover. Profile trade

Chapter 3
The Legal Framework for Mobile Telecommunications Companies and Social Media Platforms to Disclose Location Information

3.1 The Compelled Disclosure of Location Information

The Telco has the general duty to protect both the non-contents of a communication and the contents of a communication. As such, the Telco is prohibited from disclosing location information. A key exception is that the Telco is allowed to disclose location information if the disclosure is authorised by law, or if the disclosure is required under the law. The Telco is required to disclose the information that relates to the affairs of the customer. Location information is considered information that relates to the affairs of the customer. This information is legally described as '... any information or document that ... relates to ... the contents or substance of a communication' (*TA 1997* s 276 (1)). The Telco is required to disclose the location information it is legally required to retain. The Telco is also legally required to disclose the location information the Telco is not required to retain but chooses to retain for commercial, cybersecurity and network maintenance purposes. This retention may be for any period of time (AGD Submission No 27 2015: 42; *TA 1997* ss s 275A, 276, 280, 313(3), (4), 3131(7); *TIA Act 1979* ss 174(1), 175(1), 176 (1), 177(2), 178(1), 179(1), 180(1)).

The disclosure of the information to the Agencies must be 'reasonably necessary' to safeguard national security. The Telco is also required to give such help as is 'reasonably necessary' to enforce the criminal laws. Giving such help as is reasonably necessary means allowing the Agencies to intercept the contents of a communication. It also means to disclose information or documents under a stored communications warrant. The Agencies may issue authorisations and notifications in terms of the *CAC Determination 2018* to request access to location information. Disclosing information or documents about location information, as requested under such authorisations and notifications issued by the Agencies under the *CAC Determination 2018* is another way of giving help to the Agencies, which help is reasonably necessary (*TA 1997* ss 313(3), 313(7)(d), (e)); *TIA Act 1979* s 183; *CAC Determination 2018* ss 8–12).

© Springer Nature Switzerland AG 2020
S. Shanapinda, *Advance Metadata Fair*, Law, Governance and Technology Series
44, https://doi.org/10.1007/978-3-030-50255-3_3

The request for location information must follow the procedures as set out in the *CAC Determination 2018*, instead of following a judicial warrant process. The need to access existing or prospective location information without a warrant was defended by the Attorney-General's Department (AGD). The AGD argued 'certain hurdles', as limitations, would be put in place for the Agencies to access metadata. The hurdles the AGD referred to includes the *CAC Determination 2018*. The *CAC Determination 2018* outlines the authorisation and notification process the Agencies must follow to request access to location information. The *CAC Determination 2018* is held up as the appropriate governance tool for access to location information because location information is legally described as 'telecommunications data'. The AFP may request access to historical location information and prospective location information for the enforcement of the criminal law. The Telco is required to disclose the location information under those requests from the Agencies (Department of Parliamentary Services 2007, p. 14; *CAC Determination 2018*; *TIA Act 1979* ss 174(1), 175(1), 176(1), 178(1), 179(1), 180(1); *TIA Act 1979* s 178, 180).

3.1.1   The AFP

The *CAC Determination 2018* requires the authorisations issued by the AFP to include:

a. Details of the information or documents to be disclosed;
b. the statement that the authorised officer is satisfied that the disclosure is reasonably necessary:

   i. for the enforcement of the criminal law, or

c. a statement that any interference with privacy that may result is justifiable and proportionate having regard to the gravity of any conduct, the seriousness of the offence, ...

   i. the likely relevance and usefulness of the information and documents; and
   ii. the reason why the disclosure or use is proposed to be authorised, amongst others (*CAC Determination 2018* section 10 (1)).

Regarding prospective location information, the limits appear stricter. The authorisation must include a statement that the authorised officer is satisfied that the disclosure is reasonably necessary for the investigation of a serious offence or an offence against a law of the Commonwealth, a State or a Territory that is punishable by imprisonment for at least 3 years. The statement must include short statements of the particulars of the offence. The Agencies must include in the authorisations '... details of the information or documents sought to be disclosed'. There is no indication what these details may include, except for the types of metadata outlined in section 187AA(1) items 1 to 6 of the *TIA Act 1979*, which includes location information (*CAC Determination 2018*).

3.1.2   ASIO

The *CAC Determination 2018* requires the authorisations issued by ASIO to comply with the following formalities, amongst others:

a. cite relevant sections of the empowering legislation,
b. contain details of the information or documents that are requested to be disclosed, and
c. a statement that the disclosure would be in connection with the performance of the functions of ASIO (*CAC Determination 2018* ss 8–9).

ASIO may simply state the location information is required because it is 'in connection with' the performance of its functions.

The authorisation and notification in terms of the *CAC Determination 2018* guarantees ASIOs' access to the telecommunications data. The contents of a communication are instead accessed with a domestic preservation notice (*TIA Act 1979* s 107J (2)). The authorisation and notification in terms of the *CAC Determination 2018* provides the information ASIO can use to complete the application for a judicial warrant or a warrant to be issued by the Attorney-General (AG). If the Agencies would be required to access location information in terms of a domestic preservation notice or a stored communications warrant, the Agencies would lack the details to complete the applications for domestic preservation notices and stored communications warrants. This could complicate ongoing investigations.

3.1.3   Power to Collect 'Technical Information' From Social Media Tech Giants

Social Media Platform companies (SMPs) like Microsoft, Facebook, Google, Adobe, Dropbox, Zoom allows the use of their online cloud-based software applications. This is referred to as software as a service (SaaS). Other applications include the likes of Telegram, Signal, Facebook FaceTime, WhatsApp, referred to as over the top applications (OTT). With the introduction of the metadata retention regime, the Telco complaint about regulatory asymmetry—the SMP, as an OTT service provider was not regulated (Shanapinda 2016). SMPs, along with the Telco and ISPs, are now required to assist the Agencies. They do not have the specific legal obligation to retain metadata as the Telco but is required to comply with request to disclose metadata.

The Telco, ISPs and SMPs are all legally referred to as designated communications providers (DCPs). DCPs develop software to provide an electronic service that has one or more end-users in Australia. Social media applications like Facebook, WhatsApp and Instagram are electronic services with registered users in Australia. DCPs may be requested to assist and give help voluntarily to the Agencies under what is called a Technical Assistance Request (TAR) and a Technical Capability

Notice (TCN). The organisation must not, in any way, whether directly or otherwise, be a party to a contravention of the duty to comply with the notices. The DCP may be liable for financial penalties if it takes an action or makes an omission to ensure it is not able to comply with the notices. Any failure to comply is subject to an enforceable civil penalty. This raises the question about exactly how voluntarily the assistance actually is if non-compliance is met with penalties. It is also ironic that the assistance is phrased as a 'request', if the DCP has no option but to comply and non-compliance is penalised (*AAA 2018* ss 317C Items 4, 6, 317D, 317G(2), 317MAA, 317E, 317HAA, 317L, 317LA, 317M, 317ZM, 317ZH (9), 317S, 317T, 317TAAA, 317TAA, 317ZA, 317ZB, 317ZC, 317ZD).

In this way location information is collected from every player in the social media and mobile communication services ecosystem, to close all the gaps—the communications services provided by mobile telecommunications providers AND the services from SaaS providers.

3.1.3.1   The List of Things to Assist with: Disclosing Technical Information

The TAR will contain a list of *acts or things* the DCP may carry out voluntarily. This list of acts or things are also referred to as 'listed help' (*AAA 2018* ss 317E, 317HAA, 317T).[1] The organisation may be requested to provide 'technical information'. The term 'technical information' is not legally defined and may therefore be broad. The term may arguably include the types of metadata retained under the *TIA Act 1979*, which may include the pool of location information (*AAA 2018* s 317E (1) (a)–(j)). Technical information may be information about the voice, SMS, email, chat, forum and social media communications. These communications may be provided by means of the following types of technologies: Asymmetric digital subscriber line (ADSL), Wi-Fi, VoIP, cable, General Packet Radio Services (GPRS), VoLTE, LTE (4G and 5G).

The TCN is issued by the Attorney-General (AG) with the approval of the Minister, on behalf of the Director-General of Security of ASIO. The aim of the notice is to ensure the organisation is capable of giving 'listed help' to enforce laws about serious offences in Australia or a foreign country; or to safeguard national security. The act or thing must be done within a specified period, in a manner that is specified or in a way that meets the conditions that are specified in the notice. The AG must first consult with the organisation for 28 days before issuing the notice, unless there is urgency, it is impractical to wait 28-days, or the organisation waives the right to the 28-day consultation period. The organisation must ensure that, in terms of the TCN, the said capability is developed, installed and maintained (*AAA 2018* ss 317T (2), (3), 317TAAA, 317U, 317W, 317ZGA (2)).

---

[1]The Home Affairs Minister may issue additional acts or things to be done, but in a legislative instrument (see section 317T(5) – (6)).

In response to an issued consultation notice or a proposed change to a notice, the organisation may request that it carry out an assessment, in 28 days, whether the TCN the AG intends to issue should be issued to the organisation. The AG will then appoint 2 persons, a judge and a technical person, to carry out the assessment, who must consult with the DCP (*AAA 2018* ss 317WA, 317YA, 317WA (2)–(5), 317YA).

Unlike access to metadata under the *TIA Act 1979*, the TCN and TAN are restricted to serious offences. These are offences that have a prison sentence of 3 years or more (*AAA 2018* ss 317E(1)(j), 317G(5)(d)(i), 317L(2)(c)(i), 317T(3)(a), 317ZS(1)(d)).

3.1.4   The Self-Certification Process Under the TIA Act 1979

The statutory internal authorisation process under the *CAC Determination 2018* has been critiqued as being a 'self-certification process'. The Agencies use a self-certification process without an independent third party approving the authorisations and notifications, to determine whether the location information, its size and the period for which it is collected, is reasonably necessary (Leonard 2015; Evidence to PJCIS 2015, p. 31 (Leonard)). As such, location information is accessed under less stringent requirements than the requirements to access the contents of a communication, that requires a preservation notice and a judicial warrant to access. This, despite the equally personal and sensitive nature of location information.[2]

SEDNode is an electronic interface used by the Agencies to request access to the telecommunications data from the Telco (Evidence 2007, p. 19 (Harrison). The internal governance measures of ASIO include access logs used to trace the use of the location information collected from the Telco (IGIS 2016, pp. 19–20). The *ex-ante* check is conducted in-house and has been criticised as being a low threshold (Evidence to PJCIS 2015, p. 31 (Leonard)). The Councils for Civil Liberties across Australia submitted to the PJCIS that '[i]t is clearly unacceptable for the "enforcement agencies" or ASIO to be their own authorisers of access to such Personal Information (PI)' (PJCIS *Advisory Report* 2015, pp. 231–232). ASIO is applying the tests itself and approving its own compliance thereto. Any non-compliance with the legal obligations may only be detected by the Inspector-General of Intelligence and Security (IGIS) after the fact, when it has already occurred, and not able to be prevented.

---

[2]See Sect. 6.3.4 in Chap. 6.

3.1.5   The Self-Certification Process Under Section 280 of the TA 1997

In addition to collecting location information under the *CAC Determination* 2018, the Agencies and other public bodies that are non-law enforcement agencies, may collect location information and other metadata under section 280 of the *Telecommunications Act 1997 (TA 1997)*.

Under section 280, metadata is released to more law enforcement bodies and to non-law enforcement bodies than originally expected, and for non-serious crimes. These agencies include: 'Report Illegal Dumping (NSW)', city councils and the taxi services commission (Communications Alliance Submission 27 2019, pp. 12–13). There is also no independent third-party pre-approving the collection of location information under section 280, thereby bypassing existing privacy protections under the *TIA Act 1979* (Telstra 2019a, p. 3).[3]

Telstra is still not clear on what types of data it may legally disclose to the various agencies under section 280, stating that trying to make this distinction is complicated (Telstra 2019a, p. 3). Under section 280, the types of metadata retained to comply with the retention obligations are not covered. In other words, metadata retained for the purposes of complying with the retention obligations are not meant to be disclosed under section 280 to non-law enforcement agencies. However, it is challenging for the Telco to distinguish between the types of metadata they are required to retain and the types of metadata they may retain voluntarily, so they only disclose the types of metadata they voluntarily retained to the non-law enforcement agencies and the other public bodies. Applying the Exclusions, does it mean the Telco is only required to disclose the location information retained prior to, during and after the voice or social media message communication has started; and the location information of the cell tower that did not handle the voice or social media message?[4] This gets very confusing. The law is therefore not clear nor predictable. This happened despite recommendations to ensure clarity about the types of data the Telco's are required to retain and disclose: '. . .that clear and narrowly defined language be used in the Regime, particularly to describe the kinds of information that service providers are required to collect and store under the metadata retention and disclosure regime to effectively implement the intentions of the scheme and reduce uncertainty for service providers that collect and retain data' (OAIC 2019, p. 4).

The Telco may voluntarily retain and then voluntarily disclose the voluntarily retained location information. The oversight obligations for example for record keeping for inspections, only apply to the mandatory retention and mandatory disclosures under the *CAC Determination 2018* authorisations and not directly to

---

[3]For a discussion on the Privacy Tests the Agencies must comply with but that these non-law enforcement agencies and public bodies are not required to comply with see Sect. 5.1.2, in relation to the AFP and 5.2.1 in relation to ASIO, in Chap. 5.

[4]See Sect. 2.3.2 in Chap. 2.

the voluntary retention and voluntary disclosure of location information. In this manner, section 280 location information avenue of collecting location information bypasses the privacy protections and oversight build into the regime under the *TIA Act 1979* as contained in the *CAC Determination 2018.*

The Commonwealth Ombudsman reported some other law enforcement agencies also collect metadata under section 280. Similar to the voluntary disclosures of location information, location information disclosed and accessed under section 280 is not under the oversight jurisdiction of the Commonwealth Ombudsman. The Commonwealth Ombudsman only has the power to inspect location information mandated to be stored and mandated to be collected under the *TIA Act 1979* and the *CAC Determination 2018* (Commonwealth Ombudsman Submission 20 2019, p. 7). As such, the AFP (when it comes to voluntarily retained metadata) and other public bodies are not legally required to report on the location information collected (whether voluntarily retained or mandated to be retained) under section 280 (AFP Submission 15 2019). Section 280 allows for forum shopping and creates an accountability gap. The AFP is therefore not held fully accountable. Only location information retained and collected under the *TIA Act 1979* are inspected and subject to the *Privacy Act 1980,* but the same location information collected under section 280 by the AFP and other public bodies are not held accountable by the Commonwealth Ombudsman under the *TIA Act 1979.* The privacy tests under the *TIA Act 1979* are not applied—to assess whether the disclosure is justifiable and proportionate. No records are required to be kept and no formal process of requesting and reporting the collection of data, as is required to be done under the *CAC Determination 2018* under the *TIA Act 1979* are prescribed, to ensure transparency and accountability (Commonwealth Ombudsman Submission 20 2019, pp. 7–8). The individual is not allowed the right to challenge the collection of this metadata under a court of law or with a complaint to the Commonwealth Ombudsman. The user is not aware of the data collection.

These public bodies may be subject to the *Privacy Act 1980* and they may be under the oversight of the Office of the Australian Information Commissioner (OAIC), to only collect personal information that they need for their business purposes. However, Telstra reported that unnecessary and irrelevant metadata is disclosed to other agencies then is necessary: 'In our experience, non-enforcement agencies and bodies often request large amounts of data and are sometimes not able to properly interpret the data provided' (Telstra Submission 35 2019b, p. 2). Telstra does not indicate whether it refuses the disclosure of this unnecessary metadata, or how it determines the level of necessity. The *TA 1997* does not grant Telstra the opportunity to refuse, access or determine what volume data requested is reasonably necessary. This space is not regulated adequately.

Telstra continued: '... [The] supply of irrelevant or unnecessary [meta]data further undermines public trust in the Regime' (Telstra Submission 35 2019b, p. 3). The oversight powers of the OAIC to ensure the collection of only information that is relevant and necessary are not clear: 'The acts and practices of intelligence agencies are not subject to the Privacy Act. Enforcement bodies, as defined in section 6 of the *Privacy Act 1988,* are broadly subject to the Privacy Act, however there are limitations to the extent to which the APPs in the Privacy Act apply to the operations of these bodies. For example, the limitation on using or disclosing information collected for a particular purpose other than the primary purpose does not apply where authorised by law or where the entity reasonably believes it necessary for an enforcement related activity' (OAIC Submission 34 2019, p. 6). In other words, the collected metadata may be re-purposed, as long as the secondary purpose is a related to law enforcement. The OAIC however recommended that these bodies be subject to the same privacy protection mechanisms under the *TIA Act 1979* as the Agencies (OAIC Submission 34 2019).

The section 280 avenue that is less stringent than the *CAC Determination 2018* process also undermines the relationship the Telco has with its customer when it comes to the protection of privacy (Telstra, Submission 35 2019b). This process has the practical impact of reducing the effectiveness of safeguards in the *TIA Act 1979* (OAIC Submission 34 2019, p. 10). There is no justifiable basis why public bodies should be allowed less oversight and accountability than the Agencies to collect the same valuable and personal information. The protection of privacy should be attached to the information and not the status of the body collecting the information. To solve this regulatory asymmetry, all public bodies accessing location information under section 280, should be required to follow the *CAC Determination 2018* process, the Privacy Tests as well as be under the oversight regime of the Commonwealth Ombudsman. Alternatively, the location information warrant process should be followed.

Clearly there is an inconsistency in the framework that results in different outcomes for the same types of metadata but based on the pathway followed to access the metadata and based on the type of body that is accessing the metadata. The process must be aligned for all types bodies and non-law enforcement agencies, to ensure fair treatment and fair outcomes in relation to privacy. There seems to be no legally justifiable rationale why city councils should not be held to the same standards as the AFP, or why they can have unfettered access to privacy to the metadata, whereas the Agencies are more restricted, given the scope of their functions and purposes.

Regarding cyber security obligations—to ensure the confidentiality, integrity and availability of the retained metadata, non-law enforcement agencies collecting huge amounts of personal metadata that they do not need to collect, are not legally required to encrypt the metadata, whereas the Telco is (Telstra Submission 35 2019b). This cyber security obligation should be applied to agencies accessing data under section 280 as well.

3.1.6   Pre-authorisation Checks

The investigation process sometimes includes a pre-check and pre-authorisation about the types of information the AFP wants to access (Evidence to PJCIS 2015, p. 17 (Hughes)).

Telstra explained the process pre-checks and a pre-authorisation checks as follows:

Mrs Hughes: . . . . There is a list of agencies that are authorised. At the moment we believe there are about 70 that are authorised by the Attorney. They request, in a particular manner, information from us, and they can reach out and do a preauthorisation check—so, if they know what they want to ask for and they are not quite sure how to ask for it, we can help them do that so that they do not give us something that we will not respond to or that is unlawful.

Mr DREYFUS: Just pausing there: you have got staff, who are dedicated staff—

Mrs Hughes: Very much so.

Mr DREYFUS: dedicated in both senses—

Mrs Hughes: Yes.

Mr DREYFUS: who are there to talk to law enforcement agencies to assist them in formulating the request?

Mrs Hughes: To assist them in understanding what we have and do not have. So: 'Don't put in a request, (1) because we will charge you for it, but (2) we may not have the information and you might be barking up the wrong tree.' So we might be able to say, 'No, we don't keep it; we can't help you with that,' or, 'The person doesn't have a service with us; you need to go and talk to another provider.' But if they proceed with an authorisation, we will receive that authorisation. It has to lay out the information very clearly as to what they are seeking. And then we have a team of people and systems to help deliver that information in the manner that they require it in. I think that there is often a lot of mystery around it. Very simply, it is often very simple metadata—the same sorts of information that you might be able to access from your bill: who you called; where you were when you made the call, by cell tower; a name and a billing address. I am sure people perceive that it is mysterious. It is actually, often—most times— very simple metadata.

Mr DREYFUS: So perhaps there is a pre-check, or perhaps not; the quickest pre-check is: 'Is this one of your subscribers?'

Mrs Hughes: Yes, that is right (Evidence to PJCIS, Parliament of Australia, Canberra, 29 January 2015, 17 (Kate Hughes, the Chief Risk Officer, Telstra).

Telstra does reject certain requests for telecommunications data if the request is invalid:

7. Does Telstra ever reject law enforcement requests?

We only disclose customer information in accordance with the law. If a request for information from an agency is invalid or seeks information that can only be obtained via a different process (e.g. requires a warrant and the requester does not have one), we will reject it. One important difference in the law enforcement environment in Australia compared to other countries is that agencies can undertake pre-warrant checks to make sure they are targeting their warrants accurately. This reduces the instances of mistakes leading to a rejection of a warrant (Telstra *Privacy*: 2017).

It is not clear whether any of the requests for location information may be rejected on the basis that the Agencies requested more location information than was reasonably necessary or more than was justifiable and proportionate, taking privacy protection into account. The Telco is not required to consider and apply the privacy standards contained in the *CAC Determination 2018* when disclosing the location information to the Agencies. These privacy standards are only applied by the Agencies (*CAC Determination 2018* ss 8–10).

The *CAC Determination 2018* authorisation and notification process makes no reference to pre-checks or pre-authorisations (*CAC Determination 2018* ss 8–10). The *CAC Determination 2018* requires the authorisations issued by the AFP to include details of the information or documents the AFP wants the Telco to disclose (*CAC Determination 2018* s 10). The *CAC Determination 2018* does not include a pre-check or a pre-authorisation procedure to first verify whether the Telco has the location information available before the AFP decides to issue the authorisation and notification, under the *CAC Determination 2018*, based on the response from the Telco. The Telco is not meant to help the AFP with completing the authorisation and notification, in doing so the AFP and the Telco do not operate at an arm's length basis. The *CAC Determination 2018* is clear, and the procedures outlined therein detail the level of independent assistance. The AFP must by itself detail the types of information it requires for the investigation. ASIO must also list the details of the information or documents sought to be disclosed (*CAC Determination 2018* s 8), and not first request it from the Agencies, or verify that the Telco has the information available. Using the authorisations and notifications under the *CAC Determination 2018* enables the AFP greater flexibility to use pre-checks and pre-authorisations to collect location information, and for less serious offences. This process seems needed. As such, the *CAC Determination 2018* must be amended to legalise the pre-check process.

The oversight exercised over access to location information is less rigid than the oversight exercised over access to the contents of a communication. For example, the Agencies may issue an authorisation and notification under the *CAC Determination 2018* to the Telco to obtain location information of an unnamed person. This allows the Agencies to collect location information in bulk from the Telco, without listing any names of the persons of interest. For the contents of a communication the Agencies are required to submit the name of the person to apply for a stored communications warrant, after having first issued a domestic preservation notice to the Telco to store the location information while waiting for the warrant to be issued (*CAC Determination 2018* ss 8-10; *TIA Act 1979* ss 109, 39, 110, 110A, 115).

The warrant must be applied for under oath whereas no oath or affirmation is required for an authorisation and notification under the *CAC Determination 2018*. The Agencies are granted access to location information that reveals personal information under less stringent requirements than the contents of a communication

(*CAC Determination 2018* ss 8–10; *TA 1997* ss 276, 280, 313(3) (4), 3131(7); Leonard 2015; *TIA Act 1979* ss 44, 174–184, 180H (2), 180J (2), 180Q).

3.1.7 Disclosure Under Journalist Information Warrants to ASIO and the Concentration of Power

The Agencies must apply for a Journalist Information Warrant (JIW) before issuing an authorisation and notification under the *CAC Determination 2018* to request location information from the Telco. A JIW may be issued by an officer of the Administrative Appeals Tribunal (AAT), but under less stringent requirements than those for accessing the contents of voice or SMS communications. In respect of ASIO, a JIW is issued by the AG (*CAC Determination 2018* s 8; *TA 1997* ss 276, 280, 313(3), (4), 3131(7); *TIA Act 1979* ss 174–184; 180G, 180H (2), 180J (2), 180L(2)(b)(iii), s180Q; AGD 2016a, p. vii, 58; IGIS 2016, p. 18).

To have the JIW issued, ASIO only needs to specify the facts and other grounds on which the Director-General subjectively considers it necessary that the JIW should be issued (*TIA Act 1979* s 180J (2)). The AG may refuse to issue the JIW to ASIO—if the AG is not satisfied about the extent to which that information or those documents would be likely to assist in the performance of ASIO's functions (*TIA Act 1979* s 180L(2)(b)(iii)).

The process of accessing location information only protects location information about a mobile device used by a journalist and its employer.[5] The general populace, nor the whistle-blower itself is granted the same protection. The journalist is protected based on the public interest to protect journalist sources and to uphold a free press (Explanatory Statement 2015, p. 7 [36]). In respect of ASIO, the JIW is a non-judicial warrant, like a stored communications warrant, which is also issued by the AG (*TIA Act 1979* s 180L(2)(b)(iii)). The functions of ASIO are exercised as per the AG's Guidelines issued by the AG (AGD 2016b). The Communications Access Coordinator (CAC), who moved from the Attorney-General's Department and is now located in the Home Affairs Department, and is part of the same executive arm of Government as the AG, is the same body that limits the exercise of power in terms of the new *CAC Determination 2018*. Although the AG also exercises oversight over ASIO by issuing the JIW, this a concentration of power in the hands of the executive branch of government.

---

[5]Note that the journalist's source is also not directly protected by the JIW process, it only applies to and offers direct protection to the journalist; see discussion below at '3 The Ambiguity of the JIW Process'.

See Revised Explanatory Memorandum, Telecommunications (Interception and Access) Amendment (Data Retention) Bill 2015 (Cth), 6–7 [31].

3.1.8   Disclosure Under Journalist Information Warrants to the AFP

A total of 58 warrants were issued during 2017 and 2018 in respect of journalist's metadata (AFP, Submission 15 2019, p. 6). The AFP must apply for a JIW to a Judge, a magistrate, or a person appointed to the AAT, who is a legal practitioner enrolled for at least 5 years.[6]

The AAT is a quasi-judicial body that reviews administrative decisions under Federal law (*AATA 1975*; AAT 2017). The issuing authority is appointed by the AG. The application for a JIW is made under oath or affirmation. The JIW is only issued if the JIW is reasonably necessary, inter alia, to issue an authorisation and notification in terms of the *CAC Determination 2018* and may be affected by the extent to which that information or those documents would be likely to assist an investigation (*TIA Act 1979* ss *6DC*, 180S, 180T(2)(a)(iii). ASIO must simply state the facts on which basis the JIW must be issued. This creates an inconsistency between issuing a JIW to the AFP and issuing a JIW to ASIO. ASIO does not need to make a statement under oath. ASIO and AFP cooperate on inquiries and investigations that touches on national security. The question is whether ASIO would use its powers on behalf of and at the request, whether directly or otherwise, to collect a Ministerial warrant and pass the information collected on to the AFP, to benefit the AFP. The benefit being that the AFP does not need to follow its stringent requirements such as making statements under oath if it can use ASIO to fill the gaps. There appears to be no publicly known guidelines on how ASIO and the AFP cooperate in carrying out inquiries and investigations that are interrelated or over which they have concurrent jurisdiction, roles overlap, when it comes to gathering information that can serve as evidence of wrongdoing. The 2014 Ministerial Direction and the updated Ministerial Direction regarding the investigations of leaks to journalist of secret information and the obligation to consider the greater public interest, do not seem to cover this area (Dutton 2019; Keenan 2014; *AFP Act 1997* s 8(1)(bf)(ii)). It is not clear how ASIO would assist the AFP with its intelligence gathering role, so the AFP is able to carry out its law enforcement role. Publicly available guidelines that outlines the level of cooperation may provide much needed public trust in the joint and collaborative operations of the Agencies. This is particularly important given the AFP raids of a journalist's home and the and the Australian Broadcasting Corporation (ABC) in 2019, regarding reporting on the Afghanistan war, that was investigated as a matter threatening national security (Lyons 2019).

---

[6]Section 6DC was added by the Telecommunications (Interception and Access) Amendment (Data Retention) Act 2015 (Cth) (Data Retention Act 2015) on 13 April 2015. *TIA Act 1979* s 6DC.

3.1.8.1   The Ambiguity of the JIW Process in Relation to Whistle-Blowers

Section 180H of the *TIA Act 1979* requires the AFP to obtain a JIW to identify a whistle-blower. According to the Commonwealth Ombudsman: 'Agencies have the power to internally authorise access to this information, however, if an agency wishes to access telecommunications data that will identify a journalist's information source, the agency must apply to an external issuing authority for a warrant.' (Commonwealth Ombudsman 2018, p. 1).

The Commonwealth Ombudsman identified AFP's non-compliance in a number of key areas. These included:

a. adherence to the Journalist Information Warrant (JIW) provisions;
b. inability to sufficiently demonstrate required privacy considerations; and
c. access to unauthorised telecommunications data (Commonwealth Ombudsman 2018, p. 2).

The Commonwealth Ombudsman does not report an issue of non-compliance unless it considers it to be serious (Commonwealth Ombudsman 2018, p. 5). AFP officials are required to obtain JIWs to identify sources but are not held accountable, if it fails to obtain JIWs. In April 2017, an AFP official that was investigating a leak of secret information obtained the metadata of a journalists without a warrant, as required by the *TIA Act 1979*. The AFP indicated no action was taken against the officer (Royes 2017). The Commonwealth Ombudsman referred the issue of non-compliance to Parliament in 2017 but there is no indication of what happened to the referral (Commonwealth Ombudsman 2017). In November 2018 the Commonwealth Ombudsman reported it continues to monitor the AFP's compliance. The Commonwealth Ombudsman did not report on exactly what happened to the AFP official or what action Parliament took to hold the AFP accountable (Commonwealth Ombudsman 2018).

On the other hand, the AFP argued that in terms of section 180H it only needs to apply for a JIW if they need the metadata of the journalist to help them identify the source. Given the quote of the Commonwealth Ombudsman above, it seems the AFP and the Commonwealth Ombudsman interpret section 180H differently. If they can identify the whistle-blower with other information, they do not need to apply for the warrant. This means, the source may be identified without a warrant. A warrant is only required if identifying the source will be aided by the journalist's metadata. The AFP can therefore bypass this requirement. The effect is that the AFP officials can identify the source without having to first obtain a JIW. The JIW process is a vague and ambiguous process that is open to interpretation. The investigation by the Commonwealth Ombudsman revealed that poor training and lack of awareness of the new framework was to blame. The AFP officers did not fully appreciate their obligations. Training has since been offered to the officers, and the manuals and guidelines updated. The telecommunications data was destroyed and not used. The officers were not clear on when it was permissible to access the telecommunications data of a journalist (Royes 2017; Commonwealth Ombudsman 2017, pp. 1–2, 8 [2.9]; Shanapinda, S.: Advance metadata fair: The retention and disclosure of location information as metadata for law enforcement and national security, and the impact on privacy – An Australian story. Dissertation, UNSW Sydney (2018).

The question is whether this was the intention of the protections that were worked into the law, or whether it is a gap in the law. If it is a gap, this gap is being exploited. The JIW process is therefore not effective, is poorly constructed and must be strengthened. If the intention is to identify the source, the AFP officials must in all instances first obtain a JIW. Not only should the metadata of the journalist be protected by default by the JIW, as is currently the case, but also the metadata of the source. In other words, even if the journalist's metadata is not required to identify the source, but if the intention is to identify the source, the JIW must first be obtained in every situation. The JIW process should solely be based on the purpose of identifying the source and not on whether the journalist's data would aid the investigation of identifying the source. Such an amendment will require the AFP to obtain a JIW in all instances where the aim is to identify the source: (i). whether the AFP decides to use the journalist's metadata to identify the source; or (ii). whether the AFP uses other means, but still has the same aim of identifying the source. The AFP will not have the discretion to choose not to apply for JIW where it does not need the journalist's metadata. Under such an amendment a JIW would always be required when violations of secrecy laws are investigated and when the source must be identified.

3.1.8.2   The Public Interest Advocate

A JIW is not to be issued unless it is reasonably necessary to enforce the criminal law (*TIA Act 1979* s 180T(2)(b)).

The Judge or AAT member issuing the JIW must state that he or she is satisfied that '. . . the public interest in issuing this warrant outweighs the public interest in protecting the confidentiality of the source . . . .' (*Regulations 2017*: Schedule 1, 29). Form 7 in the relevant Regulation indicates the intervention that is allowed by third parties, such as the Public Interest Advocate (PIA) to appear in front of the Judge when the JIW is requested and the Judge or AAT member assesses the application. A Public Interest Advocate may make submissions to the Judge about the decision to issue or refuse to issue the JIW, or any of its conditions (*Regulations 2017*: Schedule 1, 29; *TIA Act 1979* s 180X (2)(b)).

Except for under the JIW, under the *CAC Determination 2018* there is no role for a PIA, Judge, AAT member or a Judge to independently verify, prior to collecting the location information that the proposed interference with privacy is justifiable and proportionate, reasonably necessary, and is based on a suspicion of an offence, based in turn on reasonable grounds. A Judge can issue a JIW with necessary restriction and conditions. Other than in applications for JIW's in journalist-source investigations, no third party is allowed to assess the information that the Agencies use to request the location information from the Telco. In a JIW, the Judge or AAT member is required to assess any privacy considerations. The Judge or AAT member is required to be satisfied, based on the information submitted, that the interference with privacy is justifiable and proportionate, considering the seriousness of the offences. After receiving a JIW the Agencies then issue an authorisation under the *CAC Determination 2018*, and still address the privacy considerations internally, after the involvement of the AAT or Judge as the third party. This is a second level of consideration of these issues. The AAT member's or the Judge's roles are not restricted, and the jurisdiction covers privacy considerations. The absence of a third party to collect location information, except when it comes to JIW's, presents an opportunity that can be used to better protect privacy and to instil public confidence (*TIA Act 1979* s 180T; *Regulations 2017*: Schedule 1, 29).

The AG (in respect of ASIO), Judge or AAT member can issue a JIW without the involvement of a PIA. The Parliamentary Joint Committee on Human Rights Human (PJCHR) objected to this on privacy grounds (PJCHR 2016, pp. 18, 24–25 [2.47] – [2.48]). Based on these objections, the PIA was granted the following powers in order to safeguard privacy better and more fairly:

a. to receive the proposed JIW requests made by the Director-General of Security;
b. to receive the proposed JIW applications made by an enforcement agency;
c. to deal with proposed JIW requests and applications;
d. to prepare submissions;
e. to attend a hearing of oral application by an enforcement agency for a proposed JIW; and
f. to receive further information, or a copy or summary of information (*Regulation 2015*: ss 11–16).

Despite the personal nature of location information, location information is requested directly from the Telco without the involvement of an independent external authority such as the PIA, Judge or AAT member. The Telco may choose to disclose the location information of a journalist, a source or any individual voluntarily, without the consent of the individual and without being required to follow any privacy safeguards.

The original PIAs were criticised for not specialising in representing journalists or in media law. At least one warrant was dropped due to omissions and errors in the application and another application was opposed. The whole scheme is clouded in secrecy and no journalist knows about the warrants applied for to collect their location information to try and identify their sources (*Regulation 2015*: s 13).

3.2 Voluntary Disclosure of Location Information

The Telco may also choose to voluntarily disclose any of the location information, without having the legal duty to do so. The Telco may voluntarily disclose location information to ASIO. The voluntary disclosure must be about ASIO performing its functions. The Telco may voluntarily disclose location information to the AFP. The disclosure must be reasonably necessary to enforce the criminal laws. If the AFP initiates the request, it is not considered a voluntary disclosure (*TIA Act 1979* s s174, 177).

The Telco may disclose the location information to the Agencies without the consent and knowledge of the individual, and without having to follow privacy safeguards required in some other processes. Only an estimated nine per cent of disclosures were made with the knowledge or consent of the individual. Disclosing the information without consent means the person is not informed that the location information has been disclosed to the Agencies, whether voluntarily or under a *CAC Determination 2018* authorisation and notification (*Privacy Act 1988* Schedule 1, APPs 6.1, 6.2); *TIA Act 1979* ss 175(3); *Gant court case* [2006] FCA 1475, 12 [42]; *Re Nanaimo court case* [1944] 4 DLR 638, 639; *TA 1997* s 289; ACMA 2017, p. 97.

3.2.1   Privacy Protections Are Subject to the Discretion of the Agencies and the Telco

Under the *CAC Determination 2018* authorisation and notification procedures, the Agencies are entitled to request the location information, whether retained under the law or whether retained voluntarily. The Agencies are not restricted from requesting the location information of the neighbouring Cell-ID or the location information generated at any time, whether a communication took place or not. The Telco may not have yet disclosed this location information, as confirmed by Telstra, or the Agencies may not have yet requested this location information. However, by law, the Telco is still obliged to disclose this location information when requested and the Agencies would still be within their legal powers to request it in future (*TA 1997* ss 276, 280, 313(3), (4), 3131(7); *TIA Act 1979* ss 174(1), 175(1), 176(1), 177(2), 178 (1). If the Telco has the information available the Telco may be requested to share the information, or even do so voluntarily. Throughout the lifespan of the location information in the databases of the Telco, the location information remains legally available and at the disposal of the Telco and the Agencies to collect and use in terms of their broad commercial and law enforcement functions. Under these circumstances, the lack of compulsion to retain location information prior to or during a communication is a limited protection for privacy, one that is subject to the discretion of the Telco and the Agencies in a situation where they may both have reasons and a law enforcement or commercial interest to retain and seek access to such location information that is not compulsorily retained.

The fact that the Telco may collect location information for its business purposes and may store location information for as long as it considers necessary, throughout which time the location information remains available to the Agencies, demonstrates the broad access and use powers of both the Agencies and the Telco beyond the scope of compulsory retention. The Agencies and the Telco each seek to collect or use the location information for their own objectives. The *TIA Act 1979* contains no restrictions that clearly prohibit the collection of location information apart from the Exclusions. The Agencies are also not prohibited to only collect location information stored at the start and at the end of the communications. There are no legal penalties for either the Agencies or the Telco if they were to collect, store, disclose and use location information prior to, during and after the communications ended (ACMA 2018, p. 58). This allows the Agencies and the Telco broad discretion for access to and the use of location information. The use of location information by the Telco for other commercial interests keep the location information at the disposal of the Agencies to request and use the location information. This negatively impacts the individual's freedom of movement. The Exclusions are the privacy safeguards. These privacy safeguards are however subject to the discretion of the Telco to retain location information, and the discretion of the Agencies to request access to the location information that is voluntarily retained. As a result, the Exclusions made under the *TIA Act 1979* that the Telco is not required to retain location information, that is not used to provide the service or that is generated during a voice or SMS communication, rather than at its start and end, are not effective privacy protection mechanisms, as they might appear to be.

3.3 Conclusion

The Telco has the discretion to disclose location information to the Agencies that the Telco is not legally required to retain and this undermines the privacy protections embodied in the limited scope of compulsory retention. The Telco is not required to follow privacy safeguards when disclosing location information voluntarily and under section 280 to other public bodies. Social media companies are also required to 'voluntarily' disclose technical information. Failing to do so may lead to penalties. In this manner the Agencies are guaranteed access to metadata from the digital services ecosystem, filling all the gaps. The requirements under the JIW protect privacy, but these requirements can be bypassed by using alternative interpretations of section 180H of the *TIA Act 1979* arising from its ambiguity. This vagueness undermines the newly introduced privacy protections. The voluntary and the mandatory disclose of location information should be subject to the same privacy protections. To close this privacy protection and accountability gap, the voluntary disclosure of location information should be subject to a judicial warrant process, to ensure customer trust and confidence in the Telco when it comes to the protection of their privacy.

References

ACMA (2017) Communications Report 2016–17

ACMA (2018) Communications Report 2017–18

Administrative Appeals Tribunal (AAT) (2017) What we do. http://www.aat.gov.au/about-the-aat/what-we-do. Accessed 27 Aug 2019

Administrative Appeals Tribunal Act 1975 (Cth) (AATA 1975)

AGD (2015) Submission No 27 to the Parliamentary Joint Committee on Intelligence and Security, Inquiry into the Telecommunications (Interception and Access) Amendment (Data Retention) Bill 2014, 16 January 2015

AGD (2016a) Telecommunications (Interception and Access) Act 1979 Annual Report 2015–16

AGD (2016b) Attorney-General's Guidelines in relation to the performance by the Australian Security Intelligence Organisation of its function of obtaining, correlating, evaluating and communicating intelligence relevant to security (including politically motivated violence),' 2016 (Attorney-General's [AG's] Guidelines)

Attorney-General's Department (AGD), *Telecommunications (Interception and Access) Act 1979 Annual Report 2015–16*, (2016)

Australia Federal Police (AFP) (2019) Submission 15 to the Parliamentary Joint Committee on Intelligence and Security (PJCIS), Review of the mandatory data retention regime, July 2019

Australian Information Commissioner (OAIC) (2019) Submission 34 to the PJCIS, Review of the mandatory data retention regime July 2019

Commonwealth Ombudsman (2017) A report on the Commonwealth Ombudsman's inspection of the Australian Federal Police under the Telecommunications (Interception and Access) Act 1979. Access to journalist's telecommunications data without a journalist information warrant (October 2017) https://www.ombudsman.gov.au/__data/assets/pdf_file/0021/78123/Commonwealth-Ombudsman-AFP-JIW-report-PDF-FOR-WEBSITE.pdf. Accessed 2 Sept 2019

Commonwealth Ombudsman (2018) A report on the Commonwealth Ombudsman's monitoring of agency access to stored communications and telecommunications data under Chapters 3 and 4 of the Telecommunications (Interception and Access) Act 1979. For the period 1 July 2016 to 30 June 2017

Commonwealth Ombudsman (2019) Submission 20 to the PJCIS, Review of the mandatory data retention regime, July 2019

Communications Access Coordinator's (CAC) Telecommunications (Interception and Access) (Requirements for Authorisations, Notifications and Revocations) Determination 2015 (Cth) (at 9 October 2015). (CAC Determination 2015)

Communications Alliance (2019) Submission 27 to the PJCIS on the Review of the mandatory data retention regime, July 2019

Department of Parliamentary Services (Cth), *Bills Digest*, No 10 of 2007–08, 3 August 2007

Dutton (2019, August 8) Minister for Home Affairs - Ministerial Direction to Australian Federal Police Commissioner relating to investigative action involving a professional journalist or news media organisation in the context of an unauthorised disclosure of material made or obtained by a current or former Commonwealth officer. https://www.afp.gov.au/sites/default/files/PDF/Ministerial-Direction-signed-2019.pdf. Accessed 20 Sept 2019

Evidence to Parliamentary Joint Committee on Intelligence and Security (PJCIS), Parliament of Australia, Canberra, 29 January 2015 (Kate Hughes, the Chief Risk Officer, Telstra)

Evidence to Parliamentary Joint Committee on Intelligence and Security, Parliament of Australia, Canberra, 30 January 2015, 31 (Peter Leonard Guildford, Chairperson of the Media and Communications Committee, Business Law Section of the Law Council of Australia)

Evidence to Parliamentary Joint Committee on the Australian Crime Commission, Canberra, 6 July 2007, 19 (Tony Harrison, Assistant Commissioner

Explanatory Statement, Telecommunications (Interception and Access) Act 1979 Telecommunications (Interception and Access) Amendment (Public Interest Advocate and Other Matters) Regulations 2015 (Cth)

Gant v Commissioner Australian Federal Police [2006] FCA 1475, 12 [42]

Home Affairs and Integrity Agencies Legislation Amendment Act 2018 (Cth)

IGIS (2016) Annual Report 2015–2016

Inspector-General of Intelligence and Security (IGIS), *Annual Report 2014–2015*, (2015)

Keenan M (12 May 2014) Ministerial Direction. https://www.afp.gov.au/about-us/governance-and-accountability/ministerial-direction. Accessed 27 August 2019

Leonard P (2015) Mandatory Internet Data Retention in Australia – Looking the horse in the mouth after it has bolted. https://www.gtlaw.com.au/sites/default/files/Mandatory-Internet-Data-Retention-in-Australia_0.pdf. Accessed 27 Aug 2019

Lyons J (2019, July 15) AFP raid on ABC reveals investigative journalism being put in same category as criminality. ABC. https://www.abc.net.au/news/2019-07-15/abc-raids-australian-federal-police-press-freedom/11309810. Accessed 16 Sept 2019

Parliamentary Joint Committee on Human Rights (PJCHR), Parliament of Australia, Human rights scrutiny report Thirty-fifth report of the 44th Parliament (25 February 2016)

PJCIS (2015) Parliament of Australia, *Advisory Report on the Telecommunications (Interception and Access) Amendment (Data Retention) Bill 2014* (27 February 2015)

Privacy Act 1988 (Cth)

Re Nanaimo Community Hotel Ltd [1944] 4 DLR 638

Revised Explanatory Memorandum, Telecommunications (Interception and Access) Amendment (Data Retention) Bill 2015 (Cth)

Royes L (2017, April 29) AFP officer accessed journalist's call records in metadata breach. ABC. http://www.abc.net.au/news/2017-04-28/afp-officer-accessed-journalists-call-records-inmetadata-breach/8480804. Accessed 27 Aug 2019

Shanapinda S (2016) The retention and disclosure of location information and location identifiers. Aust J Telecommun Digit Econ 4(4):Article 68. https://doi.org/10.18080/ajtde.v4n4.68

Telecommunications (Interception and Access) Act 1979 (Cth) (TIA Act 1979)

Telecommunications (Interception and Access) Amendment (Data Retention) Act 2015 (Cth) (DRA 2015)

Telecommunications (Interception and Access) Amendment (Public Interest Advocates and Other Matters) Regulation 2015 (Cth) (Regulations 2015)

Telecommunications (Interception and Access) Regulations 2017 (Cth) (Regulations 2017)

Telecommunications (Interceptions and Access) (Requirements for Authorisations, Notifications and Revocations) Determination 2018 (Cth) (at 20 November 2018) (CAC Determination 2018)

Telecommunications Act 1997 (Cth) (TA 1997)

Telecommunications and Other Legislation Amendment (Assistance and Access) Act 2018 (AAA 2018)

Telstra (2017) *Privacy*. https://www.telstra.com.au/privacy/transparency. Accessed Feb 2018

Telstra (2019a) *Privacy*. https://www.telstra.com.au/privacy/transparency. Accessed 20 Aug 2019

Telstra (2019b) Submission 35 to the PJCIS, Review of the mandatory data retention regime, July 2019

Chapter 4
The Powers of the Agencies to Collect and Use Location Information

4.1 The Powers of the AFP to Use Location Information

The law enforcement and investigatory powers of the AFP include providing police services in relation to the laws of the Commonwealth and safeguarding the Commonwealth's interests (*AFP Act 1979* s 8). Police services include crime prevention, the protection of persons from injury or death, and property from damage, whether arising from criminal acts or otherwise (*AFP Act 1979* s 4(1) (definition of 'police services'). The AFP cooperates with ASIO on investigations (*AFP Act 1979* s 8 (1) (bf)(ii). The AFP also has the following predictive national security role: '. . . identifying emerging criminal threats to the national interest' (Keenan 2014). In this sense, the AFP and ASIO are granted the power to 'use' the historical and prospective location information collected from the Telco (*TIA Act 1979*) s 181).

The word 'use' means, accessing and reading personal information; searching records for personal information; making a decision based on personal information; and passing personal information from one department of the AFP to another (OAIC 2015: 28–29).[1]

The word 'use' includes the handling of information and how the information is managed. It includes the staff members of the Telco and the AFP accessing, reading, exchanging, searching the information and making decisions based on that personal information. The unauthorised access of personal information by a staff member also amounts to the 'use' of the information The collection and access of location information is also a 'use' of the personal information (OAIC 2015: 14, 28–29).[2]

In terms of Australian Privacy Principle (APP) 6, the AFP may 'use' personal information disclosed by the Telco for the law enforcement purposes for which it was disclosed (*Privacy Act 1988* Schedule 1, APP 6.1). It follows that the use of the information must only be to enforce the criminal law; to enforce the law imposing a

---

[1] The word 'use' is not defined in the *TIA Act 1979* nor in the *Privacy Act 1988* (Cth).

[2] See that describes location information as personal information.

© Springer Nature Switzerland AG 2020
S. Shanapinda, *Advance Metadata Fair*, Law, Governance and Technology Series 44, https://doi.org/10.1007/978-3-030-50255-3_4

pecuniary penalty; to investigate a serious offence; or to investigate an offence against a law of the Commonwealth, a State or a Territory, that is punishable with a 3-year minimum prison sentence, and is reasonably necessary for that purpose (*TIA Act 1979* s 178(3), 179(3), 180 (4)). Serious offences include theft, fraud and money laundering (*Crimes Act 1914* s 15GE(2)(a), (b), (1)).

Location information serves various investigatory purposes. The Agencies request and receive location information to apply for warrants and to identify and pursue criminal inquiries (Evidence to PJCIS 2014: 17 (Hartland). The Agencies request and receive location information and use it to apply for warrants and to identify and pursue criminal inquiries (Evidence to PJCIS 2014: 17 (Hartland).

Location information is used for prospective law enforcement strategies. In using location information, the AFP is expected to deliver on key strategic priorities. These include:

(a) where possible, identifying emerging criminal threats to the national interest;
(b) advising on approaches, to counter threats;
(c) being responsive to any requests for information by the Minister of Home Affairs and the Attorney General's Department (AGD); and
(d) alerting the Minister of Home Affairs and the AGD to any significant events related to the AFP's activities through clear, comprehensive and timely advice (Keenan 2014).

Location information is used to identify existing as well as potential criminal links between persons (PJCIS, *Advisory Report* 2015: 97 [3.93]). Access to telecommunications data is seen as a critical tool and investigatory source for the Agencies, used primarily at the commencement of an investigation. It is usually the first lead information. It lays the basis for further investigations as it is used to identify inquiries and to pursue them. Telecommunications data is used to associate and disassociate persons and relations. It helps to eliminate potential suspects. Telecommunications data is used to apply for search and interception warrants. It is used to identify criminal networks. Telecommunications data provides intelligence that then leads to evidence which can be used for prosecutions. The analysis of the interlinkages with other data sources is considered vital for various types of investigations. Location information is used for both 'pro-active and reactive investigations' and is analysed with other information collected from other sources to determine if there are any links (Evidence to Parliamentary PJCIS, 2014: 17 (Hartland); Revised Explanatory Memorandum 2015: 2 [3]; Evidence to PJCIS 2014: 17 (Hartland); Evidence to PJCIS 2014: 3 (Colvin); Revised Explanatory Memorandum 2015: 6 [24], 7 [35]). The terms 'pro-active and reactive investigations' appear to cover a spectrum of investigations, whether initiated by the Agencies or those based on allegations from a witness reporting a crime or security, or at the behest of the Agencies, for serious and non-serious offences.

Table 4.1 The number of authorisations to collect metadata since 2015

Offences	Number of authorisations to collect metadata between 2015 and 2018
Miscellaneous offences	1010
Property damage and environment pollution	161
Public order offences	105
Serious damage to property	199
Theft and related offences	1957
Traffic and vehicle regulatory offences	110
Unlawful entry with intent/burglary, break and enter	269

AFP 2019, Submission 15: 4-5

4.1.1 Statistics About the Use of Metadata

During the periods 2016, 2017 and 2018, the AFP issued a total of 67703 authorisations to collect historic metadata. The figures totalled 25811; 22256 and 19636 respectively. This indicates a decreasing reliance on historic metadata. During the periods 2016, 2017 and 2018 the AFP collected 2592; 3045 and 3701 prospective metadata respectively (AFP 2019, Submission 15: 4). This indicates an increasing reliance on prospective metadata. The volume of metadata collected is unknown—it is not clear whether the metadata collected would have been for an hour, day, weeks, months or years. This statistic may be needed to assess the proportionality and reasonableness of the data collected, in relation to the seriousness and the nature of the offence. No such statistics are publicly available in relation to ASIO (Telstra 2016).

4.1.2 Access to Location Information in Respect of Non-serious Offences and the Low Threshold

The metadata is collected to investigate a criminal offence such as trespassing, public disorder, theft and damage to property. The AFP reported metadata was collected for the following (Table 4.1):

Other non-serious crimes for which location information may be stored and collected include: trespassing on agricultural land and inciting trespassing via social media (*CCA 1995* ss 474.46, 474.47). The specific mention of social media is worth noting. It sets the Telco and DCP up for having to require the disclosure of the technical information, location information and other social media to inquire into and investigate the protest actions of climate change and environmental activist. These offences were introduced after the Aussie Farms website which maps the commercial farms, led to animal rights activist trespassing on farm properties. One of the aims was to equally protect the environment—the risks harm to public health through the contamination of food, and the breach of biosecurity protocols (Explanatory Memorandum 2019: 3-4 [7] – [9]).

The metadata retention regime was originally introduced as government policy to address the threat of terrorism. Once the law was passed it was clear non-serious offences would also be investigated and inquired into under the retention scheme. The collection, access, and use of location information is not restricted to serious offences (*TIA Act 1979* s 5D). The AFP may access existing historical location information for non-serious offences to enforce the criminal law (*TIA Act 1979* s 178). The Office of the Australian Information Commissioner (OAIC) noted that the powers of the Agencies involve the investigation of minor offences because the Agencies are not prevented from accessing location information in respect of investigating minor offences (OAIC Submission No 92 to the PJCIS 2015: 21). Historical location information can be collected for offences that have a prison sentence of less than 3 years, such as giving false or misleading information, for which the penalty is imprisonment for 12 months (*CCA 1995* s 137.1).[3] The offences include harassment, bribery, cybercrimes and inciting trespassing on agricultural land via a website or social media (AFP 2019, Submission 15: 4-5; *CCA 1995* ss 474.46, 474.47).

The Law Council of Australia highlighted that the case for mandatory data retention has not been made because the access and use of metadata is not limited to national security or serious crime (PJCIS, *Advisory Report* 2015: 38). The Australian Human Rights Commission (AHRC) continues to comment that historical location information access and use should be restricted to serious crimes because the Data Retention Bill 2015 did not make a distinction between serious offences and non-serious offences. The AGD commented that access to location information remains vital in respect of all investigations, whether serious or otherwise as most crimes are apparently facilitated, enabled or carried out via communications technology. The serious crime limitation would impact investigations of crimes the Agencies are able to conduct immeasurably (PJCIS, *Advisory Report* 2015: 246, 248; AHRC Submission 8, 2019). The AGD clarified that telecommunications data is used to across the board in respect of non-serious offences (Evidence to PJCIS 2014: 29 (Clare) and (Harmer)). The AGD claims that excluding non-serious offences would go against its international law obligations under the Cybercrime Convention. On the contrary, the AHRC refutes this claim, stating that Australia's obligations under article 14 of the Budapest Cybercrime Convention apply only to serious offences (AHRC Submission 8, 2019: 12–13 [41]–[44]). The metadata retention regime was originally introduced as government policy to address the threat of terrorism. Once the law was passed it became clear non-serious offences would also be investigated under the retention scheme. The OAIC continues to

---

[3]This compilation includes commenced amendments made by Act No. 59, 2015. Amendments made by Act No. 60, 2015 have not commenced but are noted in the endnotes.

demand that access be limited to serious crime and national security (OAIC 2019, Submission 34).

4.2   The Powers of ASIO

The broad scope of ASIO's function is national 'security'. ASIO's powers are to obtain, correlate and evaluate intelligence relevant to security. ASIO has the power to communicate such intelligence in a manner that is appropriate for security (*ASIO Act* s 17(1)(a), (b), (f)). A simplified process of accessing location information may be described as follows:

> When an individual comes to ASIO's attention, there are a range of methods that can be applied to establish whether that person's activities are relevant to security or not. Requesting historical communication data is often one of the most useful as well as one of the least intrusive methods of establishing those matters of fact. In many cases a simple subscriber check on a phone number is sufficient to determine that there is actually no investigation required and the matter can be put aside. This data that we are talking about is collected lawfully in all cases. I as well as my officers understand the sensitivity of these holdings. The holdings are strictly controlled. They are well managed, and access is highly accountable. In my organisation we strictly adhere to the need-to-know principle, and in addition we have numerous internal accountability mechanisms to ensure the protection of the data.

> We use more intrusive collection methods only where there is a warrant and where it is warranted by the level of threat to Australia's national security. In these cases, ASIO is careful to ensure that the level of intrusion into individual privacy remains proportionate to that threat and in accordance with the guidelines that were provided by the Attorney General. It is not and will not be the case that ASIO automatically requests the maximum amount of data available. Should this bill become law, ASIO will continue to request access to historical communication data needed only for the purpose of carrying out our function, regardless of the length of time that data may be available for. We abide by the law (Evidence to PJCIS 2015: 65 (Edward) cited in PJCIS, *Advisory Report* 2015: 54 [2.43]).

ASIO considers accessing location information as less intrusive than accessing the content. However, the PJCIS accepted that location information is sensitive (PJCIS, *Advisory Report* 2015: 97 [3.92]).[4]

4.2.1   Investigatory Powers and the Powers Performed in Connection with the Functions

Not only does ASIO investigate known threats to security, ASIO also endeavours to identify persons, groups or entities that *may* present future new and unknown risks to security that have not been identified before and as they evolve. ASIO implements

---

[4]See Sect. 6.2 in Chap. 6.

measures or arrangements, as far as reasonably possible, to ensure that the information it relies upon is reliable and accurate. ASIO carries out investigations, which means a concerted series of inquiries in relation to a subject, where the activities may be relevant to security (AGD 2016 ss 3.2, 3.3). The national security function is anticipatory in nature:

Communications data was also used by ASIO to identify new people of interest and leads to further investigations. For example, it showed us who called whom and when (Evidence to PJCIS 2014: 5 (Hartland)).

In carrying out its functions, ASIO must:

a. . . . *undertake inquiries to determine whether a particular subject or activity is relevant to security*;
b. . . . investigate subjects and activities relevant to security;
c. . . . develop and maintain a broad understanding of the security environment; [and]

    . . . analyse and assess information obtained, and . . . provide intelligence and advice to relevant authorities; ASIO's security functions are concerned with protection and are anticipatory in nature. ASIO therefore investigates known threats to security, and endeavours to identify persons groups or entities that may present a risk to security that previously have not been identified

d. collect, maintain, analyse and assess information related to inquiries and investigations;
e. collect and maintain a comprehensive body of reference material to contextualize intelligence derived from inquiries and investigations; and
f. maintain a broad database, based on the above, against which information obtained in relation to a specific inquiry or investigation can be checked and assessed (emphasis added) (AG's Guidelines ss 3.2, 6.1 - 6.2).

The commencement of investigations is based on what is already known about the subject's activities, associations and beliefs, and the extent to which those activities, associations and beliefs are, or are likely to be, relevant or prejudicial to security; the immediacy and severity of the threat to security; the reliability of the sources of the relevant information; and the investigative techniques that are likely to be most effective (AG's Guidelines s 9).

The information may also be relevant to determine that the activities of a subject are *not* relevant to security. Information may be considered relevant to security if it helps to determine a connection or possible connection between a person, group, or entity other than the subject, or a connection or possible connection to activities that are relevant to security (AG's Guidelines s 10.1; AGD Submission No 27, *Inquiry* 2015: 5). The intentions and capabilities of a person or group are also relevant to security. The access to and use of location information is not required to be targeted only at an identified subject or a group of persons. Under the terms of the AG's Guidelines, ASIO may try and identify if a person is of interest to the Agencies (AG's Guidelines ss 6, 10.2). Inquiries and investigations may or may not be targeted. This depends on the request made in a particular case, and the details of the approval granted. Generally, the AG's Guidelines and the requirements support a position that access to the location information is not targeted.

4.2.2   Defining the Term 'Security'

The Agencies investigate matters that are of 'security' interest. 'Security' is defined to include protection from espionage, sabotage, politically motivated violence, acts of foreign interference, and border protection. ASIO conducts inquiries and investigations in respect of 'activities relevant to security' and 'activities prejudicial to security'. The phrase 'activities relevant to security' means 'not only physical acts of the sort specified in the definition of security, but also includes the acts of conspiring, planning, organising, counselling, advising, financing, or otherwise advocating or encouraging the doing of those things'. The phrase 'activities prejudicial to security' means 'activities that are relevant to security and which can reasonably be considered capable of causing damage or harm to Australia, the Australian people, or Australian interests, or to foreign countries to which Australia has responsibilities' (AG's Guidelines, s 3.2 and 3.3; *AFP Act 1979* s 8(1)(b)(3); *ASIO Act 1979* ss 4.1 (a)–(b), 17).

The term 'security' is broad and may include the economic interests of the country. National security means '. . .Australia's defence, security or international relations.' International relations means '. . .political, military and economic relations with foreign governments and international organisations' (*SCIA 2018*).

Also, under the *Assistance and Access Act 2018 (AAA* 2018), in considering whether a Technical Assistance Request (TAR) is reasonable and proportionate the Agencies must have regard to: i.) the interests of national security. The Agencies may therefore collect 'technical information' from social media technology companies, the Telco and ISPs, to safeguard national security and Australia's national economic well-being (*AAA* 2018 ss 317JC (a), (b), (g), (h), 317RA, 317ZAA, 317E (2)(iii), 317G(5); *TIA Act 1979* s 34AAA (2)(vi).

It is clear that the meaning of the term 'security' keeps changing. *AAA* 2018 clearly links the economy and activities that may impact the economy to national security. This blurs the lines between where national security starts and where the economy ends, as these interests are seen as overlapping and inseparable—two sides of the same coin. This creates uncertainty as to how these terms may be interpreted and applied in practice, when it comes to investigating and inquiring into activities that may be considered as related to security, creating potential surveillance risks for various individuals and groups, such as climate change activists and animal rights protesters.

4.2.2.1   The Courts Accept the Broad Definition of 'Security'

Courts have been reluctant to limit the definition of 'national security' and recognised the discretion of the executive branch of government to decide what is in the national interest, to safeguard national security. The courts have generally 'allowed' the government to decide what it considers to be a matter of national security.

The *Farrel court case* rejected the assertion that the term 'security of the Commonwealth' should be confined only to activities of a warlike nature, even if the term is one that fluctuates (*FIA 1982* s 33(a)(i); the *Farrell court case* 16 [49]).

In the *Jaffarie court case* Mr. Jaffarie alleged that the Director-General of ASIO erred in his construction and application of the term 'security'. Mr. Jaffarie challenged the interpretation of the word 'security', arguing that the meaning must be confined (the *Farrell court case* [52], 20 [54]). Honourable Justices Flick and Perram decided against Mr. Jaffarie, (the *Farrell court case* 24 [66], 39 [116]) stating that the Commonwealth legislature is not limited to adopt a confined meaning of the term 'security' (the *Farrell court case* 23 [64], 21 [59]).[5]

The *Jaffarie court case* concluded that a confined meaning of 'security' would be a high bar and frustrate the ability of ASIO to properly monitor and assess threats (*Jaffarie court case* 23–24 [65]).[6] The *Jaffarie court case* notes that Parliament rightfully uses the term security, despite an objection that it may be too broad. The case indicates there was no misuse of power under the guise of 'security'. In respect of collecting location information about the individual, further precaution may need to be taken, given the broad meaning of 'security' and the confidential nature of the investigations of the Agencies. Greater privacy protection, such as a requirement for the prior approval of a third party for access to and the use of location information, may be an appropriate safeguard.

In the *Church of Scientology court case* (60), Mason J stated: '... security is a concept with a fluctuating content, depending very much on circumstances as they exist from time to time'. The meaning of 'security' is not fixed but is unpredictable. Many actions may be seen as a potential threat to security. The courts have refused to limit the meaning of the term 'security', thereby confirming the broad powers of the government to decide what actions qualify as a threat to national security, but with no clear prior guidelines how possibly to take such a decision, when times change. For example, climate change protests qualifies as a national security issue, thereby justifying the collection of location information, without becoming a misuse of power.

The courts are likely to dismiss any challenge that the powers of ASIO to collect location information for security reasons are too broad, given the imprecise and fluctuating meaning of 'security'. The question is how privacy is best protected in these circumstances. The answer clearly does not lie with challenging the broadness of the power based on what the terms 'security', 'activities relevant to security' and 'activities prejudicial to security' mean, and to try and limit their meaning. The answer may lie with how the location information is collected in the first place to enable an investigation and an inquiry into 'activities relevant to security' or 'activities prejudicial to security'. While the AFP requires reasonable suspicion to

---

[5]Also see *RZBV and Director-General of Security and Anor* [2015] AATA 296 (5 May 2015) 7 [17].

[6]The case cited *Suresh v Canada (The Minister of Citizenship and Immigration)* [2002] SCC 1 at [88], [2002] 1 SCR 3, 50–51.

conduct an investigation, ASIO does not. The question is perhaps whether, to justify the interference with privacy, the speculative nature of the inquiries should be limited by also requiring a standard of reasonable suspicion and approval of a third party through the authorisation and notification process under the *CAC Determination 2018* for named and unnamed persons (AG's Guidelines 4.1(a)-(b); *TIA Act 1979* s 6A, 6B).

To collect a person's metadata, the person does not need to have committed a crime. Their actions only need to be relevant to security—that is the test. As long as it is relevant to security, at the discretion of government then the metadata may be collected by the Agencies. The broadness of that term raises concerns about where the limits are, where the oversight is and what the criteria is under which certain types of actions may qualify as posing security risks. Greater clarity and pre-defined criteria and exclusions are needed.

4.2.3 ASIO Still Yields Tremendous Power, Despite the Privacy Safeguards

Privacy is used as a tool to restrict the powers of the Agencies under the data retention and collection scheme. However, the Agencies are simultaneously targeting the private and personal details of the individual. The collection and analysis of location information reveals personal and sensitive information about the individual. The privacy protections are provided for under section 180F of the *TIA Act 1979*. However, the decision to decide how the privacy of the individual is impacted is also left to the discretion of the Agencies. The same Agencies also decide on the activities related to their functions and based on their public safety interests and strategic directions issued by the executive branch of the government (Shanapinda, S.: Advance metadata fair: The retention and disclosure of location information as metadata for law enforcement and national security, and the impact on privacy—An Australian story. Dissertation, Shanapinda (2018: 178, 305). ASIO thus exercises tremendous power over the personal information of people, and with only executive oversight, which is conducted *ex post facto* (Goldman and Rascoff 2016). This is however a clear conflict of interests.[7]

4.2.4 Confidentiality

The Agencies do not disclose the operational use of location information as this is confidential. This lack of transparency about operational matters contributed to the critique of and poor trust in the Agencies because there is no independent

---

[7]See Chap. 6.

mechanism to look at how investigations are being conducted (Evidence to PJCIS 2015: 31 (Leonard).

This lack of transparency is one of the major criticisms about the powers of the Agencies to access and use location information (Bennett and de Koker 2017; Clarke 2016; Hardy and Williams 2014; Williams 2016; Rix 2013; Casanovas Romeu et al. 2017. Bennett and de Koker (2017) and de Koker et al. (2018) raised the negative impact poor transparency has on public trust, arguing that trust be instilled via transparency, thereby leading to public accountability when it comes to algorithmic decision-making. Bennett and de Koker (2017) further argued that secrecy of operational activities should only be maintained if necessary.

The authorisations and notifications issued under the *CAC Determination 2018* to the Telco to collect location information are confidential. It is a criminal offence to inform any third party about the existence, the making or the issuing of an authorisation and notification (*TIA Act 1979* s 181A). Telstra indicated in its privacy policy, that it is not allowed to disclose figures about requests for telecommunications data by ASIO (Telstra 2016). Given the lack of transparency, it is almost impossible for the individual to challenge the actions of ASIO to collect location information from the Telco. In the *Jaffarie court case*, the Federal Court of Australia (FCA) noted that individuals may not always be able to challenge adverse national security assessments of ASIO on merit:

> The existing difficulties confronting those who seek to challenge such assessments, including the inability to seek merits review, and the absence of an ability to invoke the *ADJR Act 1977* (Cth), are well recognised (the *Jaffarie court case* 19 [48]).

Location information may be collected for security assessments before a person can even approach the court for judicial review. At the stage the location information is collected, the person is not able to challenge the interference with their privacy or have another advocate on his or her behalf. The Judge continued:

> Notwithstanding such constraints, the Courts – it is respectfully considered – should be vigilant to ensure that those who exercise power should keep within the limitations of their powers and equally vigilant to ensure the rights of citizens are protected (the *Jaffarie court case* 19 [49]).

When location information is collected, the individual is unaware that a security assessment has been made using his or her location information. ASIO may act on what it considers as necessary, but that is still a subjective judgment made by ASIO where, unlike in this court case, no independent third party can advocate on behalf of the individual or assess whether adequate justification exists for the intrusion. The Federal Court also noted that a certain level of judicial involvement might be needed in respect of national security issues, stating:

> So, too, may considerable attention to detail be directed to reasons provided which affect the liberty of the subject – even in a context where questions of national security are said to be of relevance. The days have long gone when (for example) it was able to be said:
>
> Those who are responsible for the national security must be the sole judges of what the national security requires. It would be obviously undesirable that such matters should be

made the subject of evidence in a Court of law or otherwise discussed in public: *The Zamora* [1916] 2 AC 77 at 107 per Lord Parker.

Although courts remain 'sensitive' to claims being made, it is now accepted that they will not act on 'mere assertions that questions of national security [are] involved': *Council of Civil Service Unions v Minister for the Civil Service* [1985] AC 374 at 420 per Lord Roskill. The imperative to have some degree of judicial supervision is manifest; to preclude judicial supervision would be a 'draconian and dangerous step': *R v Secretary of State for the Home Department; Ex parte Ruddock* [1987] 2 All ER 518 at 526 to 527 ((the *Jaffarie case* 16 [44]).

The Judge stated that ASIO's reasons for the security assessment of Mr. Jaffarie should be 'read with care' (the *Jaffarie court case* 19 [50]). It is not clear how such care should be applied in relation to the privacy of the individual.

The procedures outlined above are very different between ASIO and the AFP, given ASIO's security mandate. ASIO is for example not subject to the *Privacy Act 1988*. ASIO must consider privacy in terms of the AG's Guidelines, which is not a legislative instrument. The rules appear generally flexible in respect of ASIO. This cannot be because of the seriousness of the security mandate, and the national interest to be protected—both Agencies practically have the same power to investigate national 'security' concerns. ASIOs secrecy provisions may work to the benefit of the AFP in their cooperation's. The Agencies may practically 'outsource' to the other, what the other may be more effective at carrying out, based on the transparency disclosure and power dynamic.

4.3   The Likely Impact of 'Security' on Young People Protesting Inaction on Climate Change

Since the Occupy Sydney protests in 2011, in March 2019 young people have taken to the streets, this time to protest climate change, a politically sensitive issue. It seems young people will continue with their protest efforts in the future (ABC 2011, 2019a; Feldman 2019). This is especially so given how scarce natural resources such as fresh drinking water may become and may need to be managed differently, as evidenced by the Mass fish die-off in the Darling River (Hanifie and Isa 2019). Also, in 2010, surveillance concerns were raised about environmental activists who opposed the Victorian desalination plant. In this case the protesters opposed the use of collected photo recordings by the police in future inquiries and investigations, by demanding that the wordings be deleted (Victorian Government 2010). Environmental issues thus keep coming up. They have also taken their views to national television On the QandA TV talk show that aired on the Australian Broadcasting Corporation (ABC) on Monday 15 April 2019, at 9:35pm, climate change and the Adani coal mine were discussed. The Adani coal mine project is a project with great national economic value and therefore of national economic interest, despite its potential negative impact on the environment—it is stated the project will provide much needed jobs in Queensland, and for this reason the project must go ahead. This is because a project such as this, is said to be '. . .about securing Australia's future' (ABC 2019b). Senator James McGrath, Liberal Senator, in his official capacity as Senator, highlighted the Adani project as being of national security interest because of its economic significance. Below is an extract from the show:

ETHAN MOLDRICH

Thanks, Virginia. My question is to Senator McGrath. Does the LNP have a plan to win over **Liberal-minded young people who oppose Adani** and offshore detention, but support the Coalition's economic plan? Or is the LNP ceding these votes to other parties this election?

LARISSA WATERS

Great question.

JAMES McGRATH

In terms of what the Liberal National Party, in terms of our pledge and our manifestos and **our values that we're taking to the coming election is based on what Scott Morrison, as the leader of the Liberal Party, and Michael McCormack, as leader of the National Party, are talking about, and that's about a stronger future, and it's about securing Australia's future.** That's why we've got a range of tax cuts, that's why we've got a range of...of **infrastructure projects coming to Queensland**.

In terms of **Adani**, you've heard me answer that question before in terms of that **I'll always support jobs, especially in regional Queensland.** And I think it is wrong to use Adani as... which the panel has already sort of sussed, as an exemplar, in terms of other issues. **Adani** is a project that will deliver to parts of Queensland that don't have the wonderfulness of Brisbane and, say, the Sunshine Coast and the Gold Coast. **It will deliver jobs to disadvantaged communities**.

VIRGINIA TRIOLI

James, I'm just going to jump in, because the question actually... The questioner said **Adani is something that he opposes**, so you're not going to be able to persuade him tonight.

JAMES McGRATH

I know. What I'm trying to do... And what I'm trying to do is say that...that **Adani's actually more than just a coalmine. It's about helping people get on.** And for **those who are liberally minded, the best way, I think, you can help people get on with life is actually having a job**, in terms of **helping breaking that welfare cycle** (emphasis added) (ABC 2019b).

The gist of the extract is that the questioner opposes the Adani coal mine project, demonstrating his political activity and liber-minded ideology, as is normal in a free and democratic society. However, the project is politically seen as a national security issue. The question is what this legally means with regards to the possible collection and use of the location information and other metadata of the caller, that opposes a project that is politically seen as being of national economic interest.

The Greens political party also opposes the construction of Adani, lobbying that it be stopped altogether (Greens Queensland 2019).

4.3.1   The Greens Political Party Activities Are Described As a National Security and Economic Threat to Australia

Senator McGrath stated:

> ...our [the Liberal Party] values that we're taking to the coming election is based on what Scott Morrison, as the leader of the Liberal Party, and Michael McCormack, as leader of the National Party, are talking about, and that's about a stronger future, and it's about securing Australia's future (ABC 2019b).

In May 2019, as leader of the Liberal Party and as the Prime Minister, Mr. Morrison seems to have suggested that these protest activities are an issue of national security. Mr. Scott Morrison warned that the Greens political party are a threat to economic and national security, by opposing the Adani coal mine project. It must be noted that these statements were recorded on the 11th of May 2019, a mere 4 days after the early release of the Lowy Institute Poll, before the election. The polls preferred the Liberal-National Coalition over the Labor party in relation to maintaining the alliance with the United States and in regard to national security. The poll was conducted between 12 and 25 March 2019 (Kassam 2019).[8]

In clear response to the polling results, the news reports quoted Mr. Morrison as saying:

> The Greens represent the greatest **threat (to the economy and national security)**, and the Labor Party only moves closer and closer and closer to the Greens, (National Tribune 2019)

And,

> It's **infesting their economic policy**, it's **infesting their national security outlook**. (National Tribune 2019)

And,

> ...a **danger to the economy** and they are **a danger to national security** ... I think that is a fairly unremarkable statement, (National Tribune 2019)

And,

> **"They want to abolish the US -alliance and remove every area of co-operation**. The Greens' agenda has only **become more extreme**, particularly over this last term. They are more **unabashed** when it comes to **activism**," he said.' (National Tribune 2019)

And,

> '... the **Greens policies pose a clear and present danger to the Australian economy'** (National Tribune 2019).

And,

> Mr. Morrison told The Weekend Australian that it was **weakening Australia's investment future when activists turned any mine into a totemic campaign against all mining and industry** (emphasis added) (National Tribune 2019).

---

[8]See Sects. 5.1.2.2.1 to 5.1.2.2.3.1 in Chap. 5.

The statement about abolishing the US-alliance is about Australia's international relations, which is included in the definition of security (*SCIA 2018*).

In terms of the court decisions discussed earlier, the political statements of the Senator and the Prime Minister are legally acceptable statements—opposing the Adani coal mine and protesting against it, on climate change or ideological bases, may therefore legally be categorised by the government as posing a threat to national security, if the government wanted to, because of its economic and job creation value.

To bring about water policy reform climate change protests and demonstrations by tech-savvy and 'environmentally-woke' young people may be needed, thereby putting themselves at risk with security authorities given the political statements that equate climate change protests to national security threats.

4.3.2   Tech-Savvy and Politically Active Young People As Potential Targets of the Data Retention and Disclosure Scheme

Young people use more mobile services whereas seniors use more fixed line telephone services, which services are declining. These use patterns indicate that young people are more mobile. Mobility means that their locations are tracked. Given the differences in the usage patterns between fixed and mobile services, it means that young people, their location information, habits, profiles and personal information are more at risk of being collected, stored and revealed to ASIO and the AFP than those of senior citizens. This, while younger people are showing signs of political activism. This means young people are more at risk simply because they are digital natives, born into the digital age and in an age where fixed-line communications are less popular and foreign to them. The younger generation is therefore put at greater risks by the metadata retention and disclosure regime, simply for using mobile communications that seems 'natural' and obvious to them. It is not simply that they choose to, but because of the ubiquity of mobile communications that is entrenched in everyday living—banking, shopping, ordering meals, travel, dating, spending time with friends and family. Just doing these obvious day-to-day activities that young people take for granted and that have become their way of life may expose them to dragnet surveillance. The question is how free young people are to use mobile communications if they are faced with the risk of surveillance—and have their locations tracked and profiled—versus not living their daily normal life's for fear of being tracked and exposed. These risks get bigger as young people show signs of political activism and use social media applications like WhatsApp and Telegram, and other online communities to discuss climate change, organise protests and marches. Young people are becoming 'environmentally-woke' because they see how climate change will impact their generation. They therefore demand urgent action to start rolling back the effects of climate change.

Australian young people are therefore likely to be discriminately impacted by Australia's surveillance laws, simply because they are politically active and tech-savvy. The statements by the Prime Minister risk equating political activity and the freedom of expression by opposing a mining project on the basis of climate change, as being a threat to national security. As per the above court decisions, describing a protest action as a threat to national security is possibly in the remit of the government. As such, under the law enforcement and national security laws, the activities of the young people and an opposition political party, does theoretically qualify as 'activities relevant to security' (AG's Guidelines 2016: 4.1(a)) or 'activities prejudicial to security', because 'they pose a clear and present danger to the Australian economy' (AG's Guidelines 2016: 4.1(b)). Online chats about climate change related to the Adani coal mine would therefore qualify as being of interest to the Australian Defence Force (ADF), ASIO and the AFP. This is because projects such as the Adani coal mine are politically, and therefore may legally, be considered a national security issue given its economic significance. It will have a chilling effect on young people that intend on participating fully in political activities, especially about the environment, for which they demonstrate such passion. In 2016, the AFP announced plans to harvest online location data from social media platforms, as open source intelligence (Shanapinda 2016). Online discussions about protests may then be collected by the Agencies to inquire into.

The political statements that equate the right to protests climate change and youth activism the national security threats potentially have the impact of intimidating the political opposition and young people to exercise their political rights. This has a chilling effect on free speech, the right to protests and to express different political views by political parties, counter to what should be the norm in a democratic society and under Australia's international civil and political right obligations such as those under the International Covenant on Civil and Political Rights (ICCPR). It is therefore no surprise that the head of ASIO, Duncan Lewis, asked politicians to tone down on the rhetoric so as not to ostracise the Muslim community and threaten their cooperative relationship with ASIO (PlayerFM 2019).

There are no public reports about the collection of young people's 'metadata' or location information, or those of political parties opposed to the policies of the government. This book does not imply that this has occurred. The book simply argues that the actions of young people, that are frequent users of mobile technologies and who are passionate about protesting climate change inaction, are the likely targets of the metadata retention and disclosure regime, given the rhetoric. This is concerning despite the fact that the Agencies are obliged to prevent undue influence, there is no clear publicly available guideline on how government may refer matters to the Agencies to investigate and inquire into. The rhetoric flags and identifies the protesters as potential individuals and groups of interest to the Agencies. The actions of these young people and of the political parties are branded as threats to national and economic security. As a result, under these surveillance laws, the metadata of young people and political opponents may be lawfully collected and used, without a judicial warrant. as independent oversight. If those actions were to happen, in future, and were challenged in court, the courts are likely to rule that the exercise of those powers are lawful, despite the lack of independent oversight at the time of collection and use of the metadata of young people and political opponents. The other question is what guidelines the government would use to make such a decision, if it wanted to make that decision. The political rhetoric sets a dangerous trend and clears the way for a legal basis to potentially inquire into and investigate the actions of politically and tech-savvy young people and opposition political parties under the metadata retention and disclosure scheme, and with no prior judicial oversight. The question is whether the collection and use of the location information of these groups, as matters of national security—if it were to happen under the current laws—would be considered as ok and acceptable to the community at large. This book argues that there must be clear independent oversight guidelines, that are outward looking, under which such surveillance activity may be undertaken in a manner that is more transparent and the rules are clearer, in terms of the legitimate privacy expectations of the public, balanced against national interests, in a democratic society.

4.4   Conclusion

ASIO may either access historical or prospective location information, for both serious and non-serious offences. The AFP may also access existing location information for non-serious offences, to enforce the criminal law. The Agencies have the power to identify persons that were not previously on the security 'radar' on the basis of the broad security interests, defined in the sole discretion of the government of the day. The Agencies are reliant on the telecommunications data, but their self-certification of access and use raises privacy concerns. Whether ASIO properly balances privacy and public safety interests is not and cannot be known, as the process lacks transparency. Given the demands for changes to the climate change agenda, young people who are politically and technologically savvy, planning civil disobedience protests, are potentially at risk of their location information being targeted in the name of 'security'.

References

Australian Broadcasting Corporation (ABC) (October 24 2011) Despite arrests, Occupy protesters won't give up. https://www.abc.net.au/news/2011-10-24/occupy-protesters-vow-to-continue/3597178. Accessed 3 Sept 2019

ABC (March 16 2019a) Climate change strikes across Australia see student protesters defy calls to stay in school. https://www.abc.net.au/news/2019-03-15/students-walk-out-of-class-to-protest-climate-change/10901978. Accessed 3 Sept 2019

ABC (2019b) Election 2019: the battle for Queensland. Broadcast: Monday 15 April 2019, 9:35pm. https://www.abc.net.au/qanda/2019-15-04/10988470. Accessed 3 Sept 2019

Administrative Decisions (Judicial Review) Act 1977 (Cth) (*ADJR Act 1977*)

Attorney-General's Department (AGD) (2015) Submission No 27 to the Parliamentary Joint Committee on Intelligence and Security, Inquiry into the Telecommunications (Interception and Access) Amendment (Data Retention) Bill 2014, 16 January 2015

AGD (2016) Attorney-General's Guidelines in relation to the performance by the Australian Security Intelligence Organisation of its function of obtaining, correlating, evaluating and communicating intelligence relevant to security (including politically motivated violence), 2016 (Attorney-General's [AG's] Guidelines)

Australian Federal Police (AFP), Submission 15 to the Parliamentary Joint Committee on Intelligence and Security, Review of the mandatory data retention regime, 2019

Australian Federal Police Act 1979 (Cth) (*AFP Act 1979*)

Australian Human Rights Commission (AHRC), Submission 8, to the Parliamentary Joint Committee on Intelligence and Security, Review of the mandatory data retention regime, 2019

Australian Security Intelligence Organisation Act 1979 (Cth) (*ASIO Act 1979*)

Bennett ML, de Koker L (2017) Open secrets: balancing operational secrecy and transparency in the collection and use of data for national security and law enforcement agencies. Melb Univ Law Rev 41(2):530. http://classic.austlii.edu.au/au/journals/MelbULawRw/2017/32.html

Casanovas Romeu P, de Koker L, Mendelson D, Watts D (2017) Regulation of big data: perspectives on strategy, policy, law, and privacy. Health Technol 7:335–349

Church of Scientology Inc v Woodward [1982] HCA 78; (1982) 154 CLR 25

Clarke R (2016) Privacy impact assessments as a control mechanism for Australian national security initiatives. Comp Law Secur Rev 32:403–418

Communications Access Coordinator's (CAC) Telecommunications (Interception and Access) (Requirements for Authorisations, Notifications and Revocations) Determination 2015 (Cth) (at 9 October 2015) (*CAC Determination 2015*)

Council of Civil Service Unions v Minister for the Civil Service [1985] AC 374

Crimes Act 1914 (Cth)

Criminal Code Act 1995 (Cth) (*CCA 1995*)

de Koker L, Chan J, Mendelson D, Bennett Moses L, Maurushat A, Vaile D, Gaffney M, Sadler G, Grierson P, Cater D (June 2018) Australia report. Big data technology and national security. Comparative international perspectives on strategy, policy and law. Law and Policy Program. Data to Decisions Cooperative Research Centre. https://uploads-ssl.webflow.com/5cd23e823ab9b1f01f815a54/5cff12f563db55c367e6c7ca_Big%20Data%20Technology%20and%20National%20Security%2C%20Comparative%20International%20Perspectives%20on%20Strategy%2C%20Policy%20and%20Law%20-%20AUSTRALIA%20REPORT.pdf

Evidence to Parliamentary Joint Committee on Intelligence and Security (PJCIS), Parliament of Australia, Canberra, 30 January 2015, 65 (Lewis Duncan Edward, Director-General of Security, Australian Security Intelligence Organisation) cited in Parliamentary Joint Committee on Intelligence and Security, Parliament of Australia, Advisory Report on the Telecommunications (Interception and Access) Amendment (Data Retention) Bill 2014 (Cth) 2015

Evidence to Parliamentary Joint Committee on Intelligence and Security, Parliament of Australia, Canberra, 30 January 2015, 31 (Peter Leonard Guildford, Chairperson of the Media and Communications Committee, Business Law Section of the Law Council of Australia)

Evidence to Parliamentary Joint Committee on Intelligence and Security, Parliament of Australia, Canberra, 17 December 2014, 3 (Andrew Colvin, Commissioner, Australian Federal Police)

Evidence to Parliamentary Joint Committee on Intelligence and Security, Parliament of Australia, Canberra, 17 December 2014, 17 (Kerri Hartland, Acting Director-General, ASIO)

Evidence to Parliamentary Joint Committee on Intelligence and Security, Parliament of Australia, Canberra, 17 December 2014, 29 (Jason Clare, Member of the PJCIS)

Evidence to Parliamentary Joint Committee on Intelligence and Security, Parliament of Australia, Canberra, 17 December 2014, 29 (Anna Harmer, Acting First Assistant Secretary, Attorney-General's Department)

Explanatory Memorandum (2019) Criminal Code Amendment (Agricultural Protection) Bill 2019

Farrell; Secretary, Department of Immigration and Border Protection (Freedom of information) [2017] AATA 409 (31 March 2017)

Feldman H (May 2 2019) Young people won't accept inaction on climate change, and they'll be voting in droves. *The Conversation.* https://theconversation.com/young-people-wont-accept-inaction-on-climate-change-and-theyll-be-voting-in-droves-116361. Accessed 3 Sept 2019

Freedom of Information Act 1982 (Cth) (*FIA 1982*)

Goldman ZK, Rascoff SJ (eds) (2016) Executive oversight of intelligence agencies in Australia. Global intelligence oversight: governing security in the twenty-first century. Keiran H, and Williams G. UNSW Law Research Paper No. 2016–35 (7 June 2016). https://ssrn.com/abstract=2804835. Accessed 27 Aug 2019

Greens Queensland, The (2019) The Plan to Stop Adani. https://greens.org.au/qld/platform/plan-to-stop-adani. Accessed 3 Sept 2019

Hanifie S, Isa N (January 15 2019) Mass fish die-off in Darling River could impact fish numbers in other states. https://www.abc.net.au/news/2019-01-15/mass-fish-kill-in-darling-river-to-impact-other-states/10715640. Accessed 3 Sept 2019

Hardy K, Williams G (2014) National security reforms stage one: intelligence gathering and secrecy. Law Soc NSW J 6(November):68. https://search.informit.com.au/fullText; dn=20151952;res=AGISPT

Jaffarie v Director General of Security [2014] FCAFC 102 (18 August 2014)

Kassam K (May 07 2019) Polling. Press Release - 2019 Lowy Institute Polling: Australian Attitudes Towards Foreign Policy Issues Ahead of the 2019 Federal Election. https://www.lowyinstitute.org/publications/press-release-2019-lowy-institute-polling-australian-attitudes-towards-foreign-policy. Accessed 16 Sept 2019

Keenan M (12 May 2014) Ministerial Direction. https://www.afp.gov.au/about-us/governance-and-accountability/ministerial-direction. Accessed 27 Aug 2019

National Tribune (May 11 2019) PM Politics. Greens 'a greater threat than Palmer'. https://www.nationaltribune.com.au/greens-a-greater-threat-than-palmer-pm/. Accessed 3 Sept 2019

Office of Australian Information Commissioner (OAIC), Submission No 92 to the Parliamentary Joint Committee on Intelligence and Security, to Inquiry into the Telecommunications (Interception and Access) Amendment (Data Retention) Bill 2014, January 2015

OAIC (2015) Australian privacy principles guidelines chapter B: key concepts', Version 1.2 ed., vol B

OAIC (2019) Submission 34 to the Parliamentary Joint Committee on Intelligence and Security, Review of the mandatory data retention regime, July 2019

Parliamentary Joint Committee on Intelligence and Security (PJCIS) (2015) Advisory Report on the Telecommunications (Interception and Access) Amendment (Data Retention) Bill 2014', (February 2015)

Privacy Act 1988 (Cth)

PlayerFM (2019) An address by ASIO Director-General Duncan Lewis. 11 days ago 1:00:02. https://player.fm/series/the-lowy-institute-live-events/an-address-by-asio-director-general-duncan-lewis. Accessed 16 Sept 2019

Revised Explanatory Memorandum, Telecommunications (Interception and Access) Amendment (Data Retention) Bill 2015 (Cth), 2015

Rix M (2013) Security without secrecy? Counter-terrorism, ASIO and access to information. In: Baldino D (eds) Spooked: the truth about intelligence in Australia, 2013, pp 240–263, 240

R v Secretary of State for the Home Department; Ex parte Ruddock [1987] 2 All ER 518

RZBV and Director-General of Security and Anor [2015] AATA 296 (5 May 2015)

Security of Critical Infrastructure Act 2018 (Cth) (*SCIA 2018*)

Shanapinda S (2016) The types of telecommunications device identification and location approximation metadata: under Australia's warrantless mandatory metadata retention and disclosure laws'. Commun Law Bull 35(3):17–19. http://www.camla.org.au/communications-law-bulletin/. Accessed 23 July 2017

Shanapinda S (2018) Advance metadata fair: the retention and disclosure of location information as metadata for law enforcement and national security, and the impact on privacy-an Australian story. Dissertation, UNSW Sydney

Suresh v Canada (The Minister of Citizenship and Immigration) [2002] SCC 1 at [88], [2002] 1 SCR

Telecommunications (Interception and Access) Amendment (Data Retention) Bill 2015 (Cth)

Telecommunications (Interceptions and Access) (Requirements for Authorisations, Notifications and Revocations) Determination 2018 (Cth) (at 20 November 2018) (*CAC Determination 2018*)

Telecommunications (Interception and Access) Act 1979 (Cth) (*TIA Act 1979*)

Telecommunications and Other Legislation Amendment (Assistance and Access) Act 2018 (AAA 2018)

Telstra (2016) Privacy. https://www.telstra.com.au/privacy/transparency#top. Accessed 4 June 2016

The Zamora [1916] 2 AC

Victorian Government (2010) Inquiry into arrangements for security and security information gathering for state government construction projects. Final report of the Victorian Parliament Law Reform Committee. October 2010. Authority Victorian Government Printer Parliamentary Paper No. 394, Session 2006-2010. https://www.parliament.vic.gov.au/papers/govpub/ VPARL2006-10No394.pdf. Accessed 3 Sept 2019

Williams G (2016) The legal assault on Australian democracy. QUT Law Rev 16(2):19

Chapter 5
Limits to the Powers of the Agencies to Collect and Use Location Information

5.1 Privacy as a Limit to the Powers of the AFP

The AFP is legally required to consider privacy when making authorisations and issuing notifications under the *CAC Determination 2018* to collect location information.

5.1.1 Increased Privacy Protections

Section 180F of the *TIA Act 1979* specifically requires the AFP to consider privacy. The section was introduced in 2012.[1] The 2012 wording read:[2]

> Before making an authorisation under Division 4 or 4A[3] in relation to the disclosure or use of information or documents, the authorised officer considering making the authorisation *must have regard to whether any* interference with the privacy of any person or persons that may result from the disclosure or use is justifiable, having regard to the following matters:
>
> (a) the likely relevance and usefulness of the information or documents;
> (b) the reason why the disclosure or use concerned is proposed to be authorised (emphasis added) (*CLAA 2012* (Cth) 2012 s 180F).

In 2015, when the telecommunications data retention regime was introduced, the words: 'have regard to whether any interference with the privacy of any person or persons that may result from the disclosure or use is justifiable' (*CLAA 2012* s 180F)

---

[1] The *Cybercrime Legislation Amendment Act 2012* (Cth) was made to implement the Council of Europe *Convention on Cybercrime*. It was assented to 12 September 2012.

[2] The parts underlined have been deleted in 2015.

[3] Division 4 or 4A refers to the disclosure of metadata that is retained under section 187AA of the *TIA Act 1979*.

© Springer Nature Switzerland AG 2020
S. Shanapinda, *Advance Metadata Fair*, Law, Governance and Technology Series
44, https://doi.org/10.1007/978-3-030-50255-3_5

were deleted. These words were subsequently substituted with the words: '... be satisfied on reasonable grounds that any interference with the privacy of any person or persons that may result from the disclosure or use is justifiable and proportionate' (*CLAA 2012* s 180F). The April 2015 wording reads:[4]

> Before making an authorisation under Division 4 or 4A in relation to the disclosure or use of information or documents, the authorised officer considering making the authorisation must [*be satisfied on reasonable grounds that*] any interference with the privacy of any person or persons that may result from the disclosure or use is justifiable [*and proportionate*], having regard to the following matters:
>
> [(aa) *the gravity of any conduct in relation to which the authorisation is sought, including:*
>
> (i) *the seriousness of any offence in relation to which the authorisation is sought*; and
>
> ...]
>
> (a) the likely relevance and usefulness of the information or documents;
> (b) the reason why the disclosure or use concerned is proposed to be authorised (emphasis added) (*TIA Act 1979* s 180F).

To be satisfied on 'reasonable grounds' that the interference is 'justifiable and proportionate', is a higher standard to meet than the standard that requires the AFP to 'have regard to whether the interference is justifiable'. This standard applies to the collection of historical and prospective location information (*CAC Determination 2018* ss 8–12).

No longer must the interference to privacy only be justifiable, but it must be proportionate as well. Inserting the words '...be satisfied on reasonable grounds ...' and '...proportionate ...' in section 180F *TIA Act 1979* and confirming this in the *CAC Determination 2018* strengthened the privacy protections to be complied with (*CAC Determination 2018* ss 10, 12). These words introduced the objective test and introduced the concept of proportionality between the offence and the interference with privacy (Selvadurai 2017, p. 36; AFP 2015, p. 2). The question is how the higher standard is applied in practice after 2015, compared to before.

5.1.2   The Privacy Tests

Privacy is a tool used to limit the collection, access and use of location information. The AFP must comply with the 'Privacy Tests' prior to authorising the disclosure of location information. The 'Privacy Tests' applicable to the AFP are:

a. the 'Justifiable and Proportionate Privacy Test'
   (*TIA Act 1979* s 180F);
b. the 'Reasonable and Proportionate Privacy Tests'
   (*AAA 2018* ss 317JC (a), (b), (g), (h), 317RA; 317ZAA); and

---

[4]The italic parts in brackets were inserted in 2015.

c. the 'Reasonably Necessary or Directly Related Tests'
   (*TIA Act 1979* ss 177(1), 178(3), 179(3), 180(4); *Privacy Act 1988* (Cth)
   Schedule 1 Part 2 s 3).

5.1.2.1   The Justifiable and Proportionate Privacy Test

Before making an authorisation in relation to the disclosure or use of the location information, the AFP must be satisfied, on 'reasonable grounds', that any interference with the privacy of any person or persons that may result from the disclosure or use is 'justifiable and proportionate'. Privacy is not an absolute right—it has limits, but if privacy is interfered with, the interference must simultaneously be 'justifiable and proportionate' (Selvadurai 2017; *TIA Act 1979* s 180F; *CAC Determination 2018* ss 10, 12).

5.1.2.2   The Reasonable and Proportionate Privacy Tests

Under the *Telecommunications and Other Legislation Amendment (Assistance and Access) Act 2018 (AAA 2018),* the Agencies may issue a Technical Assistance Request (TAR), Technical Assistance Notice (TAN) and a Technical Capability Notice (TCN) to collect technical information from the Telco and the SMP. These requests must be reasonable and proportionate, considering aspects of national and economic security (*AAA 2018* ss 317JAA, 317JA, 317JB, 317JC, 317P, 317V, 317X, 317XA, 317Y, 317ZAA).[5]

Considering the Legitimate Expectations Relating to Privacy
and Cybersecurity

In considering whether a TAR, TAN and TCN are reasonable and proportionate the Agencies must have regard to whether the requests are necessary (*AAA 2018* ss 317JC (a), (b), (g), (h), 317RA; 317ZAA). To determine whether the requests are necessary, the Agencies must also consider the availability of other means to achieve the objectives of the notice, amongst other interests (AAA 2018 ss 317JC (c), 317RA (c); 317ZAA(c)). If no other means exists to enforce the laws, the requests may then be considered as being necessary.

---

[5]See sections 317JC and 317RA about what it means for the request to be 'reasonable and proportionate'.

Considering the Legitimate Expectations Relating to Privacy
and Cybersecurity

The requests for assistance must be reasonable and proportionate. That means the Agencies must consider the 'legitimate expectations of the Australian community relating to privacy and cybersecurity' (*AAA 2018* ss 317JC (a), (b), (g), (h), 317RA; 317ZAA; Revised Explanatory Memorandum 2018). This however does not mean that privacy can be used as a shield against unearthing a crime. It instead relates to maintaining personal privacy in general—it is about protecting the individuals private life (DoH 2019, p. 5).

Determining what the legitimate expectations are, as they relate to privacy and cybersecurity, is a process that is guided by the resolutions of Parliament that puts limits on the powers of the Agencies—the extent to which the individual's private life can be interfered with (DoH 2019, p. 5).

These limits create the legal requirements the Agencies must comply with before collecting the technical information by means of the TAR, TAN and TCN. The Agencies may then justify their operational investigatory, inquiry activities and decisions based on having considered these expectations. The TAR, TCN and TAN process is what constitute such procedural limits by which privacy may be interfered with. The public can legitimately expect that the TAR, TAN, TCN and TAN procedures are followed. The legal requirement that the requests for assistance must be reasonable and proportionate may be referred to as the 'Reasonable and Proportionate Privacy Tests'.

The legitimate expectations principle is specifically referred to in regard to the Privacy Tests under the *AAA 1979* as per a law made by Parliament. As such, the legitimate expectations doctrine, as contained in the Reasonable and Proportionate Privacy Tests, under the broader Privacy Tests that the Agencies must comply with, is specifically applicable to, and only under statutory law, to the collection of technical information from the Designated Communications Provider (DCP), when using the TAR, TAN and TCN processes.

Practically, applying the legitimate expectations doctrine means the relevant decision-maker in the given Agency or the Attorney-General, before deciding to collect technical information from the DCP, owes a procedural fairness duty to the DCP and indirectly to the affected individual. The legal duty is for the Agencies to consider the legitimate expectations of the Australian community relating to privacy and cybersecurity before exercising the discretionary decision to collect the technical information.

This statutory recognition of the legitimate expectations doctrine appears to somewhat be an acceptance of the principle, under Australian statutory law, and in the context of privacy and cybersecurity. Previously court cases considered the doctrine in the context of migration. The latest court case where the doctrine was raised, stated that it would not be helpful to discuss the doctrine (*the WZARH court case [30]*). The *WZARH court case* instead took the view that the core principle is that administrative decision-makers must grant procedural fairness to those that are affected by their decisions. Moreover, what is required in order to ensure that the decision is made fairly and in the circumstances is to look to the legal framework within which the decision must be made (*the WZARH court case [30]*). The question for any person whose privacy may be impacted by a technical information request is then whether the Agencies followed the procedures outlined in the TAR, TAN or TCN, as reflected by the Reasonable and Proportionate Privacy Tests. The decision-maker has the duty to demonstrate that the request for and the collection of the technical information was reasonable and proportionate. The Agencies must give a written copy of the TAN, TAR to the DCP (*AAA 2018* s 317L, 317M (3) and (4)). The notice must also be given to the Inspector-General of Intelligence and Security (IGIS) (*AAA 2018* s 317MAB). It is not clear whether the contents of the notice must include statements about the assessment of the legitimate expectations of the Australian community relating to privacy and cybersecurity, and the extent to which the Agencies have practically considered these expectations, in order to demonstrate their compliance with the duty to the DCP and the individual whose privacy has been affected by the decision to collect the technical information. The procedural fairness doctrine would generally operate where the duty is exercised and the person affected by the decision, to whom the duty is owed, has knowledge about the exercise or the non-exercise of the duty. The person would then be able to lodge a complaint claiming the duty was not exercised as legitimately expected. In this instance, the DCP is informed that it has the right to complain to IGIS and has a copy of the notice (*AAA 2018* s 317MAA). The DCP is also consulted about the requests and the notices and a report is issued on the assessment about the extent to which the DCP may assist (*AAA 2018* s 317PA, 317YA). All these are requirements that create legitimate expectations for the benefit of the Telco and the SMP, to be complied with by the Agencies, based on procedural fairness.

There is however a limitation to the doctrine's statutory introduction—it has limited applicability. The doctrine only operates to establish a benefit in respect of the Telco and the SMP, and practically none for the ordinary citizen. As regards the individual whose location information and telecommunications data are collected, the core principle of the doctrine of legitimate expectations, as provided for under the common law would apply—that is to say that the Agencies must grant procedural fairness to the individual affected by the decision to collect technical information according to the *WZARH court case*. The principle is applicable under the *TIA Act 1979* as well as the *AAA 2018*. The affected individual can therefore legitimately expect that the Privacy Tests, the Reasonable and Proportionate Privacy Tests and the Connection Tests would be applied, because legitimate expectations are at their core about procedural fairness. As such, administrative decision-makers must grant procedural fairness to those affected by their decisions, who are the persons to whom the procedural fairness is owed to (*the WZARH court case [30]*; *the Kioa court case*). As far as it concerns the inclusion of the doctrine under the *AAA* 2018, it would only apply to the Telco and the SMP. In instances were any of the requirements under the Privacy Tests are not met, as highlighted by the concerns of IGIS and the

Commonwealth Ombudsman,[6] the legitimate expectations of the public may have been breached and such a fault on the part of the Agencies may not be procedurally fair. The practical effect or practical injustice is that the individual's privacy has been interfered with—decisions would have been made collecting personal and sensitive information about the person and thereby impacting their privacy; decisions would have been about investigating the person; about prosecuting the person; obtaining an interception warrant. In all instances it is based on the facts, as a defect that occurred as a result of the expected procedures not being followed, resulting in unfairness (*the WZARH court case [58]*; Moss 2015). The question is whether individual may under the common law, complain that they were not afforded procedural fairness, by lodging an application in favour of judicial review. However, there is unfairness at play here. The individual has no legitimate expectation that they will be notified and consulted and is not able to lodge a complaint to IGIS, the Commonwealth Ombudsman or for judicial review. Moreover, decisions by the Agencies under the *AAA 2018* and the *TIA Act 1979* are not reviewable as administrative decisions under judicial review legislation (*ADJR Act 1977* Schedule 1 s 3 (daaaa)). For the individual that is of interest to the Agencies or under investigation, there is therefore nothing practically to expect in a court of law, let alone anything legitimate. The individual whose privacy is impacted is not protected in a court of law. The individual is not notified, does not obtain copies of the notices and is not able to complain to IGIS or the Commonwealth Ombudsman either. At the end of the day, the affected individual is owed a procedural duty when both location information and technical information is collected and has an expectation that such procedures will be complied with, even though the individual does not have an avenue to raise any concerns of procedural unfairness. The procedural duty owed to assess the legitimate expectations of the public via public reporting and opinion polling is a duty that is owed to the Telco and the SMP, when deciding to collect technical information, even if it is about the privacy of the affected individual. The DCP may lodge a complaint and has copies of the relevant documents to assess the procedural compliance or the failure to comply, of the Agencies. If the DCPs are concerned about individual privacy, they may raise concerns about how procedures are flawed, for the indirect benefit of and in the interest of the affected individual. The individual may perhaps raise that there is an indirect duty owed—that in all instances, the Agencies must demonstrate, and to the individual as well, that the legitimate expectations were considered, but this is simply likely to be theoretical when it comes to judicial review proceedings and oversight by public bodies such as IGIS.

The doctrine and its accompanying principle however may have impact within the internal workings of the Agencies. The Agencies have a legal duty to comply with the Privacy Tests, the Reasonable and Proportionate Privacy Tests, and the Connection Tests procedures under the telecommunications retention and disclosure scheme and owe that duty to the affected individual and perhaps indirectly to the Telco. The Agencies also owe the Telco and the SMP, jointly referred to as the DCP,

---

[6]See Sects. 7.3.3, 7.4.2 and 7.11 in Chap. 7.

the procedural duty to consider the legitimate expectations of the Australian community, when collecting technical information. In the latter, the individual is perhaps owed the duty indirectly. The Agencies will see to it that they comply with these procedural duties, under their own internal processes. However, as the Commonwealth Ombudsman and IGIS reported, it is not always that the Agencies comply with similar procedural duties. Given this lack of compliance, the affected individual should be afforded the opportunity and the avenue to challenge this non-compliance, based on the expectation they have that the Agencies would follow the procedures. However, this principle can only be enforced under a court of law, under judicial review. Given that judicial review is not available to the affected individual, there is no way the individual can enforce the legitimate expectation that they possess under the common law, in a court of law, on the basis of the doctrine. These circumstances where all avenues are closed to enforce the legal duties owed to the individual, does not adequately protect privacy.

The metadata retention and disclosure framework and the technical information disclosure scheme are both confidential and non-transparent to the individual concerned. Given that inquiries and investigations are confidential, there is little to no chance of such a complaint being raised to enforce the legitimate expectations of the public about ensuring that the outlined process by which their privacy may be restricted have indeed been followed, especially given the serious issue of privacy and the risk of a legal penalty. All individuals whose metadata was collected and who were subjects of inquiries and investigations, were the non-compliance of the law was raised by the oversight bodies, must, as a matter of natural law, be owed the legal remedy of review.[7] It is only right that affected individuals be afforded such an opportunity. Under these circumstances, Australia cannot be said to adequately protect privacy under the metadata retention and disclosure laws and the technical information disclosure framework, if outlined procedures such as the requirement to obtain a Journalist Information Warrant (JIW) are not followed, despite expectations by journalist and whistle-blowers that these procedures should be followed. In that instance, the individuals were not granted procedural fairness, because they legitimately expect, as a matter of natural law, that the JIW process should be adhered to, but that decision is not subject to judicial review in any event.

Given the that the person is not required to be informed about the collection of their metadata, under both the *AAA 2018* and the *TIA Act 1979*, as per the process described in the *CAC Determination 2018*, that their legitimate expectations to privacy and cybersecurity have been considered; that the Privacy Tests have been complied with; that the JIW process was complied with; that only the metadata that is reasonable and proportionate has been collected and used, there is no procedural fairness principle to speak of. The Commonwealth Ombudsman stated that it is not able to verify how privacy requirements are practically applied (Commonwealth Ombudsman 2018, p. 10). This is an indication of how poorly privacy is protected—given how revealing metadata is and the unrestricted access to automated Big Data

---

[7]See Sects. 7.3.3, 7.4.2 and 7.11 in Chap. 7.

analytics capabilities, the individual has no right of redress, to receive documents, to be informed, to verify that the Privacy Tests and the Reasonable and Proportionate Privacy Tests have been complied with.[8]

Partially Entrusting National Security to Polling Data

Determining what the legitimate expectations are as they relate to privacy and cybersecurity, is a process that is also guided by public reporting and opinion polls:

> Public reporting, polling data and other public material can also inform legitimate expectations (DoH 2019, p. 5).

Public Reporting By this policy, public reporting is officially opened as a conduit for direct influence on the operational decisions of the Agencies. The Agencies may use public reporting as a basis to justify their decisions as it relates to privacy and cybersecurity. Public reporting includes news reports and articles. Public reporting is generally based on public interest news articles, that can be based on leaks of secret government information.[9] In this regard, gauging the attitude of the public to such reporting may positively influence how the Agencies can go about doing its work, whether a certain operational activity has general public support or not. The negative aspect of this is the extent to which the media is divided into political camps of 'the left' and 'the right'. If a report is meant to influence either side of the political spectrum, then care may need to be taken, about the extent to which such reporting will influence the decisions of the Agencies. There is also the use of the media by foreign countries to influence a policy position on a given issue. There is also the rise of fake news, where care should be taken, and the Agencies must verify news reports and question underlying motivations. Any particular individual that has an interest in the work of the Agencies, looking to influence their functions, may use their relationship with the media to exert such influence or to sway public opinion in a given direction, and that shaped opinion may be what is then reflected in opinion polls. Caution must be taken about how journalists are engaged by the Agencies, the departments, and interests bodies, to prevent conflict of interests, if public reporting is going to be relied on in shaping the operational activities of the Agencies to collect and use technical information from social media companies.

Polling Data The Agencies may also use public polling as a basis to justify their decisions as it relates to privacy and cybersecurity. This means polling is used as a source to recognise the legitimate expectations, whatever those may be, regarding law enforcement and national security plans and priorities. This raises concerns because of the methodological issues about opinion polling.[10] However, as a far as this statement is included in an official government document of the Department of

---

[8]See Sects. 7.3.1, 7.3.3, 7.4.2 and 7.6 in Chap. 7.
[9]See Sect. 3.1.7 in Chap. 3.
[10]See Sect. 5.1.2.2.3.

Home Affairs (DoH), to whom the Agencies report to, this creates a policy obligation, which may in turn be creating a legitimate expectation, the public and the DCP can rely on.

A positive aspect of this policy decision is one that relates to substantive law. Prior to the statutory introduction of the doctrine of legitimate expectations, the doctrine was only considered as part of Australian law as far as it relates to procedural fairness and not when it comes to substantive matters of the law, such as a right (Robertson 2015; Groves 2008, pp. 514, 517).

Beyond the procedural law aspects of the doctrine discussed earlier, the introduction of opinion polls as a policy tool under the legitimate expectation doctrine to gauge popular public opinion on privacy and cybersecurity may partly be based on the principles of natural justice. Natural law may be defined as: 'the natural sense of what is right and wrong' (the *Voinet court case (1885):* 41 cited in Robertson 2015). By introducing this doctrine DoH is looking to guide the decisions of the Agencies to look for a sense of doing the right thing by the Australian people—doing what they expect is the right thing for their law enforcement and national security agency to do as it relates to their privacy and cybersecurity.

The decisions of the Agencies under the *AAA 2018* may not be subject to judicial review under *ADJR 1977*. So, the doctrine may not raise technically legal issues and no person may be able to claim legal relief based on it. However, it may serve as an expression of public policy and a voluntary willingness to consider principles of natural justice. The metadata retention scheme is however not subject to a public polling of legitimate expectations. The doctrine is broad. As such, public opinion can demonstrate a strong desire and wish for a particular type of process—an expectation—that if enough people agree to in an opinion poll, may be fairly considered a legitimate expectation. It may then translate into the rationale for a given inquiry or investigative decision, such as the collection of the technical information in order to meet the legitimate expectations of privacy and cybersecurity of the Australian community. In this non-common law, non-*ADJR 1997* sense, DoH appears to be creating a legitimate expectation, and not in the traditional sense that the judiciary would apply the doctrine, about the merits of the decision by the Agencies—the merits will consider the polling results of the majority. If the majority are concerned about cyberattacks from foreign countries and express an expectation to be protected from it, then a decision will be based on that expectation. This decision may never be tested in a court of law, and the judiciary may never express itself on the procedural aspects of the decision or the merits of the decision, but DoH seems to be expressing a desire for its discretionary decision-making powers to be limited to a social sciences method (polling) and the non-judicial application of the doctrine of legitimate expectation, but as a matter of a non-reviewable administrative decision-making process. It is an interesting move that seeks to strengthen the privacy protections, while at the same time retaining administrative discretionary power but not yielding to the judiciary. It is an interesting dynamic, one that is quite moderate—not progressive because it does not open itself up to judicial review, but its not too conservative either, it does maintain the traditional separation of powers split, but it recognises the need to introduce certain elements found under judicial review to bear upon its decision-making. In this latter sense, it's an expression of independence—to do it at its own terms. The same can be said for the introduction of the Privacy Tests under section 180F of the *TIA Act 1979* and the inclusion of the principles to protect privacy a little better under the AG's Guidelines as it relates to ASIO. It is the jealous guarding of its executive realm, but at the same time a subtle compromise by adopting the types of principles that are likely to be considered under judicial review, by the independent judiciary, but on its own terms without surrendering to the judiciary.

As such, opinion polls can check Australians attitudes on this specific question, seeing that opinion polls are legitimised as a procedural step owed to the Australian public, to check the polls in setting and deciding on the legitimate expectations of the Australian community relating to privacy and cybersecurity, in addition to and balanced against national security and law enforcement interests. Location information warrants and authorisations are generally said to require approval by an independent third party, such as the Office for the Communications Data Authorisations (OCDA) and judicial warrants in the UK and the USA, based on national constitutions, charter of rights and international human rights instruments that are similar to Australia's international legal obligations under the privacy protections under Article 17 of the ICCPR, as ratified by Parliament,[11] a relevant polling question may be whether Australians can be said to have a legitimate expectation that the procedural fairness to interfere with their privacy, is also only done by means of a judicial warrant. Does it then follow, that the departure from this expectation, by the metadata retention and disclosure framework, can be said to constitute procedural unfairness of the legitimate expectations? The question must be answered in the affirmative. Australians expect to enjoy rights that are materially similar to those enjoyed by citizens of its allies so much so that these rights may only be limited with materially the same procedures in order to ensure the maximum enjoyment of these rights. It is for this reason that benchmarking exercises are continuously taken with allied countries and comments are made about how Australia may be lagging behind.[12]

The *Lam court case* generally questioned the source of a legitimate expectation, raising questions about how expectations are created. Other questions included the legitimacy of expectation; what the expectations include; those whose expectations are considered relevant versus those whose are not; and how objective versus subjective the standard is. Given the statutory introduction of the doctrine, these questions may again become relevant. As per the policy of DoH, polls may help in answering these questions, at least within the inner workings of the Agencies. However, polls themselves raise questions about legitimacy, accuracy and the suppression of minority interests, that must be countered if any law enforcement and security assessment weight is to be attached to an opinion poll.

---

[11]See Sect. 6.1 in Chap. 6 and Sect. 8.4 in Chap. 8.
[12]See Sect. 8.4 in Chap. 8.

Opinion Poll on Cybersecurity

Cyber-attacks have been a growing concern since 2014. According to the 2019 Lowy Institute opinion poll cyberattacks are topping the list of threats to Australia's vital interests having risen five points since 2014, to 62%. Climate change tops the list for the first time. Young people aged between 18 and 29 years are more concerned about climate change at the rate of 83%, than they are about cyberattacks at 47%, whereas 66% of older Australians are concerned about cyberattacks (Lowy Institute 2019).

Overall, in 2019, 64% of Australians consider climate change as a critical threat, whereas 62% of Australians consider cyberattacks from other countries as a critical threat. Privacy was not polled. In 2018 however, cyberattacks from other countries were seen as a critical threat by 57% of the population (Lowy Institute 2019). It would appear as if these types of polling is what DoH seeks to legitimise. The Agencies may then justify their operational investigatory and inquiry activities and decisions based on these results.

There is however a clear divide between the opinions of older Australians versus those of younger Australians. The *Lam court case* raised concerns about the legitimate expectations doctrine in general, that may relevant to consider in the opinion polling context as well, given the policy direction by DoH: How will these differences be addressed when the Agencies are making their decisions to collect technical information? How will the minority views of young people be reconciled by the Agencies, against those of the elderly given the 47%, and 66% split in opinion? Where do the Agencies draw the line and what guidance is given to decision-makers on assessing and relying on polling opinions?

Others like the Essentials, Ipsos, Newspoll and Galaxy polls, test attitudes about nativism, populism, the threats immigration pose and economic threats.

Indirectly Legitimising Opinion Polls

Opinion polling is generally the playground for politicians and marketers to improve sales. The policy guidance given by DoH to the Agencies, state law enforcement agencies and the message to the Telco, the SMPs and the individual citizen and resident, is that the Agencies will also adopt a political tool in their operational activities.

Opinion polling raises its own concerns. Polls may create feedback loops, creating what is referred to as 'spirals of silence'—minority views are drowned out because people fear being isolated. It may also lead to peer pressure where people adopt majority views because they want to be on the winning side, but they do not principally agree with, referred to as the 'bandwagon effect' (Arnesen et al. 2018). Political slogans may also steer public opinion in a given direction, creating a feedback loop. The question is then what came first—the chicken or the egg—the poll or public messaging? These risks must be addressed to ensure opinion polling can be used to influence public policing.

The question is exactly how opinion polls, given their broad sentiments, their methodological and reliability challenges, will translate into actual decisions of the Agencies about collecting technical information to the Telco and the SMP specifically, and generally about metadata collection to set law enforcement and national security agendas and priorities.

Another question is just the extent to which the Agencies intend on being swayed by opinion polls in making law enforcement and national security decisions, given that general public opinion may see certain minority groups as particularly criminal and expect a tougher stance on what may be perceived as crime ridden communities, as it relates to collecting metadata from social media tech giants. This is especially so given newspaper headlines like 'African youth crime wave' that can shape public opinion and skew the reality. Headlines such as these raised concerns about criminal activity by Australians of South-Sudanese origin, and a concern that crime has gotten worse, whereas the state of Victoria was much safer now than it was in a decade (Hutchinson et al. 2018; DCA 2018).

The Lowy Institute Poll 2019 showed growing concern about cyber-attacks and foreign influence from foreign countries. The notable example are concerns about hacking of Australian political bodies and Parliament websites, and foreign influence donor activities by organisations and person linked to the China, and its communist party (Laurenceson 2019; Packham 2019). It is now reported that many Chinese-Australians feel being distrusted based on these broader concerns. The Muslim community had similar feelings of distrust at the height of terrorist attacks in 2015 and 2016, of a police officer in Paramatta in Sydney and at the Sydney Lindt Café siege in December 2015. These fears filtered into subsequent Lowy Institute Polls (Lowy Institute 2018, 2019). The key question is how these opinions will come to be certified as legitimate, if and when they happen to lead to law enforcement, public safety and national security priorities, investigatory and inquiry activities about collecting and using telecommunications data and technical information from the Telco and the SMP. How will a given strategy be justified as necessary; and reasonable and proportionate, in the circumstances, in a manner that does not marginalise and alienate minority groups? Moreover, how will IGIS and the Commonwealth Ombudsman supervise such decisions?

These concerns are relevant to polls and raise concerns about efforts to legitimise polls, in the manner DoH is doing. Through this policy position of the DoH and linking it to the *Assistance and Access Act 2018*, opinion polls are indirectly being elevated to the same legal standard and given the same legal weighting as integral parts of the Privacy Tests. These do not replace existing traditional methods of national security and law enforcement decision-making, but is added to the equation, with quasi-legal influence.

Mentioning polls as a source of the legitimate expectations of the public sets to validate and endorse polling data as policy shaping tools, to help measure and set law enforcement and national security priorities, operations and strategies, in collecting technical information from DCPs. In other words, polls, as selected by DoH or the Agencies, will help shape the operations of ASIO and the AFP, when collecting metadata from a company like Google. This, despite criticisms about polling methodologies—how polling questions are phrased; issues about how participants are selected, whether at random or otherwise; issues of potential bias; issues about reliability; how representative the samples are and the shifting nature of public opinion. More importantly, if polls are assumed to be reliable, how concerns about 'the tyranny of the majority'; the rise of nationalism; the rise of populism; the rise of tribalism; white extremism; racial prejudice, from polling results may be neutralised and balanced against equally legitimate expectations and the interests of the minority. Legitimising polling results places legal weight on polling data and makes it influential in an unprecedented fashion. This is particularly alarming given the use of fake news to sway public opinion; the role of foreign interference by the use of social media to influence public opinion which may in turn be what the opinion of the individuals that part take in a poll may be based on; and how unreliable polls were in predicting a Labor victory in the 2019 election and got it wrong. One of the issues identified by Peter Lewis of Essential, a polling company, was that responses from undecided voters were disregarded because it was seen as statistical noise and respondents were not engaged enough with the political process. There were calls to introduce and improve protocols on how data is analysed, to improve accuracy (The Guardian 2019, June 7).

Generally, there is also the use of automated polling, referred to as robocalls, and the rise of deep fakes, that disrupts traditional polling, and that may create more uncertainty, tainting reliability. It is interesting to note that polls are legitimised at this point in time. Given all these credibility issues, polls who are traditionally political tools, are now legalised as a yardstick in order to offer a window into the legitimate expectations of the people, or at least of the majority, on whose opinions national and cybersecurity policy decisions can be based.

Polls may not be able to ask the correct questions, or the results may be misinterpreted to fit a particular narrative and justify particular decisions of the decision-maker. The correct outcomes of polls depend on asking the right questions and these at times can be complicated, involving issues of technology, politics and public safety concerns. The public may not expect to be followed in the virtual world while protesting climate change inaction—the expectation would be that they should be free to protests and not have their locations tracked, recorded and stored indefinitely by the police and used for other criminal inquiries where they are not suspected of crimes that are based on reasonable grounds and without a judicial warrant. The ultimate question is whether the community accepts that their near-precise locations be tracked and recorded by the police without a judicial warrant, and without a reasonable suspicion of committing a crime. There may be no legitimate expectation by the public of this except in unusual circumstances such as where a state of emergency is declared.

Regarding access to journalist and whistle-blower metadata, opinion polls can ask whether the Australian community have a legitimate expectation that this metadata should be collected without first having obtained a judicial warrant. The other matter that can be tested in polls is whether there should be publicly available procedures that outline how investigations that relate to public interest investigations, leaks by whistle-blowers and that relate to national security and law enforcement are and should be conducted.

A more evidence-based approach may be required, asking such detailed and complex questions, perhaps a well-designed focus group methodology can be a good start. These questions can better canvass what the public's legitimate expectations are about interference with their privacy, that may deserve the label 'legitimate'.

For example, a poll and other research methods could instead ask whether the public expects to have their prospective locations tracked, by the AFP, ASIO or the Australian Signals Directorate (ASD) in near-real time, whilst they are using their social media applications commenting on various topics, tweeting and retweeting, in order to predict if they are likely to commit a crime in future, such as protesting and thereby trespassing, without a court order. This question may need to be tested against another question, as a control question: how different this will be to the police following a person in public with just a few meters behind them, watching their every move, without identifying themselves. What polls may do is to play one part of community against another, and both may have 'legitimate expectations', based on their specific interests based on what poll is followed, based on what news media report is relied on. This may proof to be more divisive than anticipated. The commendable part about this policy is its move towards an evidence-based-type policy making direction. True evidence-based decision making is more nuanced than newspaper reports and polling data. It is based on proven scientific methods to assess all the available evidence, it is systematic and a rational approach (ABS 2010). Unlike polls and news media reports it is more divorced from sensationalism and emotions such as fear but based on rationality. The government may need to consider introducing a documented policy-making process that is more evidence-based than not, to obtain greater public trust and confidence, in a manner that demonstrates leadership to manoeuvre the unprecedented globalised issues, largely based on the ubiquity of the Internet, that are of national interests. Leadership also requires shaping public opinion based on facts, balanced against the interests of the minority, instead of simply following that which is popular for now. Polls may simply reflect popular public opinion.

The Department of Home Affairs and ASIO Endorse the Use of Opinion Polls

It is clear that DoH and ASIO agree with the position that polling data can be the basis for determining what the legitimate expectations of the public are. The Lowy Institute has been running polls for over 15 years. Before passing the torch to Mike Burgess at the end of September 2019, Duncan Lewis gave a nod of approval, endorsement and acceptance of the work of the institute and citing the results of the Lowy Institute Poll of 2019, on the 4th of September 2019 (PlayerFM 2019).[13]

---

[13] See subsection titled: "Partially Entrusting National Security to Polling Data".

The Agencies should generally guard against the tacit acceptance of polling results as irrefutable and an indirect acknowledgement of being influenced by polling results. Poling is one part of the intelligence equation and must not skew decisions in order to justify a pre-determined action. There must be a critical analysis of the mixed bag of all polling results. In terms of section 20 of its enabling legislation, the Director-General ASIO must take all reasonable steps to ensure that ASIO is kept free from any influences or considerations that are not relevant to ASIOs functions and nothing is done that might lend colour to any suggestion that ASIO is concerned to further or protect the interests of any particular section of the community, or with any matters other than the discharge of its functions. When incorporating opinion polls into the discharge of its functions, the polls may feed into making decisions about security, so it will not be outside the scope of its function. What section 20 however does not address is the possibility of opinion polls being influential to protecting the interests of the majority and carry out its functions but at the same time marginalising the interests of the minority. Opinion polling may justify the use of stronger policing tactics, to ensure public safety, but may result in intimidation and surveillance of low-income communities, or migrant communities, that end up being targets of such tactics, because of their perceived propensity to crime and posing security threats.

The Agencies must guard against external influence, even if it relates to exercising its functions and purposes. This is equally applicable to the reliance it places on polling data, to the extent that it influences the national security agenda, operations and strategies. The Agencies must adopt guidelines about where they will draw the line about the extent of influence polls can have. The Agencies may need to outline criteria about how polls are considered and limit its potential influence and giving prominence to the evidence on the ground. The Agencies must then inform, educate and speak out about the hard-core evidence if polls lean in a skewed direction, that may marginalise minority groups. These guidelines must be built into the Big Data strategies of the Agencies.

The Lack of the Personal Privacy and Free Speech Rights Versus Parliamentary Sovereignty and the Proportionality Principle

In the *Comcare court case* a public servant lost her job because of anonymous tweets, that were seen as unacceptable, and critical of the immigration department she worked in. The reason for her dismissal was that the tweets did not meet acceptable conduct standards for members of the public service. The Administrative Appeals Tribunal (AAT) wrongly approached the issue by equating the implied freedom of political communication to a personal right to free speech. The issue was whether the termination of the employment of the public servant was a reasonable action balanced against the implied freedom of political communication. The issue was not whether her personal right to free speech was violated, as the latter was irrelevant under Australian law—Australians do not have the right to free speech, as Americans may have under the First Amendment.

Parallels can be drawn between to the lack of a common law right to free speech and the lack of a common law right to privacy under the Australian law. In the *Comcare court case* it was essentially a lack of a common law right to free speech that made it impossible for the Court to study the public service rules and come to a conclusion that the employees personal right to free speech was violated. The earlier decision of the *AAT* was based on the reasoning that the employee had a personal right to free speech, which the employee clearly did not have (the *Comcare court case [18] – [21]*). The employee possessed the implied freedom of political communication, but this freedom was not a personal right that she could claim and rely on to defend her tweets. This is because Australian law does not expressly recognise the right to free speech, as it may be recognised in the United States, for example, under the First Amendment (Griffiths 2005). The implied freedom of political communication is not a personal right of free speech (*Comcare court case [20]*). This, despite Australia having adopted the ICCPR. In the absence of the personal common law right to free speech granted to the individual employee, she could not claim that the public service rules violated her right to free speech. The implied freedom of political communication is based on the fact that Australia is a representative democracy under its Constitution, where political communication is the basis and such communication is therefore implied. The freedom is therefore applied to test the validity of a law that seeks to restrict this freedom. It restricts the powers of the executive branch of government. The freedom may be restricted by means of reasonable limits (*Comcare court case [20]*; Griffiths 2005, p. 2; Caisley 2019). In the *Comcare court case* the Court decided that the public service rules, as prescribed in section 10 of the *Public Service Act 1999* (Cth) did not impose an unjustified burden on the employees implied freedom of political communication. As such, the action to terminate her employment was reasonable and taken in a reasonable manner, for breaching the code of conduct that required her to be impartial and professional. The law was therefore reasonably appropriate and adapted to serve a legitimate purpose, which was to ensure impartiality and professionalism: '. . .even if a law significantly restricts the ability of an individual or a group of persons to engage in political communication, the law will not infringe the implied freedom of political communication unless it has a material unjustified effect on political communication as a whole'(the *Comcare court case [20]*). The action of Parliament to pass section 10 was justified, it did not have a material unjustified effect on political communication as a whole, because Australian law does not recognise the personal right to free speech. The part in the *Comcare court case* that confirmed the absence of a personal right to free speech is worth noting, because if there were a personal right to free speech, like in Canada, perhaps it could be said that section 10 of the *Public Service Act 1999* (Cth) was unjustified:

Before the Tribunal, the parties were agreed that the only issue for the Tribunal was:

whether or not the termination of the [respondent's] employment with the Commonwealth falls outside the exclusion in s 5A(1) of the Act, having regard to the implied freedom of political communication.[38]

It is unfortunate that the issue was framed in those terms for it appears to have led the Tribunal to approach the matter, wrongly, as if the implied freedom of political communication were a personal right like the freedom of expression guaranteed by ss 1 and 2(b) of the Canadian Charter of Rights and Freedoms or the freedom of speech guaranteed by the First Amendment to the Constitution of the United States. Thus, in their reasons for decision, the Tribunal spoke [39] in terms of the impugned provisions imposing a "serious impingement on Ms Banerji's implied freedom", and stated[40] that "[t]he burden of the Code on Ms Banerji's freedom was indeed heavy". The Tribunal reasoned [41] that Canadian jurisprudence as to the balance to be struck between an individual government employee's "duty of fidelity and loyalty" and the "countervailing rights of public servants to take part in a democratic society" was "illuminative of the appropriate balance to be struck between the implied freedom and the fostering of an apolitical [Australian] public service". And, ultimately, the Tribunal decided [42] the matter, erroneously, on the basis "that the use of the Code as the basis for the termination of Ms Banerji's employment impermissibly trespassed upon her implied freedom of political communication".

As has been emphasised by this Court repeatedly, most recently before the Tribunal's decision in this matter in Brown v Tasmania [43], the implied freedom of political communication is not a personal right of free speech. It is a restriction on legislative power which arises as a necessary implication from ss 7, 24, 64 and 128 and related sections of the Constitution and, as such, extends only so far as is necessary to preserve and protect the system of representative and responsible government mandated by the Constitution [44]. Accordingly, although the effect of a law on an individual's or a group's ability to participate in political communication is relevant to the assessment of the law's effect on the implied freedom, the question of whether the law imposes an unjustified burden on the implied freedom of political communication is a question of the law's effect on political communication as a whole [45].

More specifically, even if a law significantly restricts the ability of an individual or a group of persons to engage in political communication, the law will not infringe the implied freedom of political communication unless it has a material unjustified effect on political communication as a whole.

For that reason, the way in which the Tribunal decided the matter was misconceived and the Tribunal's decision must be set aside (the *Comcare court case* [18]–[21]).

The Court also assessed whether the legal restriction was proportional to the purpose of having an effective and efficient public service. The decision was that the legal restriction was reasonably necessary and therefore proportional to that purpose, despite the heavy restrictions it placed on the employee. The restriction was also reasonably balanced to ensure that Parliament policy was implemented, and that it was respected. And so, the restriction was proportional for the purpose of implementing government policy (the *Comcare court case* [165] – [166], [188] – [189]).

From the *Comcare court case* it is clear that no Australian resident or citizen, whether a public servant or private citizen has the personal right to free speech. From the *Comcare court case* the following principle and impact is clear: if an Australian does not have a personal common law right, the principle of proportionality (which includes the principles of 'reasonable and necessary') will be used to assess whether the restrictions on the right the individual claims to have, are justified. More importantly, no Australian citizen or resident can claim a right they do not possess, even if they think they may possess it. In that instance, there is no legitimate claim to enforce such a right.

In subsequent media reporting there was a sense of surprise that Australian law does not recognise the personal right to free speech. The union for public service employees labelled the social media policy as 'draconian' and as 'bad for democracy' (Byrne 2019, August 8; Whitbourn 2019, August 7). It shows a lack of public awareness of their rights, versus what rights they may think they possess. If the public is tested in an opinion poll and asked if they think they have the right to free speech, they may respond in the affirmative, even after this decision, or if asked whether they should have a personal right to free speech.

Coming to the lack of a common law personal right to privacy, no Australian citizen or resident can claim the common law right to privacy. The right to privacy is as prescribed in the *Privacy Act 1988* (Cth) and is applauded as an adequate protection of the right to personal privacy under Australian law. It however has its limits. The question about proportionality is whether the common law right to privacy, if it did exist was reasonable and necessary and justified, by allowing the Agencies the administrative act of issuing authorisations and notifications under the *CAC Determination 2018*, to self-certify and collect metadata that is personal and sensitive, without a judicial warrant. Simply put, is the mandatory and voluntary retention of bulk location information of every person, with precision in meters and revealing personal information metadata; and the subsequent mandatory and voluntary disclosure and collection, without a judicial warrant reasonable and proportional in relation to individual privacy? In the UK and the USA this question was generally answered in the negative, based on the personal right to privacy of their citizens under their Constitution, human rights laws, as recognised by common law.[14] In Australia, there is no personal right to privacy to use as a limit to the powers of Parliament to make laws that restrict this right because the right does not exist. The only limit are the principles of proportionality, reasonableness and necessity. Given the *Comcare court case,* the decision in a theoretical court case about privacy is likely to be that the restrictions imposed on privacy, by the powers of the Agencies to collect personal information without a warrant, is firstly the ambit of Parliamentary and executive power in accordance with the separation of powers principle, and that secondly, that those laws are subject to proportionality and reasonableness and necessity, and that these powers are proportional to the purpose of enforcing laws, safeguarding the national interest and generally to keep the community safe—public safety. As such, collecting location information without a judicial warrant is a reasonable and justifiable limit to privacy, to serve the public safety purpose.

Regarding legitimate expectations, if a poll were to determine that Australians wish for a judicial warrant to be issued to access metadata and technical information and use it in automated Big Data analytics databases, powered by machine learning and artificial intelligence, would the Agencies reconsider their notices and authorisations, and allow for judicial warrants? Is this what DoH would do in

---

[14]See Sect. 8.4 in Chap. 8.

meeting the legitimate expectations of the Australian community as it relates to privacy? Opinion polling may serve as a benefit in this regard, seeing that no review decision about the collection and use of metadata or technical information is likely to see its day in any court, given such decisions are not up for judicial review. It is therefore no surprise that there have been three attempts in 2001, 2017 and 2019 to introduce an Australian Bill of Rights, to give effect to the ICCPR (Explanatory Memorandum 2019).

Australians have no common law personal right to free speech and to privacy. The risk of this is that the courts are not able to come to the rescue, to protect free speech and privacy, even though Australians may legitimately expect to possess the right to free speech and privacy. The courts are not able to restrict Parliaments power to unfairly interfere with rights Australians do not have. There are no limits to set to the sole discretion of Parliament, to a right that does not exists. The absence of these rights should be the headline and it is a cause for alarm. The statute cannot be reined in for going too far—there is no going too far. Parliament sets the bar in the law, only subject to the principle of 'implied freedom of political communication, high or low and only answerable to itself, as there is no avenue for judicial review. Moreover, national security is a bipartisan issue, and so the strength of Parliament is amplified, and there are fewer voices to serve as a check on Parliament's exercise of its near-absolute power. The exercise of the power in this context is: legitimising the use of polling data as a tool to assess the legitimate expectations of the Australian community as it relates to privacy and cybersecurity, in order to influence national security and law enforcement activity—to help determine whether the TARs are necessary to collect technical information from the DCP. This is a risk for the democracy of a multicultural Australian community, where the public opinion of the majority culture may override the interests of the minority. The multicultural democracy is placed at further risk by the absence of a bill of rights in the form and fashion as seen in Canada and the United States. There is no constitutional check—everything rests with Parliament. Given this, reserving public opinion, that is aimed at moving the needle, with polling data, where opinions of the majority are the basis of a political and then a policy decision, without a common law right or a constitutional foundation, puts the minority's interest at greater risk—subject to the will of the majority. Minority interests in this context refers to those that agree that the metadata retention and disclosure, and the disclosure of technical information without a judicial warrant, is an unfair restriction of the universal human right to privacy even if they are discriminatorily impacted by the law. The majority that agrees that it is necessary to protect public safety, rules the day.

Relevance to the Civil Disobedience

Crimes of trespassing and inciting others to trespass agricultural land by using social media, on the basis that farming methods violate animal rights,[15] may only be

---

[15]See Sects. 4.1.1 and 4.1.2 in Chap. 4.

challenged under the implied freedom of political communication, as described above (Explanatory Memorandum 2019, p. 18 [127] – [130]). Any person charged with the offence may not be able to successfully raise that they were expressing their personal right to free speech. The proportionate purpose is to prevent biosecurity risks and protect the privacy of personal households, which may be considered a justified limit to the freedom and a reasonable exercise of Parliamentary power. Any person challenging the retention and collection of their location information, technical information and other metadata, without a judicial warrant, as an unreasonable limit to free speech will not be successful, nor if the base of their claim is the implied freedom of political communication. This is because the power to collect metadata without a judicial warrant is exercised for the reasonable aim of protecting biosecurity, and the implied freedom of political communication would not trump this justified aim. It would therefore be an adequately balanced restriction of the implied freedom, for which personal information may be stored and collected, without a judicial warrant, and for a crime the public may not consider a serious crime or threat.

5.1.2.3   The 'Reasonably Necessary or Directly Related Tests'

Prospective location information that is authorised to be disclosed must be 'reasonably necessary' for an 'investigation'. Historical location information must be reasonably necessary to enforce the criminal law, or be reasonably necessary for or directly related to the functions and activities of the AFP (*TIA Act 1979* ss 176, 177(1), 178(3), 179(3), 180(4); *Privacy Act 1988* (Cth) Schedule 1 Part 2 3.1, 3.4(d) (ii); *CAC Determination 2018* ss 8–12).

The tests allowing for the collection of this personal information are referred to as the 'Reasonably Necessary or Directly Related Tests'. The 'Reasonably Necessary or Directly Related Tests' are in turn divided into four sub-tests.

The APP consists of 13 principles which the AFP must adhere to, unlike ASIO. This is because the AFP is legally classified as an APP entity (OAIC 2019, p. 5 [B.8]). APP 3 refers to the collection of solicited personal information. APP 3.1 states:

> If an APP entity is an agency, the entity must not collect personal information (other than sensitive information) unless the information is reasonably necessary for, or directly related to, one or more of the entity's functions or activities (*Privacy Act 1988* Schedule 1 Part 2 3).

In terms of APP 3, four tests must be applied by the AFP prior to it collecting location information. APP 3 is a contributing source for the 'Reasonably Necessary Tests'.

a. The 'APP 3.1 Reasonably Necessary or Directly Related Personal Information Test' (*Privacy Act 1988* (Cth) Schedule 1 Part 2 APP 3.1.); and
b. The 'APP 3.5 Lawful and Fair Means Test' (*Privacy Act 1988* (Cth) Schedule 1 Part 2 s 3.5).

Sections 177(1), 177(3), 179(3) and 180(4) of the *TIA Act 1979* also contribute to the 'Reasonably Necessary or Directly Related Test', by creating the following two sub-tests:

c. The 'Reasonably Necessary to Enforce the Criminal Law Test' (*TIA Act 1979* ss 177(1), 178(3), 179(3)); and
d. The 'Reasonably Necessary to Investigate an Offence Test' (*TIA Act 1979* s 180 (4)).

These four 'Reasonably Necessary or Directly Related Tests' are described and critically analysed below.

The APP 3.1 Reasonably Necessary or Directly Related Personal Information Test

The 'APP3.1 Reasonably Necessary Personal Information Test' can be unpacked into four elements. The AFP must only collect personal information if it is either:

a. Reasonably necessary for the AFP's functions;
b. Reasonably necessary for the AFP's activities;
c. Directly related to a function of the AFP; or
d. Directly related to an activity of the AFP

(*Privacy Act 1988* (Cth) Schedule 1 Part 2 APP 3.1).
Personal information must not be collected for any purpose that is outside the scope of the functions and powers of the AFP. As an example, collecting personal information about previous injuries that took place while on duty, but that did not have anything to do with the job the person is required to do, was not regarded as related to the activities of the organisation (Own Motion Investigation v Australian Government Agency 2007, p. 4). The connection between the personal information and the location information must be clear and direct, or the collection must be reasonably necessary in the opinion of a reasonable person—the reasonable person that is suitably informed. This reasonable person must agree that the collection of the personal information is reasonably necessary. The onus rests on the AFP to prove that the collection of the personal information was reasonably necessary.

The AFP is authorised to collect sensitive information if the AFP 'reasonably believes' that the collection of the location information is 'reasonably necessary' for, or 'directly related' to, one or more of the entity's functions or activities (*Privacy Act 1988* (Cth) Schedule 1 Part 2 s 3.4). As an example, taking photos of patients to file was also not considered related to the function of providing a health service if the picture was not related to the treatment (M and Health Service Provider 2007, p. 15). The related term 'reasonably belief' closely relates to the term 'reasonably believes'.[16]

---

[16]The *Carratti court case*, the *Day court case*, and the *George court case*.

The above tests are wide. The tests do not limit the location information to be collected for the investigation or inquiry at hand. The collection does not need to be reasonably necessary for, or directly related to the specific function or the specific activity that is the actual ongoing investigation or inquiry into an offence, suspected on reasonable grounds, and in good faith.

The Term 'Reasonably Necessary' Versus the Term 'Directly Related'

The application of the words 'reasonably necessary' in APP 3.1 and APP 3.4 and the words 'directly related' in APP 3.1 and APP 3.4 are open to interpretation. There is no telling under what circumstances which alternative part of the test is to be used, which one is preferred, or whether one overrides the other. The location information may be 'reasonably necessary', 'directly related' or be both. Either way, it may result in forum shopping. Based on the facts and circumstances at hand the AFP may choose to adopt the term that may best suit the situation, in order to take the easiest route and meet the minimum legal requirement. The AFP can choose the explanation that the collection of the location information was justified because it was directly related to a policing function, if it finds it more challenging to explain why the collection of the location information was 'reasonably necessary'. Under the 'directly related' principle, the AFP does not need to prove that the collection of the location information was crucial. The AFP just needs to state that the collection of the location information is for or connected to a law enforcement activity, such as an investigation or an inquiry. If the AFP decides to collect the location information of all mobile devices in the area served by one particular cell tower where a protest group usually meets, location information may be collected because it is 'directly related' to the police activity of conducting inquiries about activities that may lead individuals to commit an offence, whether minor or serious. The AFP would then have details of the members' movements, visitors and residents in the neighbourhood, how often they met, and their identities once the location information is analysed—all of which may not be necessary to prove a potential charge of say, illegal public assembly. The meeting times, dates and durations may be re-used for other police activities and be shared with other partner agencies. This affords the AFP wide discretion (*CAC Determination 2018* ss 10–12; Williams 2005; Golder and Williams 2006).

The term 'reasonably necessary' is a higher standard. The term 'directly related' is a lower standard, there just needs to be a direct connection, but the location information need not be necessary because it can simply be desirable to collect the location information. The 'directly related' standard is a way of guaranteeing the AFP will always have 'open access' to the location information if the necessity standard cannot be satisfied. This allows the AFP a backdoor to continue collecting location information.

The APP 3.5 Lawful and Fair Means Test

The location information must be collected by lawful and fair means (*Privacy Act 1988* Schedule 1 Part 2 s 3.5). In authorising the disclosure of the location information, the AFP must comply with the limitations imposed by the APP3.1 and APP3.4 tests, as well as the *CAC Determination 2018*. In the event the AFP does not abide by these provisions, the location information can be alleged not to have been collected by lawful and fair means.

The AFP does not need to conduct an investigation to collect location information (*CAC Determination 2018* ss 10–12). Location information may be collected to monitor whether people working at airports may be in the same area as known suspects, as indicated by the enhanced Cell-ID (E-CID), and how often they gather in the same vicinity (ETSI 2017, p. 5 [3.1]). The aim is not an investigation, but an inquiry, to see links between individuals. This activity of monitoring the locations of these individuals can be justified as a law enforcement activity. The AFP does not require suspicion of an offence on reasonable grounds to start to monitor the activities of these individuals. The number of times and the period over which their movements can be analysed are not restricted (*Privacy Act 1988* Schedule 1 Part 2 3.1, 3.4(d)(ii)). The AFP may request historical location information about the individuals every 30 days, for example. The unlimited continued analyses are not prohibited by law and would therefore be lawful. There is no limit to the number of times a new request can be made (*TIA Act 1979* ss 175–178). The continued tracking and monitoring start to border on being unjustifiable as no publicly available limit is set which would allow for a process to review whether to renew the monitoring by re-approval based on the possibility of valuable information being obtained from the monitoring.

The Reasonably Necessary to Enforce the Criminal Law Test

Historical location information may also be authorised for disclosure by the AFP if the authorised officer is satisfied that the disclosure is reasonably necessary for the enforcement of the criminal law (*TIA Act 1979* ss 175, 178). Historical location information may be collected, disclosed and used by the AFP to enforce all types of criminal offences, as long as it is reasonably necessary for its law enforcement related activities.

The Reasonably Necessary to Investigate an Offence Test

In terms of the 'Reasonably Necessary to Investigate an Offence Test' prospective location information may only be collected and disclosed on the basis that the AFP is satisfied that the disclosure is 'reasonably necessary' to investigate a serious offence. In the event it is not a serious offence, the AFP must be satisfied that the disclosure of the location information is 'reasonably necessary' to investigate an offence that carries a minimum three-year prison sentence (*TIA Act 1979* s 180(4)).

Police activity by the AFP may also be referred to as an 'enforcement related activity' (OAIC 2015: Chapter B, B.71–B.73), and include intelligence gathering and monitoring (Addendum 2012, p. 3). Collecting location information for activities to prevent, detect and investigate criminal offences would be related to the law enforcement activities of the AFP, whereas collecting location information to locate a romantic partner would not be (OAIC 2019, p. 16 [B.71]–[B.73]). This is an obvious example of potential misuse. The challenge arises when the enforcement of the criminal law is done with the help of location information that when analysed reveals personal information about a sector of the community, such that the enforcement may lead to unintended consequences of, for example, ethnic prejudice or discrimination, or racial profiling. In terms of this test, if the law is being enforced and the investigation is conducted, the location information may be collected, analysed and used. There is no specific guideline on how to address instances where the location information may reveal racial or political information that may contribute to the development of or the manifestation of biases.

The 'Reasonably Necessary' Threshold as Lacking the Requisite Degree of Precision

The last two tests allow the AFP a broad scope. The Parliamentary Joint Committee on Human Rights (PJCH) also criticized the 'reasonably necessary' threshold as lacking the requisite degree of precision. Disclosing telecommunications data to investigate 'any offence' may lead to a 'disproportionate limitation on the right to privacy' (PJCIS 2015, pp. 246–247 [6.178]).

Telecommunications data should only be disclosed if it is 'necessary' to do so for specified serious crimes or classes of serious crimes. The *Caratti* and the *Day court cases* will shed light on the meaning of the 'reasonably necessary' standard.

The Section below also describes another key limit to the powers of the AFP: the suspicion of an offence on reasonable grounds, to start an investigation and to collect the location information that is reasonably necessary for the investigation and to enforce the criminal law.

Suspicion of an Offence, Based on Reasonable Grounds, as a Limit to the Powers of the AFP

For an investigation to start, the individual must be suspected of an offence on 'reasonable grounds'. The need for reasonable grounds for suspecting an offence and to have suspicion of an offence, are two limits to the investigatory powers of the AFP. An offence is an offence against a law of the Commonwealth or of a State. A person is involved in an offence only if the person has committed or is committing the offence; or is suspected on reasonable grounds of having committed, of committing, or of being likely to commit, the offence (*TIA Act 1979* ss 6A, 6B, 5 (1) (definition of 'offence').

Investigations are a function of the AFP. For the AFP to exercise its investigatory powers under the *AFP Act*, under the Ministerial Direction, and to collect location information under an authorisation and notification issued under the *CAC Determination 2018*, the AFP must suspect the person is involved in an offence (*AFP Act 1979* (Cth) s 8; *TIA Act 1979* s 6B). Such suspicion may be formed with the help of the government referring a matter to the AFP to investigate. However, no publicly available guideline exists to verify how matters are referred to the AFP to request inquiries and investigations.

An 'investigation' can only be about a person that has committed, is committing or is likely to commit an offence. If there are no reasonable grounds for suspecting a past, present or future offence, the person cannot be considered as being involved in an offence, and there is no basis for an investigation to start, and there is no justification for the collection of the location information. This standard, however, applies specifically to 'investigations'. It does not apply to inquiries (*TIA Act 1979* ss 6A, 6B).

The study conducted to research this book was not able to locate a court case where the terms 'reasonably necessary', 'reasonable belief', 'reasonable grounds', 'justifiable and proportionate' or 'investigate' were discussed in relation to the collection and use of location information or other types of telecommunications data. The terms 'reasonably necessary', 'reasonable belief', 'justifiable and proportionate' and 'investigate' were inserted in the law to limit the exercise of the powers of the AFP so that the AFP does not misuse its powers and does not unnecessarily interfere with privacy.

The Section below discusses cases that interpreted the terms 'reasonably necessary', 'reasonable grounds', 'reasonable belief' and 'investigates', in different contexts not related to location information. These interpretations help to understand how the courts may view these terms and how the AFP may in turn be expected to interpret and practically apply these terms in relation to location information.

Caratti v Commissioner of the Australian Federal Police

The *Caratti court case* proposes the principle: even if the search warrant was poorly drafted, vague and broad, the search warrant is still valid if there were 'reasonable grounds' for suspecting that the premises may have evidence, as long as the search did not exceed what was justified by the material. The *Caratti court case* discussed the broad and vagueness of search warrants in complex commercial or tax-related criminal offences, which is apparently a frequent occurrence. The warrants were too long, complex and poorly drafted. The court noted that the officers lacked experience and background in the writing and execution of warrants. This created the impression that the officers did not know what they were searching for and that they seized anything that looked 'even remotely like it might be relevant to the investigation' (the *Caratti court case*: 1 [2]).

Instead of reducing the amount of private property and information to be seized, the AFP instead collected more, just in case it may be relevant. The AFP did not apply caution to limit the interference to privacy. In the same manner, the AFP is likely to collect more location information because it can, and because it may be relevant going forward. The Agencies must draft authorisations and notifications under the *CAC Determination 2018* to request location information from the Telco. The Agencies then use the location information to draft domestic preservation notices, stored communications warrants and interception warrants. In all these instances, the information submitted to the officer to authorise the request for the location information and the Judge or Administrative Appeals Tribunal (AAT) member to issue the warrants, must be sufficient so that the officer, Judge or member is satisfied that the interference with privacy is justifiable and proportionate to the offence investigated. Like the warrants, the authorisations and notifications for location information require issuance on 'reasonable grounds', even if there may be drafting errors. The Judge or AAT member may consider that the warrant complied substantially with the required standard. Upon review, the Judge is less likely to put the warrant application aside. Unlike the warrant however, authorisations for location information are not reviewed by a magistrate, Judge or AAT member.

The non-transparency of the authorisations potentially hides minor and major flaws that could be revealed and reviewed by an independent third-party providing transparency around interference with privacy, as was reviewed in the *Caratti court case*.

Day v Commissioner, Australian Federal Police

In the *Day court case,* the issues included the following:

1. whether an 'investigation or inquiry' in the relevant sense can exist unless and until a charge is laid under section s 61(2) of the *Public Service Act 1922* (Cth); and
2. whether the information was communicated for a purpose 'connected with' a relevant investigation or inquiry (the *Day court case* 2 [1]).

Mr Day's telephonic conversations from his home and office were intercepted. Mr Day was an employee of the Australian Customs Service (ACS) who requested the transcript for disciplinary proceedings which were used to develop the charges that were later laid against Mr Day. The purpose of communicating the transcript was so that it is used in connection with 'possible disciplinary action'. Based on the information obtained, Ms Williams of the ACS would then decide whether to lay charges. The decision to lay charges would be the first step in the disciplinary process. The court decided Mr Day had to prove that the powers of Ms Williams to use the transcript and lay the charges, were exercised improperly (the Day *case* 2 [1], [3] – [5], 4 [14], 5 [15]). The court decided that the word 'investigation' is taken to mean '. . . the act or process of searching or enquiring in order to ascertain facts.' (the Day *case* 4 [10]). Since Mr Day could not prove that the transcripts were used for an improper purpose, and the transcripts were just used to determine the facts to be used in the disciplinary hearing to prove his guilt, the transcripts were properly used for an investigation. The use of location information for the sole purpose of establishing facts, to determine how a criminal act took place in order to lay charges in criminal matters, for example, is the proper use of the location information. It would be 'in connection with' the purpose of law enforcement. It would however be difficult to prove whether the AFP was biased against the individual at any stage of the collection and use of the location information, based on the personal information it revealed. If the AFP did not use the location information for an improper purpose, such as when an officer inspects the location information for personal purposes related to a current or former romantic partner, then the location information is properly collected for the investigation, where an offence such as theft is suspected. This is a strong standard that protects privacy, as the interference with privacy by collecting and using location information is used in the process of establishing the facts that the person was involved in the theft. The investigation starts when the location information is collected and used to prepare any charges that may be laid against the person in future. To share location information under these circumstances would be a suitable limit to the privacy of the individual—to collect and use location information to determine what offences the person may have been involved in. The protection to privacy lies in the fact that the AFP must have suspicion on reasonable grounds, when collecting and using location information to put the facts together for an offence the person may be charged with, and to share it with another party such as the prosecutor, to lay the charges in a future hearing. The challenge to privacy also arises when the AFP collects and uses historical location information when a person is not involved in an offence, meaning there is no suspicion of an offence based on reasonable grounds, and the offence is not serious but carries a penalty of less than 3 years. The AFP is only required to act on the suspicion of an offence when it comes to serious offences and when prospective location information is involved. This is critically discussed in below.

George v Rockett

The *George court case* interpreted the terms 'reasonable grounds', 'reasonable suspicion' and 'reasonable belief', holding that there must be sufficient facts to make a reasonable person come to the conclusion that there are 'reasonable grounds', 'reasonable suspicion' and 'reasonable belief' to issue a search warrant (the *George case* 4 [8]).

The *George court case* interpreted section 679 of the *Criminal Code* (Qld). The *George court case* also stated that the 'reasonable grounds' requirement allows for judicial review to take place. It prevents the arbitrary exercise of statutory powers (the *George case* 4 [8]). The authorisation and notification issued by the Agencies under the *CAC Determination 2018* are not disclosed to the person, and the Telco is not allowed to inform the person, so there is less chance for judicial review, given the lack of transparency. The test is: based on the material given to the officer, by the applying officer, would a reasonable person have approved the request for the location information?

This 'reasonable grounds' test in the *George court case* is commendable, requiring the AFP to comply with the test, at least in theory. In practice, the individual will not get access to the authorisation to challenge the actions of the AFP, whether under judicial review or for administrative review, because the Telco is not allowed to inform the person and the Agencies conduct the collection confidentially (*CAC Determination 2018* ss 10–12). Decisions under the *TIA Act 1979* and *TA 1997* are not reviewable as administrative decisions under judicial review legislation (*ADJR Act 1977* Schedule 1 s 3 (d)).

Per the *George court case*, the term 'reasonable grounds' is taken to mean the officer authorising the collection of the location information must make sure that the information presented to him or her to approve the request contains facts that are sufficient for him or her to form the requisite belief (the *George court case* 4 [8]). If the AFP is conducting an 'investigation' and requires access to location information, the authorisation and notification under the *CAC Determination 2018* issued by the AFP must be issued on the basis of 'reasonable grounds' of suspecting a past, present or future offence. The AFP must have sufficient facts to find the suspicion that the person has committed an offence, is committing an offence or will commit an offence in the future (*TIA Act 1979* s 6A, 6B).

Under the 'Reasonably Necessary or Directly Related Test', the AFP may collect location information if the collection is reasonably necessary or directly related to the functions and activities of the AFP. It is not clear whether under these circumstances, the AFP is investigating and must therefore act, on suspicion based on reasonable grounds or not. Even if suspicion of being involved in an offence is not required, the AFP must still collect the historical location information on 'reasonable grounds' (*CAC Determination 2018* ss 10). The question is whether the AFP must comply with this limit when collecting historical or prospective location information under an authorisation and notification issued under the *CAC Determination 2018* for a 'non-investigation' activity that is related to its functions. Should the AFP always have an investigation to collect location information or must the 'non investigation' activity also be based on suspicion of an offence based on reasonable grounds? This issue is critically discussed below.

The Wording of the CAC Determination 2018

In respect of the AFP, the *CAC Determination 2018* sets out how the Telco must be notified about the authorisation to approve the collection of the location information.[17] The Section below discusses whether suspicion based on reasonable grounds is required to collect historical and prospective location information, and the impact on privacy if suspicion of an offence based on reasonable grounds is not required.

---

[17] *CAC Determination 2018* ss 10–12 lists the things that must be included in the notice handed to the Telco.

Suspicion on Reasonable Grounds Is Required to Collect Prospective Location Information for Serious Offences There is a requirement for the AFP to have an 'investigation' in order to collect prospective location information. This was described in the 'Reasonably Necessary to Investigate an Offence Test' (*TIA Act 1979* s 180(4)). If the AFP is requesting access to prospective location information for a serious offence or an offence against the law of the Commonwealth that is punishable by imprisonment for at least 3 years, the AFP needs to have suspicion of a past, present or future serious offence, based on reasonable grounds, to collect prospective location information (*CAC Determination 2018* s 12). The AFP may collect and use prospective location information. It is however only when it comes to serious offences that the AFP is required to conduct an investigation and have suspicion of a past, present or future serious offence, based on reasonable grounds (*TIA Act 1979* s 180(4); *CAC Determination 2018* ss 10–12). It follows that for minor offences, historical location information may be collected without a suspicion of a past, present or future serious offence, that is based on reasonable grounds.

It is only in respect of prospective location information for serious offences that the short description of offences is required to be stated in the authorization under the *CAC Determination 2018*, and only in respect of the AFP. It is only in respect of prospective location information for serious offences that an 'investigation' of offences is required, and only in respect of the AFP (*CAC Determination 2018* ss 12).

Collecting prospective location information is close to being real-time location tracking (OAIC Submission No 92, 2015: 41 Appendix B [5.]). The movements of the individual may also be identified from the prospective location information, and the individual may then be physically followed by a person in real time once the individual starts to travel. The individual could be followed in a car or by an officer in disguise on foot, and their actions recorded in real time, as outdated as this may sound. The tracking of the mobile device and the person in this manner, without the judiciary authorising such tracking, with the Agencies making the sole decision that tracking the persons movements in real-time is based on suspicion which is in turn based on reasonable grounds. Such tracking may be justified as an activity that is reasonably necessary to enforce the law and safeguard national security.

No Suspicion on Reasonable Grounds Required to Collect Historical Location Information for Both Serious and Minor Offences It also follows that for serious offences, historical location information may be collected without the suspicion of a past, present or future offence, based on 'reasonable grounds'. In other words, no reasonable grounds are required to collect the historical location information under the *CAC Determination 2018* for serious offences (*TIA Act 1979* s 178(2); *CAC Determination 2018* ss 10–12). The AFP does not need to have an investigation as a requirement before collecting the historical location information for a serious offence (*TIA Act* ss 6A, 6B). There seems to be no requirement for the AFP to have an active 'investigation', as defined in the *Day court case,* as a requirement to collect historical location information. It means the AFP does not need to have a suspicion of a past, present or future offense, based on reasonable grounds, to collect and search the location information when it is putting the facts together about the actions of the individual in order to allege that the person has committed a crime.

If the AFP is requesting access to historical location information, the Telco may be given the copy of the authorisation or a statement stating the details of the information or documents to be disclosed (*CAC Determination 2015* ss 8–12). To collect the historical location information to enforce the criminal law, the AFP needs to be '. . . satisfied that the disclosure of the information or documents is reasonably necessary for the enforcement of the criminal law . . .' (*CAC Determination 2018* s 10(1)(h)). The AFP must also be '. . . satisfied on reasonable grounds that any interference with the privacy of any person or persons that may result from the disclosure or use is justifiable and proportionate. . .' (*CAC Determination 2015* s 10 (1)(i)). The AFP is not required to suspect that a person is involved in an offence to collect historical location information about the person (*TIA Act 1979* ss 6A, 6B). The person does not need to be involved in an offence for his or her historical location information to be collected, and it can also be collected for both serious and minor offences. The impact on privacy that this presents is discussed below.

Voluntary Disclosure and Requests for Historical Location Information and Suspicion Based on Reasonable Grounds

The historical location information may be voluntarily disclosed '. . . if the disclosure is reasonably necessary for the enforcement of the criminal law' (*TIA Act 1979* ss 177(1), 178(3)). The wording of sections 177 and 178 of the *TIA Act 1979* makes no reference to an 'investigation'.

It appears, for the AFP to exercise its powers under the *AFP Act* and under the Ministerial Guidelines, the AFP can either conduct an investigation and collect the location information under the investigation; or the AFP can collect the location information '. . . if the disclosure is reasonably necessary for the enforcement of the criminal law.' (*TIA Act 1979* s 177(1)). The legal phrase '. . . if the disclosure is reasonably necessary for the enforcement of the criminal law' appears not to necessarily require an investigation. In collecting the historical location information '. . . if the disclosure is reasonably necessary for the enforcement of the criminal law' the collection must be reasonably necessary, but the AFP does not have to have suspicion based on reasonable grounds about a past, present or future offence. The impact on privacy is discussed below.

The Impact of the Absence of the Need for Suspicion of an Offence, on a Reasonable Grounds Standard, on Privacy

The absence of the standard—suspicion of an offence, based on reasonable grounds—to collect historical location information results in a broader power. This impacts the privacy of the individual. The location information can be collected while the person is not under suspicion of a serious offence, whereas if the location information was prospective location information, the person must be suspected of an offence. It would be fairer to collect the historical location information that has been stored for 2 years, only if the person was suspected to be involved in a serious offence, and with a judicial warrant. Any inquiry by the Agencies is a law enforcement activity. The conduct of a person may not necessarily be criminal, but the location information may be accessed to try and detect illegal conduct or make sure the person is not breaking the law, without any prior suspicion, without an investigation and that inquiry would be perfectly lawful because the inquiry is directly related to an activity of the AFP. The activity is policing, and it is reasonably necessary to collect the location information for the purposes of that inquiry. The best safeguard for privacy is the omnipresence of the standard of needing suspicion of a past, present or future offence, based on 'reasonable grounds'. The 'reasonable grounds' element forces the AFP to consider the facts and make an operational decision based on that. The absence of such a requirement for historical location information that reveals personal information, potentially allows the AFP to delve into speculation. It does not instil a culture of acting in good faith and on merit, even if it is to enforce the law. The AFP or its officers may at times be motivated to enforce the law based on bad faith—based on racial prejudice, hypothetically speaking. The lower standard of expressly requiring the AFP to act in good faith may ensure better protection of privacy.

The Section below critically discusses the 'APP3.1 Reasonably Necessary or Directly Related Personal Information Test' in relation to the 'reasonable grounds' standard.

The Likely Relevance and Useful Standard The facts that are used to collect location information only need to demonstrate that the location information is likely relevant and useful to the broad enforcement related activities and functions of the AFP (*TIA Act 1979* s 180F). This is a low threshold for allowing access to personal information. The use of the word 'likely' can cover the case where the location information may not actually be relevant and useful, but the location information can still be collected based on a prior assessment that it was 'likely' to be. It is like gambling, to see whether the location information is perhaps relevant. As discussed in the *Caratti court case*, the AFP can legally collect every detail of location information it thinks is remotely relevant (the *Caratti court case*: [2]). The AFP is not held to a higher standard that the location information will be useful and will be relevant, or that the AFP 'reasonably believes' that the collection of the location information is reasonably necessary to investigate the offence, based on sufficient facts in front of it. The AFP just needs to demonstrate to itself that the location information is 'reasonably necessary' to carry out and is 'directly related' to the activity of a Big Location Data (BLD) storage database, and is likely relevant for that purpose and activity, for example. The powers of the AFP to collect historical location information for an offence that is not classified as a serious offence is not sufficiently narrowed down to the investigation of the particular offence in question, and there does not even need to be a suspected offence to collect historical location information (*TIA Act 1979* s 178(2)). The likely relevance requirement under the 'Privacy Tests' can be met with a mere statement, from a template, that the person must be assessed to see whether the person is not a security risk, by using speculative data matching, with no factual basis or reasonable suspicion or belief at hand to commence that inquiry, and without the person having any idea about the investigation or inquiry (AFP 2015, p. 7, 57; *CAC Determination 2018* ss 8–12). Under these circumstances, privacy cannot be said to be protected effectively.

Warrants to Access Content Require Suspicion But Authorisations to Collect Location Information for Non-Serious Offences Do Not

Location information lacks the additional layer of protection that is only granted to the contents of voice and SMS communications. The warrants require that an 'investigation' be carried out. The presence of an 'investigation' means the AFP must have suspicion of a past, present or future serious offence, based on reasonable grounds, to apply for the warrant to collect the contents of a voice or SMS communication (*Regulations* 2017: Schedule 1).[18]

The *CAC Determination 2018* is the procedure used to collect location information. The privacy safeguards that are contained in the domestic preservation notices, the stored communications warrants, Part 2-2 Warrants and the Part 2-5 Warrants are absent from the *CAC Determination 2018*, in respect of the AFP (*TIA Act 1979* ss 39 (1), 107J (1), 109, 110, 110A, 115; AGD 2016, pp. 31–34)).

To collect the contents of a voice or SMS communication, the AFP must be conducting an investigation, in terms of the standard and prescribed wording of the warrants (*Regulations* 2017: reg. 1 (2) (e) Schedule 1 Form 1). The wording refers to an 'investigation', which means there must be reasonable suspicion of an offence. On the contrary, to collect the historical location information from the Telco for a minor or serious offence, the AFP does not need to have a suspicion of a past, present or future offence, based on reasonable grounds. It is only in respect of a serious offence that the AFP must have a suspicion of a past, present or future offence, based on reasonable grounds (*TIA Act 1979* ss 6A, 6B). Location information is treated less favourably than content, because it is not considered as personal as the contents of a communication. This despite the personal nature of location information. Location information is also treated unequally because it is classified as subscriber data and as

---

[18]Schedule 1 Form 1, Form 2—Telecommunications service warrant—B-party, Form 3—Named person warrant—telecommunications services, Form 4—Named person warrant—telecommunications devices, Form 5—Warrant for entry on premises and interception of communications, and Form 6—Stored communications warrant.

metadata, based on a narrow technology driven viewpoint. The aim is to downplay the nature and the value of location information compared to content, and to gain easier access to location information. This is ironic in a sense because, location information is so vital to the functions and law enforcement activities of the Agencies that telecommunications data is the lead information to start an inquiry or an investigation. This results in an inconsistent application of the law between location information and voice calls, and negatively impacts privacy.

The Various Templates to Request Telecommunications Data

The privacy standard was updated in 2015. No previous copies of templates could be obtained to assess what changes may have been made in the new wording. It appears that to comply with privacy safeguards, the AFP can simply copy and paste a standardised statement into the authorisation and notification under the *CAC Determination 2018*. The statement does not reflect how the 'Privacy Tests' and the 'Reasonably Necessary or Directly Related Tests' were practically applied, based on the facts at hand (AFP 2015, p. 57). The AFP uses various authorisation and notification templates under the *CAC Determination 2018* to request telecommunications data. The 'Historical Subscriber Request' form refers to location information because location information is classified as subscriber data (*TIA Act 1979* s 275A). Regarding accessing historical location information, the template makes formal provisions for the authorised officer to show that consideration has been given to privacy concerns (AFP 2015, pp. 74–103).[19] However, the problem is that the officer applying for the authorisation and notification to be approved is not specifically required to express an opinion, written in his or her own words, about the case at hand and how privacy is directly impacted, and how the direct impact is minimised. Also it does not appear as if the officer who is authorised to approve the collection of the location information is specifically required to express an opinion, written in his or her own words, about the case at hand and how privacy is impacted, and how the impact is minimised (AFP 2015, pp. 7, 57; *CAC Determination 2018* ss 10–12). It appears the AFP may simply tick boxes as proof that it met the 'Privacy Tests'. The templates simply repeat what the section 180F of the *TIA Act 1979* states, with a box next to it for the authorised officer to tick, that the 'Privacy Tests' were met (AFP 2015).

Figure 5.1 below illustrates the template:

---

[19]The Historical Call Charge Records (CCR) Request form, made in terms of section 178A (2) and section 179(2) of the *TIA Act 1979*; and The Historical Subscriber Request forms, made in terms of section 178A (2) and section 179(2) of the *TIA Act 1979*.

AFP Authorisation to disclose information or documents to the Organisation (ASIO) or a domestic enforcement agency

PROMIS: Insert PROMIS number

I, Insert name and rank am an authorised officer of the Australian Federal Police (the AFP) for the purposes of paragraph (a) of the definition of 'authorised officer' in subsection 5(1) of the *Telecommunications (Interception and Access) Act 1979* (the Act) covered by an authorisation in force under subsection 5AB(1A) of the Act.

Acting under paragraph 180D(1)(a) of the Act, I authorise the disclosure of the following information or documents to:

☐ the Organisation (ASIO) as I am satisfied that the disclosure is reasonably necessary for the performance by the Organisation of its functions; or

☐ Insert name of agency, an enforcement agency within the meaning of section 176A of the Act as I am satisfied that the disclosure is reasonably necessary for the Choose an item.

- List the relevant information and/or documents

The information or documents specified above has/have been disclosed by Insert name of carrier/ISP to the AFP pursuant to an authorisation given under Division 4A of Part 4-1 of the Act.

I have had regard to the circumstances in which the disclosure will be made and I am satisfied that the disclosure is appropriate in all the circumstances.

I am satisfied that any interference with the privacy of any person or persons that may result from the disclosure or use is justifiable and proportionate having regard to the matters set out in section 180F of the Act, including Choose an item.

The information or documents authorised for disclosure will likely be:

☐   relevant to the performance by the Organisation of its functions.

☐   relevant and useful to the investigation regarding Insert reference to relevant investigation in so far as it/they are likely to set out how the information is likely to assist with the investigation.

☐   relevant and useful to the investigation regarding Insert reference to relevant investigation against set out how the information sought is likely to assist with the investigation into the particular contravention of the relevant law imposing a pecuniary penalty, or with the protection of the public revenue.

_____
Signed

Click here to enter the date

Updated 13 October 2015
Owner: Telecommunications Interception Division

Fig. 5.1 The template used to request location information and show the Privacy Tests are applied

Based on the principles outlined in the *George court case,* one would assume that applications to approve access authorisations sent to authorised officers should include sufficient information to allow the authorised officer to make an assessment in terms of section 180F of the *TIA Act 1979.* In turn, the authorised officer must have sound reasoning for an approval, when challenged (AFP 2015, pp. 28, 57). However, it does not appear as if the privacy circumstances of the unique facts at hand are required to be spelt out in the authorisation and notification under the *CAC Determination 2018.* The template for prospective location information merely contains a summation of the wording of section 180F:

> I am satisfied that any interference with the privacy of any person or persons that may result from the disclosure or use of the information/documents specified above is justifiable and proportionate having regard to the matters set out in section 180F of the Act, including the seriousness of the offence[s] in relation to which the authorisation is sought (AFP 2015, p. 57).

It may become a formality to just have this wording, without the factual analysis being fully considered and properly applied. It is not clear whether the thinking of the officer making the application to request the location information and the thinking of the senior officer approving the application is required by the *CAC Determination 2018,* to be outlined in another document. The AFP is required to keep records. The records must include whether the officer approving the collection of the location information considered the 'Privacy Tests' and 'Reasonably Necessary or Directly Related Tests', and other relevant considerations (*TIA Act 1979* s 186A).

It is implied that a record must be kept of the approving officer that the collection of the location information was 'justifiable and proportionate' and on 'reasonable grounds'.

The wording in the template does not specifically require that there be an analysis of the actual interference of privacy by the collection and use of the location information, how privacy may be impacted; how the privacy impact will be minimised; the total amount of location information that could be requested and how, by considering the various 'Privacy Tests', the volume has been reduced, or less intrusive methods have been employed; and that based on this reasoning, the reduced volume of location information is 'reasonably necessary' and 'justifiable and proportionate', in the circumstances. It may best to clearly state that the AFP is required to state its reasons, based on the facts at hands and not use templates with boxes to be checked. The use of templates may lead to the risk of copying the statement but not properly applying the facts to the various tests. The AFP issues thousands of authorisations and notices to the Telco (AFP 2015, pp. 13, 57). As such the use of templates is efficient but compromises the privacy of the individual. The approving officer and the magistrate both may apply the tests to the facts and request more information to ensure there are 'reasonable grounds' to approve the collection of the location information. The difference is that the magistrate is an independent third party, while the approving officer is not an independent third party but has a vested interest in the outcome of the investigation, inquiry and enforcement of the criminal law. The magistrate, judge or member could be expected to act more objectively and to more closely scrutinise the application.

In the *George court case*, the High Court of Australia referred to *Bridgeman case* (the *George court case* [9]). A stricter requirement for search warrants was stated in the Bridgeman decision. The Bridgeman case decided that the information used to issue a warrant must state the reasonable ground for suspicion, in terms of the *Towns Police Act* ((19 Vict. No. 24) 1849 (UK)). If the information 'merely contains a statement that the deponent suspects they are concealed, for which suspicion he gives no relevant foundation',[20] in that instance, the magistrate had no power to issue the warrant as there was no 'reasonable ground' for suspicion to issue the warrant. The *George court case* stated the *Bridgeman court case* should be accepted as correct. Copying and pasting the templates into the authorisations and notifications may invalidate the authorisations and notifications, under the *CAC Determination 2019,* unless the senior employees of the Agencies who issue the authorisations and notifications study the material and based on that material are satisfied that the interference with privacy is justifiable and proportionate. The officers applying for issuance of the authorisations and notifications should be required by the *CAC Determination 2018* to record how they have applied the 'Privacy Tests' to the facts before them and come to the conclusion that the interference is indeed 'justifiable and proportionate'.

The template does not go far enough to require the latter. The approving officer should be held to a higher standard—the approving officer should state that he or she considered the facts at hand, applied the 'Privacy Tests' and the 'Reasonably Necessary or Directly Related Tests' and state how the tests were applied to the facts, and the reasons for and against issuing the authorisation and notification; and all those arguments should be included in the authorisation, available to be inspected by the oversight bodies. The role to then review the authorisation may be best exercised by a Judge or magistrate, as an independent third party.

5.2   Privacy as a Limit to the Powers of ASIO

5.2.1   ASIO Has the Special Duty to Prevent Undue Influence Over the Exercise of Its Powers

The Director-General (DG) of ASIO has the special duty to prevent undue influence and ensure ASIO focuses on what is necessary to carry out its functions. The DG must keep ASIO free from any influences that are not relevant to its functions. ASIO must not be seen to be protecting only the interest of a section of the community. ASIO must only be focussed on the discharge of its functions (*ASIO Act 1979* s 20). I was not able to identify a similar restriction in the AFP establishing law. Despite this, when the AFP raided the ABC head office in Sydney and the house of journalist Annika Smethurst of News Corp, in Canberra on the 4th and the 6th of June in 2019, the Prime Minister, Scott Morrison stated the AFP acted independently (Gagliardi 2019, June 6). This was however undermined by statements of Michael Pezzullo, the Secretary in the Department of Home Affairs. Michael Pezzullo. He informed the PJCIS that he wanted the journalist to go to jail (PJCIS 2019a, August 14: 28). This was after Michael Pezzullo, as a senior public servant called the Deputy

---

[20]*The Bridgeman case* as cited in the *George case* 5 [9]. See also *Feather v. Rogers* (1909) 9 SR (NSW) 192 and *Mitchell v New Plymouth Club (Inc.)* (1958) NZLR 1070).

Commissioner of the AFP, Neil Gaughan, to compliment him on the police raid on the home of News Corp journalist Annika Smethurst (Lyons 2019, August 29). The big question was how an individual, such as a journalist comes to ASIOs attention. The question was whether the Minister of Home Affairs or a senior government official had prior knowledge the search warrants were to be served on the ABC. Even more crucial was whether and how the member of cabinet or senior government official referred the matter to the AFP.

The head of the AFP, Andrew Colvin did confirm the existence of internal guidelines (PJCIS 2019a, August 14: 3). The Deputy Commissioner of the AFP, Neil Gaughan and other members of the AFP also did confirm the existence of national guidelines, especially as it relates to issues that of political sensitivity. The majority of investigations appear to be handled by means of referrals from government departments, and a small number are initiated by the AFP. A committee, headed by a Commissioner would then triage the referral and make a decision whether to reject the referral or to commence an investigation (PJCIS 2019b, September 20). There are no clear public guidelines that exists about how the government may refer matters to the Agencies to inquire into or investigate. In order to gain public trust, DoH may want to release public documents about how DoH and the AFP interact when it comes to investigations and inquiries. Perhaps these internal guidelines, if they are different to the publicly available Ministerial Guidelines, can be made public, in the interest of openness and transparency. If the AFP is referring to these 2014 Ministerial Guidelines and the updated guidelines regarding journalists in 2019, as to how referrals are evaluated, then these may simply be wholly inadequate insofar as they relate to how referrals are made by government departments to the AFP. The 2014 Ministerial Direction and the updated Ministerial Direction of 2019 regarding the investigations of leaks to journalist of secret information and the obligation to consider the greater public interest, do not seem to cover this area (Dutton 2019; Keenan 2014).[21]

In the *Jaffarie court case*, the Federal Court of Australia took the view that section 20 of the *ASIO Act 1979* emphasises the importance attached to ASIO discharging its purposes based on what is 'necessary', and not merely for example what ASIO itself considers to be 'desirable' (the *Jaffarie court case* 16 [17]). The case demonstrates that the individual is protected against the exercise of broad discretion. The analysis of location information to reveal movements of persons may also reveal personal information (PJCIS, Advisory Report 2015). It is not clear whether ASIO has any internal guidelines on how biases that arise when personal information is revealed is to be controlled, and ASIO is free from such influence when carrying out activities related to the its functions, such as collecting and using location information for an investigation ([3.92]; AGD, Submission No 27 to the PJCIS 2015, p. 29 cited in PJCIS, Advisory Report 2015, p. 93 [3.79]). In the Australian state of Victoria, the Assistant Commissioner Brett Guerin, the former head of Professional Standards, resigned after making online racial comments. The

---

[21]See Sect. 3.1.7 in Chap. 3.

incident was referred to an anti-corruption investigation (Houston and Vedelago 2018). ASIO nor the AFP may be immune to such biases. It is hard to determine how these biases may influence a legitimate investigation, or how an investigation may start based on such a bias but be justified as 'reasonably necessary' and related to the functions and purposes of the Agencies. BLD analysis may entrench certain biases that may cloud the judgment of even the most well-meaning of officers. In the absence of tools to reveal and address such biases, the collection and use of location information for security purposes may be influenced by irrelevant factors that are revealed by the location information.

5.2.1.1   Prevent Undue Influence From the Insider

In the *Jaffarie court case,* the court only relied on section 20 of the *ASIO Act 1979* as preventing undue influence from the outside but did not question whether any internal processes exist and are applied to address biases of officers themselves and undue influence from the outside (the *Jaffarie court case* 16 [17]). ASIO is shielded from being used for political gain. This is commendable. ASIO itself, without any outside influence, may have political biases motivated by the interest of keeping society safe, or in bad faith. The public safety interest can be abused to target individuals of a certain interest group, such as man of African descent, given the spate of criminal activities by the so-called 'African gangs' in Melbourne (Hutchinson et al. 2018). Section 20 of the *ASIO Act 1979* protects against advancing the interest of the majority, for example, but it does not specifically protect the minority and their interest in cases that can lead to racial profiling, and where location information is used for such practices whether intentionally or not. The AG's Guidelines warn against such actions by ASIO that may be politically motivated or be racially biased (AG's Guidelines, s 10.4 (b)(ii)). The use of BLD, show that such analyses reveal sensitive racial and political leanings of the individual (PJCIS, Advisory Report 2015: [3.92]; AGD, Submission No 27 to the PJCIS 2015, p. 29 cited in PJCIS 2015, p. 93 [3.79]). If these conflict with those held by an ASIO member, it may be justified as necessary to collect the location information without the bias of the officer being exposed, and with no meaningful practical safeguards in the AG's Guidelines about how to address and minimise such bias.

No third party can sift through the authorisations and notifications to ensure the use of the location information is based on good faith and will not marginalise or unfairly affect sections of the community. The AG's Guidelines do not go far enough to address how ASIO should handle such a sensitive situation, to ensure public trust that minority groups are not unfairly targeted and to give confidence that such targeting is addressed swiftly with community members and with the broader public. The AG's Guidelines simply state that inquiries and investigations into individual and groups should be done with due regard to the cultural values, mores and sensitivities of individuals of particular cultural or racial backgrounds, consistent with the national interest (AG's Guidelines 2016: s 10.4(b)(ii)). With the use of BLD, inquiries and the identification of persons as relevant to security run the risk of racial profiling, which needs to be addressed in documents that are publicly available, in order to ensure public trust and confidence.

5.2.2 The Reasonable and Proportionate Privacy Test

The Reasonable and Proportionate Privacy Test as it relates to the legitimate expectations of the Australian community relating to privacy and cybersecurity, as discussed in Sect. 5.1.2.2 in relation to the AFP, equally applies to ASIO.

5.2.3 The Connection Test

The 'use' is limited to the purpose for which, or 'in connection with', the disclosure was made (*TIA Act 1979* ss 174(2), 175(3), 176(4), 181). The voluntary or requested disclosure of historical location information and prospective location information to ASIO can only be made if ASIO or the Telco is satisfied that the disclosure would be 'in connection with' the performance of the functions of ASIO (*TIA Act 1979* ss 175 (3), 176(3)).

Personal information may only be collected, used, handled or disclosed for purposes connected with ASIO's legislative function, consistent with the performance of ASIO's functions, and be reasonably necessary for the performance of its statutory functions. This can be referred to as the 'Connection Test' (*TIA Act 1979* ss 175(3), 176(3); AG's Guidelines 2016: s 10.4). The term 'in connection with' is at the centre of the 'Connection Test' but is undefined in the law in this context.

This requirement can be referred to as the 'Connection Test'. ASIO has to demonstrate that the location information is likely to assist ASIO in carrying out its functions, such as the function to collect intelligence relating to security (*TIA Act 1979* ss 107J(2)(b)(i), 175(3), 176(3); *CAC Determination 2018* ss 8–9).

5.2.3.1 Cases Interpreting the Phrase 'in Connection with'

The court cases below refer to the AFP and not ASIO. I was not able to locate cases interpreting the words 'in connection with' in relation to ASIO (*TIA Act 1979* ss 175 (3), 176(3)). The phrase 'in connection with' is generally used in other pieces of legislation.[22] The opinions of the courts about the phrase 'in connection with' shed light on how courts are likely to interpret the phrase 'in connection with' in relation to ASIO. However, it is unlikely that such cases will be litigated, given the

---

[22]See Wilcox J in *Our Town FM Pty Ltd v Australian* Broadcasting Tribunal (1987) 77 ALR 577 at 591–592 as cited in *Gant v Commissioner Australian Federal Police* [2006] FCA 1475 12 [42].

confidentiality of the location information collection process, which is not a good sign for privacy protection.

Gant v Commissioner Australian Federal Police

The *Gant court case* addressed the interpretation of the phrase 'in connection with' (*ADJR Act 1977* s 9A; the *Gant court case* 8, [29]). The expression 'in connection with' has a broad meaning.[23] In the *Gant court case* Collier J also referred to cases that recognised that the words 'in connection with' as referring to a relationship.[24]

It simply requires a relation between connected things. That relation can be used to describe future events that are expected.[25] Things have a 'connection' if they are involved with one another and if it has something to do with the principal thing.[26]

The legislative context and purpose are also important to consider.[27] Collier J decided that the search warrant issued by the Commissioner of the AFP related to events for which Mr Gant was prosecuted, and so the relationship between the warrant, the investigation and the prosecution was clear (the *Gant court case* 14 [51]). Collier J also referred to Full Court decision in the case *Health Insurance Commission v Freeman (1998: 277)*, which noted that the fact of obtaining a search warrant and seizing the material under the warrant is conduct that is 'in connection with' an investigation (the *Gant court case* 7 [11]).[28] ASIO is permitted to collect the location information 'in connection with' the performance of its functions or directly related to its activities.

The functions of ASIO include the duty to maintain a broad database against which information obtained in relation to a specific inquiry or investigation can be

---

[23]See Wilcox J in the case *Our Town FM Pty Ltd v Australian Broadcasting Tribunal* (1987) 77 ALR 577, 591–592 cited in the *Gant case* 12 [42].

[24]See: Barwick CJ (with whom McTiernan, Windeyer and Owen JJ agreed) in *Brown v Rezitis* (1970) 127 CLR 157 at 165, Beazley and Tobias JJ in *Boylan Nominees Pty Ltd v Williams Refrigeration Australia Pty Ltd* [2006] NSWCA 100 at [68], Burchett and Marshall JJ in *Minister for Immigration and Multicultural Affairs v Mohammad* [2000] FCA 1275 (per Burchett J at [15]–[17], Marshall J agreeing with respect to this issue at [53]), the Full Court of the Federal Court in *Health Insurance Commission v Freeman* (1998) 158 ALR 267 at 273 and the Full Court in *Collector of Customs v Cliffs Robe River Iron Associates* (1985) 7 FCR 271, 275.

[25]See: Wilcox J in *Our Town FM Pty Ltd v Australian* Broadcasting Tribunal (1987) 77 ALR 577, 591–592 cited in Gant v Commissioner Australian Federal Police [2006] FCA 1475, 12 [42].

[26]See: MacFarlane J in *Re Nanaimo Community Hotel Ltd* [1944] 4 DLR 638, 639.

[27]See: Dawson J in *O'Grady* at 367, Brennan CJ, Gaudron and McHugh JJ in *PMT Partners Pty Ltd (in liq) v Australian National Parks and Wildlife Services* (1995) 184 CLR 301 at 313, *Australian Communications Network Pty Ltd v Australian Competition and Consumer Commission* [2005] FCAFC 221 at [26]–[34]) cited in the *Gant case* 14 [50].

[28]See: Judge Street in *Rebelution Pty Ltd & Anor V Commissioner of the Australian Federal Police* [2015] FCCA 338 referred to the binding decision of Collier J, and Collier J identifying the breadth of the meaning of the term 'in connection with'.

checked and assessed (AG's Guidelines ss 6.1, 6.2). This supports the development and use of BLD analytics software. In terms of the *CAC Determination 2018,* ASIO may list the detail of location information it requires to perform this function (*CAC Determination 2018* ss 8–9). ASIO may maintain a database of all the location information and analyse this database for any inquiry or investigation, both for persons under suspicion and those not, to try and identify if the person may be a risk to security in future, because there is a relationship between the collection and the use of the location information and ASIO developing and maintaining a storage database for BLD.[29] ASIO needs the location information for the database so it can identify and analyse the movements of persons that are relevant to security—this is the relationship between the location information and the security function of ASIO, as two things that are connected.[30] In this instance, location information may be checked and assessed that reveals personal information that may be of value in an investigation because it is 'in connection with' the performance of the functions of ASIO. The quantity of location information collected is not restricted to a named investigation or inquiry, with the scope defined, but may be used in other inquiries and investigations. The expression 'in connection with' is an indication of the broad discretion of the powers of ASIO, and how unlimited the access to location information, and in turn the access to location information as personal information is.

Samsonidis v Commissioner, Australian Federal Police

The term 'connected with' means that the location information obtained under one investigation can be used, where relevant, in other investigations. In the *Samsonidis court case* the AFP sent a letter dated 19 June 2007 to Greek authorities. The contents of the letter included transcripts of communications lawfully intercepted with a warrant. The AFP could communicate the information for a 'permitted purpose', which includes the communication of the information for a purpose 'connected with' an investigation (the *Samsonidis court case* [4]-[8]; *TIA Act 1979* ss 5(1) (definition of 'permitted purpose'), 67(1)).

The purpose of the letter was to disclose information that the Greek authorities could use as evidence in criminal proceedings. In terms of this definition, the connection sought is between the purpose for which a specific authority acts and an investigation being conducted by that authority. The purpose is not restricted to

---

[29]See: Barwick CJ (with whom McTiernan, Windeyer and Owen JJ agreed) in *Brown v Rezitis* (1970) 127 CLR 157 at 165, Beazley and Tobias JJ in *Boylan Nominees Pty Ltd v Williams Refrigeration Australia Pty Ltd* [2006] NSWCA 100 at [68], Burchett and Marshall JJ in *Minister for Immigration and Multicultural Affairs v Mohammad* [2000] FCA 1275 (per Burchett J at [15]–[17], Marshall J agreeing with respect to this issue at [53]), the Full Court of the Federal Court in *Health Insurance Commission v Freeman* (1998) 158 ALR 267 at 273 and the Full Court in *Collector of Customs v Cliffs Robe River Iron Associates* (1985) 7 FCR 271 at 275.

[30]See: Wilcox J in *Our Town FM Pty Ltd v Australian* Broadcasting Tribunal (1987) 77 ALR 577 at 591–592 cited in the *Gant* case 12 [42].

the investigation in question: 'A connection between the purpose and the investigation is sufficient' (the *Samsonidis court case* [9], [14], [15]). However, it must be the investigation of the agency in question. The term 'connected with' includes the discovery of new relationships in the current investigation, but also to follow the information to where it leads to discovering new relationships and new connections. The term 'connected with' is not restricted to circumstances where the aim is to assist the current investigation. The investigation is a process that goes on for periods. The aim is to discover, collect and organise and analyse information concerning facts and circumstances; discovering previously unknown relationships between facts and circumstances; discovering relationships between facts and circumstances that were not understood well. This process is carried out against listed criteria (the *Samsonidis court case* [16]-[17]).

Although the charges in Greece were similar to the investigation by the AFP, there was no sufficient connection under the definition of 'permitted purpose', and it was not connected with the AFP's investigation in relation to the appellant. As such, communicating the information was not allowed (the *Samsonidis court case* [23]; *TIA Act 1979* s 67(1)). If the decision was that the sharing of the communication was permitted, the effect would be that the information would simply be available to any other agency in the world, simply because ASIO or the AFP was involved in an investigation (the *Samsonidis court case,* Ibid [18]). The *Samsonidis court case* makes the point: if the information was shared within one organisation to perform another investigation, the organisation would be allowed to do so. The *Samsonidis court case* did not address the privacy impact of its interpretation of the term 'connected with'. The information was not able to be shared with international law enforcement agencies under the circumstances stated above, but the location information may be shared for secondary investigations, secondary offences and in respect of secondary individuals.

5.2.3.2   The Disclosure of Location Information Under the CAC Determination 2018 and the Suspicion on Reasonable Grounds

Location information may only be accessed with an authorisation and notification issued under the *CAC Determination 2018* (*TIA Act 1979* ss 175, 176, 183). The wording in the *CAC Determination 2018* is now considered to see whether an investigation and an inquiry requires suspicion of an offence, based on reasonable grounds, before location information is requested from the Telco.

Suspicion on Reasonable Grounds IS NOT a Limit to the Powers of ASIO

The AG's Guidelines defines an investigation as '. . . a concerted series of inquiries in relation to a subject where it has been determined that the activities of the subject could be relevant to security' (AG's Guidelines s 4.1(e)). ASIO may also undertake an 'inquiry'. The AG's Guidelines defines an inquiry as '. . . action taken to obtain information: (i) for the purpose of identifying a subject and/or determining whether the activities of a subject could be relevant to security; or (ii) as part of an investigation' (AG's Guidelines s 4.1(d)). The word 'inquiry' does not appear to be defined in the *TIA Act 1979* or in the *ASIO Act 1979*.

The AG's Guidelines do not appear to make any reference to suspicion of a past, present or future offence, based on reasonable grounds to start an inquiry nor do they reference the collection of location information for that inquiry based on suspicion of a past, present or future offence, on reasonable grounds. The suspicion standard may impact the operations, as it is a high standard. For a broad power such as security, there may be a need for 'reasonable grounds', based on good faith, to undertake the inquiry and investigation, of a person not suspected of an offence, and notifying a Judge of persons being actively monitored, with reports to the court and indicating whether the inquiry may continue and for how long it may be expected to continue and if useful and relevant intelligence is being obtained.

The wording in the *CAC Determination 2018* does not specifically require suspicion of an offence based on reasonable grounds to collect location information. The *CAC Determination 2018* states how the Telco must be notified about the authorisation ASIO issued, approving the collection of the location information. The *CAC Determination 2018* lists the things that must be included in the notice handed to the Telco (*CAC Determination 2018* ss 8–9). The wording of the *CAC Determination 2018* only requires that ASIO simply state that it is satisfied the disclosure of the location information would be 'in connection with' the performance by ASIO of its functions (*CAC Determination 2018* ss 8–9). The question is whether the legal phrase 'in connection with' requires suspicion of an offence, on reasonable grounds for ASIO to collect the location information. It does not appear as if suspicion is a required standard under the 'Connection Test', as demonstrated by the *Gant court case*.

BLD can be collected of any person for any purpose related to security, no prior judicial oversight is allowed, and the process is not transparent (Hardy and Williams 2014; Rix 2014). A court following *Gant court case* would likely agree the BLD would be lawful because it is 'in connection with' ASIO's broad security functions. ASIO yields tremendous power over the personal information of people, with only executive oversight conducted *ex post facto* (Hardy and Williams 2016; Williams 2016; *TIA Act 1979* s 186A; Evidence to PJCIS 2015, p. 41 (Thom)).

The phrase 'activities relevant to security' is described as including '... acts of conspiring, planning, organising, counselling, advising, financing, or otherwise advocating or encouraging the doing of those things.' It is not clear what it may mean '... to determine whether a particular subject or activity is relevant to security', and to undertake an inquiry on that basis, if one does not know of a past or present offence or suspect a future offence based on reasonable grounds. It is not clear what the term 'relevant to security' means versus suspicion on reasonable grounds (AG's Guidelines s 4.1(a)). If the person does not display obvious signs of misconduct, such as advising a person to commit a crime, then collecting location information would be an intrusive way of analysing the relationship between individuals to show that they are in contact and then to argue they are possibly advising each other. In this instance it may call for speculation, profiling and predictions based on past trends and persons displaying certain traits where security threats occurred. The question is how the collection of location information in an inquiry or investigation where no offence is suspected is considered as reasonably necessary and balanced with privacy interests.

ASIO may conduct inquiries about persons without needing suspicion of an offence based on 'reasonable grounds' (Revised Explanatory Memorandum 2015, p. 2 [3.]). In those circumstances, what informs ASIO that the inquiry is 'necessary' or security, without prior judicial oversight? What criteria is used to make the decision that it is 'necessary'? Is it only based on leads, received on reasonable grounds? Or is it only restricted to the term 'relevant to security' (*ASIO Act 1979* s 17 (1)(a), (b), (f)). If the person were not involved in an offence, how would the collection and analysis of a person's location information be 'necessary' as opposed to being 'desirable'? If a person were involved in an offence, collecting the location information would be necessary. It seems as if a broad investigatory power is not able to be limited by privacy, if ASIO can inquire into an individual's location information without judicial participation, to see if a person is relevant to security or not, and the basis for starting such an inquiry in the first place. Reasonable suspicion does not appear to be the required basis. If a person is not involved in an offence, and ASIO wants to assess if a person is a security risks, it is desirable that the location information is collected and analysed—ASIO would wish to make sure the person is not a threat. This can lead to random, trawling and speculative analyses of persons, using criteria in the broad discretion of the Agencies, with limited proof potentially not based on 'reasonable grounds', to predict the future criminal behaviour of the individual. An in-depth analysis of other internal oversight mechanisms that are confidential and not public information may address concerns regarding the limits that are imposed internally.

The location information of the person can be collected with no suspicion, and be analysed, with the aim of seeing whether the actions fall under the broad and fluctuating term 'security'. Any action of a person is subject to being relevant to security. As stated in the *Jaffarie court case*, the courts are very interested not to restrict ASIO so that it restricts ASIO's ability to properly monitor and assess threats (the *Jaffarie case* 23–24 [65], cited cf. *Suresh v Canada (The Minister of Citizenship and Immigration)* [2002] SCC 1 [88], [2002] 1 SCR 3 50–51). The court may have indirectly given a blessing to the broad powers of ASIO. The question is what standard is used to start the inquiry or investigation? It does not seem fair to privacy to covertly collect and analyse the location information of citizens without judicial involvement at some level, as may be necessary in a democratic society, to try and see if they are conspiring, as a security threat.

5.2.3.3 Balancing the Competing Interest of Privacy and the Public Interest of an Effective Criminal Justice System

The *Caratti court case* noted that search warrants are representative of balancing the competing interest of privacy and the public interest of an effective criminal justice system. Private interests are therefore overtaken by the public interest and the public interest is considered as more important by laws that allow search warrants to be issued. The *Caratti court case* states the laws allow access to location information. These laws also allow imposing conditions to ensure that valid warrants are issued. These conditions indicate the need for appropriate protections of the rights of the individual. This is however a limited protection of the individual's rights. However, to give effect to the protection of the rights, as intended by the laws, these conditions must be complied with. The law protecting the rights of the individual should not be interpreted with hostility if privacy is invaded—the invasion of privacy is inherent to the power to conduct investigations (the *Caratti court case* 10–11 [21], 15 [30]; the *George court case,* 110–111).[31]

Access to and the use of location information for inquiries and investigations is about balancing the conflicting interests of privacy, the public interest of police efficiency and the powers of the Agencies. Section 180F requires that the privacy of the individual be considered when location information is collected for an investigation. In doing so, the section seeks to balance the conflicting interests involved. In balancing these interests', challenges may arise for the investigations, such as delays ensuring that certain procedures are complied with. The interest of the Agencies is to have the flexibility to determine the quantity of the location information that may be reasonably necessary, based on the facts of a given investigation. However, the *CAC Determination 2018* grants the Agencies the sole discretion to set the level of location information and by simply requiring that the Agencies make the statement directly from the template that any interference with privacy was justifiable and proportionate (AFP 2015, p. 57). Unlike the Journalist Information Warrant (JIW) that tries to safeguard the public interest, when issuing the authorisation and notification under the *CAC Determination 2018* the Agencies are not required to give a preliminary demonstration of how the Agencies have tried to balance the privacy and the law enforcement interest to a third party such as a magistrate, Judge or AAT member. The oversight bodies such as the Inspector-General of Intelligence and Security (IGIS) and the Commonwealth Ombudsman may inspect the authorisations and notifications, but they are not specifically required to assess whether the operational activities themselves were 'reasonably necessary' to enforce the law.

---

[31]See also *Hart v Commissioner of Australian Federal Police* [2002] FCAFC 392; 124 FCR 384 [68].

5.3   Conclusion

The AFP must comply with the Privacy Tests prior to authorising the Telco to disclose location information. When conducting 'investigations' for serious offences, the AFP must act on the suspicion that the person is involved in an offence to collect the location information. However, to enforce the criminal law and for minor offences, the location information may be collected even if the person is not suspected of being involved in an offence.

ASIO must comply with the 'Connection Test' to collect the location information. The court decisions that were about issuing warrants seem to entrench the existing broad powers of the Agencies. This may set a precedent when it comes to the collection and use of location information if it is directly related to a law enforcement or security activity. However, the courts did not address privacy issues in relation to the broad powers of the Agencies. Given the non-transparent process of location information collection and use, and the absence of an obvious cause of action, there may be little chance that a court will consider how the powers of the Agencies impact privacy. The various Privacy Tests are built on the assumption that the activities of the Agencies are sound and do not question these activities but subject the protection of privacy to these broad activities. This Chapter described how this broad scope does not lend itself to protecting privacy but to advancing the powers of the Agencies to collect and use location information for its activities, which activities can easily be justified as acceptable, at the sole discretion of the Agencies. Moreover, other public bodies that collect location information under section 280 of the *TA 1997,* are not subject to the Privacy Tests, and this loophole may need to be stopped.

References

Addendum to the Explanatory Memorandum, Privacy Amendment (Enhancing Privacy Protection) Bill 2012

Administrative Decisions (Judicial Review) Act 1977 (Cth) (ADJR Act 1977)

Arnesen S, Johannesson MP, Linde J, Dahlberg S (2018) Do polls influence opinions? Investigating poll feedback loops using the novel dynamic response feedback experimental procedure. Soc Sci Comput Rev 36(6):735–743. https://doi.org/10.1177/0894439317731721

Assistance and Access Act 2018 (Cth) (AAA 2018)

Attorney-General's Department (AGD) (2016) Attorney-General's Guidelines in relation to the performance by the Australian Security Intelligence Organisation of its function of obtaining, correlating, evaluating and communicating intelligence relevant to security (including politically motivated violence)' (2016) (Attorney-General's [AG's] Guidelines)

Australia Federal Police (AFP) (2015) Processing of prospective data authorisations. https://assets.documentcloud.org/documents/3119594/AFP-Disclosure-Log.pdf. Accessed 28 Aug 2019

Australian Bureau of Statistics (ABS) (2010) 1500.0 - A guide for using statistics for evidence based policy. Latest ISSUE Released at 11:30 AM (CANBERRA TIME) 20/10/2010 First Issue. WHAT IS EVIDENCE BASED DECISION MAKING? https://www.abs.gov.au/ausstats/abs@.nsf/lookup/B214D5C2D2077A69CA2577C10011850A?opendocument. Accessed 20 Sept 2019

Australian Federal Police Act 1979 (Cth) (AFP Act 1979)

Australian Security Intelligence Organisation Act 1979 (Cth) (ASIO Act 1979)

Boylan Nominees Pty Ltd v Williams Refrigeration Australia Pty Ltd [2006] NSWCA 100

Bridgeman v Macalister (1898) 8 QLJ 151 (the Bridgeman court case)

Brown v Rezitis (1970) 127 CLR 157

Byrne E (2019, August 8) Public servant loses free speech High Court case over tweets criticising government policies. ABC. https://www.abc.net.au/news/2019-08-07/high-court-free-speech-public-service%2D%2Dbanerji-decision/11377990. Accessed 19 Sept 2019

Caisley O (2019, August 7) High Court Michaela Banerji ruling goes 'too far' on free speech: expert. The Australian. https://www.theaustralian.com.au/nation/high-court-backs-dismissal-of-public-servant-michaela-banerji/news-story/da989d40d2517392ecc0aafd5208a80f. Accessed 19 Sept 2019

Caratti v Commissioner of the Australian Federal Police [2017] FCAFC 177 (10 November 2017) (the Caratti court case)

Charter of Fundamental Rights of the European Union [2000] OJ C (364/012000/C)

Collector of Customs v Cliffs Robe River Iron Associates (1985) 7 FCR 271

Comcare v Banerji [2019] HCA 23 (7 August 2019) (the Comcare court case)

Commonwealth Ombudsman (2018) Report by the Commonwealth Ombudsman under s 186J of the Telecommunications (Interception and Access) Act 1979, November 2018. https://www.ombudsman.gov.au/__data/assets/pdf_file/0033/96747/201617-Chapter-4A-Annual-Report.pdf. Accessed 29 Aug 2019

Communications Access Coordinator's (CAC) Telecommunications (Interception and Access) (Requirements for Authorisations, Notifications and Revocations) Determination 2015 (Cth) (at 9 October 2015) Part 2 2.01 (1) Item 9 (CAC Determination 2015)

Criminal Code (Qld)

Cybercrime Legislation Amendment Act (Cth) 2012 (CLAA 2012)

Day v Commissioner, Australian Federal Police [2000] FCA 1272 (11 September 2000) (the Day court case)

Department of Home Affairs (DoH) (2019) Industry assistance under Part 15 of the Telecommunications Act 1997 (Cth). Administrative guidance for agency engagement with designated communications providers. https://www.homeaffairs.gov.au/nat-security/files/assistance-access-administrative-guidance.pdf. Accessed 29 Aug 2019

Diversity Council Australia (DCA) (2018, September 3) The facts on Victorian African Crime Position statements. https://www.dca.org.au/position-statements/facts-victorian-african-crime. Accessed 18 Sept 2019

Dutton (2019, August 8) Minister for Home Affairs - Ministerial Direction to Australian Federal Police Commissioner relating to investigative action involving a professional journalist or news media organisation in the context of an unauthorised disclosure of material made or obtained by a current or former Commonwealth officer. https://www.afp.gov.au/sites/default/files/PDF/Ministerial-Direction-signed-2019.pdf. Accessed 20 Sept 2019

European Telecommunications Standards Institute (ETSI) (2017) Lawful Interception (LI); Retained Data; Requirements of Law Enforcement Agencies for handling Retained Data

Evidence to Parliamentary Joint Committee on Intelligence and Security (PJCIS), Parliament of Australia, Canberra, 29 January 2015, 41 (Vivienne Thom, Inspector-General of Intelligence and Security, Office of the Inspector-General of Intelligence and Security)

Explanatory Memorandum (2019) Criminal Code Amendment (Agricultural Protection) Bill 2019

Explanatory Memorandum and Statement of Compatibility with Human Rights (2019) Australian Bill of Rights Bill (Cth), 2019

Feather v. Rogers (1909) 9 SR (NSW) 192

Gagliardi J (2019, June 6) Your morning Briefing: AFP raids at arm's length from government: PM. The Australian. https://www.theaustralian.com.au/news/your-morning-briefing-afp-raids-at-arms-length-from-government-pm/news-story/5a8e3375904609d63d046f380325bd13. Accessed 19 Sept 2019

Gant v Commissioner Australian Federal Police [2006] FCA 1475 (the Gant court case)

George v Rockett (1990) 170 CLR 104 20 June 1990 (the George court case)

Golder B, Williams G (2006) Balancing national security and human rights: assessing the legal response of common law nations to the threat of terrorism. J Comp Policy Anal Res Pract 8 (1):43–62

Griffiths L (2005) The implied freedom of political communication: the state of the law post Coleman and Mulholland. James Cook Univ Law Rev 5, 12:93

Groves M (2008) Substantive legitimate expectations in Australian administrative law. Melbourne Univ Law Rev 32:270–523. https://law.unimelb.edu.au/__data/assets/pdf_file/0010/1705708/32_2_4.pdf. Accessed 17 Sept 2019.

Hardy K, Williams G (2014) National security reforms stage one: intelligence gathering and secrecy. Law Soc NSW J 6(November):68. https://search.informit.com.au/fullText; dn=20151952;res=AGISPT. Accessed 27 Aug 2019.

Hardy K, Williams G (2016) Executive oversight of intelligence agencies in Australia. (June 7, 2016) In: Goldman ZK, Rascoff SJ (eds) Global intelligence oversight: governing security in the twenty-first century (2016); UNSW Law Research Paper No. 2016-35. https://ssrn.com/abstract=2804835. Accessed 3 Sept 2019

Hart v Commissioner of Australian Federal Police [2002] FCAFC 392; 124 FCR 384

Health Insurance Commission v Freeman (1998) 158 ALR 267

Houston C, Vedelago C (2018 February, 26) Top cop resigns in disgrace over link to racist and obscene posts. The Age. https://www.theage.com.au/national/victoria/top-cop-resigns-in-disgrace-over-link-to-racist-andobscene-posts-20180226-p4z1u5.html. Accessed 4 Apr 2018

Hutchinson S, Ferguson R, Urban R (2018, January 6) African Gangs Reign of Fear in Melbourne's West. The Australian. https://www.theaustralian.com.au/nationalaffairs/state-politics/african-gangs-reign-of-fear-in-melbournes-west/newsstory/deb78713fb90f132c8df28b2b163fd24. Accessed 4 Apr 2018

Jaffarie v Director General of Security [2014] FCAFC 102 (18 August 2014) (the *Jaffarie court case*)

Keenan M (12 May 2014) Ministerial Direction. https://www.afp.gov.au/about-us/governance-and-accountability/ministerial-direction. Accessed 27 Aug 2019

Kioa v West [1985] HCA 81; (1985) 159 CLR 550 (18 December 1985) (the *Kioa court case*)

Laurenceson J (2019 September 18) Creeping distrust: our anxiety over China's influence is hurting Chinese-Australians. The Conversation. https://theconversation.com/creeping-distrust-our-anxiety-over-chinas-influence-is-hurting-chinese-australians-123677. Accessed 19 Sept 2019

Lowy Institute (2018, June 20) Lowy Institute Poll. https://www.lowyinstitute.org/publications/2018-lowy-institute-poll. Accessed 16 Sept 2019

Lowy Institute (2019) Threats to vital interests. https://lowyinstitutepoll.lowyinstitute.org/themes/security-and-defence/. Accessed 16 Sept 2019

Lyons J (2019, August 29) Home Affairs Secretary Mike Pezzullo complimented AFP for raid on home of journalist Annika Smethurst. ABC. https://www.abc.net.au/news/2019-08-29/pezzullo-complimented-afp-on-journalist-raid/11460306. Accessed 19 Sept 2019)

M and Health Service Provider [2007] PrivCmrA 15.

Minister for Immigration and Border Protection v WZARH [2015] HCA 40 (4 November 2015) (*the WZARH court case*)

Minister for Immigration and Multicultural Affairs v Mohammad [2000] FCA 1275

Minister of State for Immigration & Ethnic Affairs v Ah Hin Teoh ("Teoh's case") [1995] HCA 20; (1995) 128 ALR 353; (1995) 69 ALJR 423; (1995) EOC 92-696 (extract); (1995) 183 CLR 273 (7 April 1995)

Mitchell v. New Plymouth Club (Inc.) (1958) NZLR 1070)

Moss A (2015, December 8) Refashioning 'legitimate expectations' in Australian administrative law: Minister for Immigration and Border Protection v WZARH' on AUSPUBLAW). https://auspublaw.org/2015/12/refashioning-legitimate-expectations/. Accessed 17 Sept 2019

Natural Justice or Procedural Fairness. https://www.fedcourt.gov.au/digital-law-library/judges-speeches/justice-robertson/robertson-j-20150904. Accessed 17 Sept 2019

OAIC (2019) *Chapter B: Key concepts Version 1.3, July 2019*. https://www.oaic.gov.au/assets/privacy/app-guidelines/APP-Guidelines-Chapter-B-v1.3.pdf. Accessed 29 Aug 2019

Office of the Australian Information Commissioner (OAIC) (2015) Submission No 92, Inquiry into the Telecommunications (Interception and Access) Amendment (Data Retention) Bill 2014, January 2015.

Our Town FM Pty Ltd v Australian Broadcasting Tribunal (1987) 77 ALR 577 at 591–592

Own Motion Investigation v Australian Government Agency [2007] PrivCmrA 4

Packham C (2019, September 16) Exclusive: Australia concluded China was behind hack on parliament, political parties – sources. Reuters. https://www.reuters.com/article/us-australia-china-cyber-exclusive/exclusive-australia-concluded-china-was-behind-hack-on-parliament-political-parties-sources-idUSKBN1W00VF?utm_medium=Social&utm_source=twitter. Accessed 20 Sept 2019

Parliamentary Joint Committee on Human Rights (PJCHR), Fifteenth Report of the 44th Parliament

Parliamentary Joint Committee on Intelligence and Security (PJCIS) (2015) Parliament of Australia, Advisory Report on the Telecommunications (Interception and Access) Amendment (Data Retention) Bill 2014 (Cth)

Parliamentary Joint Committee On Intelligence and Security (PJCIS) (2019a, August 14) Hansard. Impact of the exercise of law enforcement and intelligence powers on press freedom. https://parlinfo.aph.gov.au/parlInfo/download/committees/commjnt/ddce966e-26b5-4fcc-ba56-c07e51b19793/toc_pdf/Parliamentary%20Joint%20Committee%20on%20Intelligence%20and%20Security_2019_08_14_7104_Official.pdf;fileType=application%2Fpdf#search=%22committees/commjnt/ddce966e-26b5-4fcc-ba56-c07e51b19793/0007%22. Accessed 19 Sept 2019

Parliamentary Joint Committee On Intelligence and Security (PJCIS) (2019b, September 20) Hansard. Impact of the exercise of law enforcement and intelligence powers on press freedom. ??. Accessed 20 Sept 2019

PlayerFM (2019) An address by ASIO Director-General Duncan Lewis. 11 days ago 1:00:02. https://player.fm/series/the-lowy-institute-live-events/an-address-by-asio-director-general-duncan-lewis. Accessed 16 Sept 2019

PMT Partners Pty Ltd (in liq) v Australian National Parks and Wildlife Services (1995) 184 CLR 301

Privacy Act 1988 (Cth)

Public Service Act 1922 (Cth)

Public Service Act 1999 (Cth)

Re Minister for Immigration and Multicultural Affairs; Ex parte Lam [2003] HCA 6; (2003) 214 CLR 1; (2003) 195 ALR 502; (2003) 77 ALJR 699 (12 February 2003) (*the Lam court case*)

Re Nanaimo Community Hotel Ltd [1944] 4 DLR 638

Rebelution Pty Ltd & Anor V Commissioner of the Australian Federal Police [2015] FCCA 338

Revised Explanatory Memorandum, Telecommunications (Interception and Access) Amendment (Data Retention) Bill 2015 (Cth), 2015

Revised Explanatory Memorandum, Telecommunications and Other Legislation Amendment (Assistance and Access) Bill 2018 (Cth), 2018

Rix M (2014, August 26) What is the meaning and what is the use of 'metadata retention'? The Conversation. https://theconversation.com/what-is-the-meaning-and-what-is-the-use-of-metadata-retention-30350. Accessed 29 Aug 2019

Robertson A (2015, September 4) Judges and the Academy

Samsonidis v Commissioner, Australian Federal Police [2007] FCAFC 159 (5 October 2007) (the *Samsonidis court case*)

Secretary of State for The Home Department and Tom Watson MP and others [2018] EWCA Civ 70

Selvadurai N (2017) The retention of telecommunications metadata: a necessary national security initiative or a disproportionate interference with personal privacy? Comput Telecommun Law Rev 23(2):35–41

Suresh v Canada (The Minister of Citizenship and Immigration) [2002] SCC 1 [88], [2002] 1 SCR 3 50–51

Telecommunications (Interception and Access) Act 1979 (Cth) (TIA Act 1979)

Telecommunications (Interceptions and Access) (Requirements for Authorisations, Notifications and Revocations) Determination 2018 (Cth) (at 20 November 2018) (CAC Determination 2018)

Telecommunications service warrant Telecommunications (Interception and Access) Regulations 2017 (Cth)

The Guardian (2019, June 7) Why did the polls fail and how can they change? – Australian politics live podcast. https://www.theguardian.com/australia-news/audio/2019/jun/07/opinion-polls-fail-federal-election-australian-politics-live-podcast. Accessed 19 Sept 2019

Towns Police Act (19 Vict. No. 24) 1849 (UK)

Voinet v Barrett (1885) 55 LJQB 39 (Vionet court case)

Whitbourn M (2019 August 7) Former public servant loses free speech case over anonymous tweets. Sydney Morning Herald. https://www.smh.com.au/politics/federal/former-public-ser vant-michaela-banerji-loses-high-court-free-speech-case-20190807-p52enu.html#comments. Accessed 19 Sept 2019

Williams G (2005) Balancing national security and human rights: lessons from Australia. 4(1) Borderlands e-Journal. http://www.borderlands.net.au/vol4no1_2005/williams_balancing.htm

Williams G (2016) The legal assault on Australian democracy. QUT Law Rev 16(2):19

Chapter 6
Location Information as Personal Information, to Better Protect Privacy

6.1 The Right to Privacy Under Australian and International Law

As a start, the relationship between the *TIA Act 1979*, the *TA 1997*, the *Privacy Act 1988*, the Attorney-General's (AG's) Guidelines and the *CAC Determination 2018* regarding privacy; access to and the use of location information; and how these in turn relate to the Agencies requires a discussion.

As demonstrated by the Privacy Tests, privacy is a key limit to the powers of the Agencies: privacy serves as an oversight mechanism. The *CAC Determination 2018* include the privacy protections to be complied with incorporating section 180F of the *TIA Act 1979* in the location information collection process (AG's Guidelines s 13; *Privacy Act 1988* Schedule 1 Part 2 3.1; *TIA Act 1979* s 180F; *CAC Determination 2018*). In terms of section 180F of the *TIA Act 1979,* the AFP must be satisfied on reasonable grounds that any interference with the privacy of any person or persons that may result from the disclosure or use of the 'information or documents' is justifiable and proportionate. *CAC Determination 2018* is a legislative instrument, but not a source of substantive law. It establishes the machinery for issuing authorisations to collect location information under the substantive law—the *TIA Act 1979* (*TA 1997* s 276). The *CAC Determination 2018* was made by the Communications Access Co-ordinator (CAC), under the *TIA Act 1979* (s 183(2)). The CAC was previously appointed by the Attorney-General (AG), but is now appointed by the Minister of Home Affairs, both executive member of the government (*TIA Act 1979* s 6R (1), (2)).

Despite not being subject to the *Privacy Act 1988*, ASIO must comply with the AG's Guidelines, which are not made by Parliament, but by the AG, as an executive member of Cabinet. The guidelines protect privacy and uses privacy as a tool to limit the powers of ASIO. The guidelines simultaneously allow access to personal information. Personal information may only be collected, used, handled or disclosed for purposes connected with ASIO's legislative functions, consistent with the

© Springer Nature Switzerland AG 2020
S. Shanapinda, *Advance Metadata Fair*, Law, Governance and Technology Series
44, https://doi.org/10.1007/978-3-030-50255-3_6

performance of ASIO's functions, and be reasonably necessary for the performance of its statutory functions (AG's Guidelines s 10.4).

Australian common law does not protect the right to free speech (the *Comcare court case*).[1] Similarly, Australian common law is said not to recognise the general right to privacy (Watts and Casanovas 2019; Taylor 2000, pp. 238, 241; *Victoria Park court case* (1937) 58 CLR 479; *ABC court case* [2001] HCA 63: 58; Human & Constitutional Rights Resource Page 2018; the *Comcare court case*). The same principle may be applied when it comes before the court and the individual intends to demand recognition of their right to privacy, but under statutory law (the *Privacy Act 1988*). Given this, coupled with the confidentiality of the metadata disclosure scheme; the ignorance of the individual that their metadata is collected and used; and the inability to lodge complaints based on not knowing about the collection of their metadata, no individual is practically able lodge any such case in a court of law, in any event. These circumstances may be described as the privacy rights of the individual having reached a *cul-de-sac*. If somehow the individual is able to lodge such a court case under the current legal circumstances, then regard must be had to the laws passed by Parliament only, to protect privacy and applying the proportionality principle to it (the *Comcare court case*).[2]

Instead, privacy is protected as a by-product of other interests that are already protected, such as confidentiality clauses from contracts with banks (Taylor 2000, pp. 240–241; Loyd court case (1826) 2 Car & P 325; 172 ER 147; Tournier court case [1924] 1 KB 461; *Australia & New Zealand Bank court case* (1968) 88 WN (Pt 1) (NSW) 368; *Federal Commissioner of Taxation court case* (1979) 143 CLR 499; *Barclays Bank court case* [1989] 1 WLR 1066; *Winterton Constructions court case* (1992) 39 FCR 97, 114-15; *Robertson court case* [1994] 1 WLR 1493; *Christoj court case* [2000] 1 WLR 937; Laster 1989: 31,424).

Customers of the Telco are protected by privacy policies and standard terms and conditions that contain clauses to protect the privacy of the customers such as the privacy policy of Telstra and of Vodafone, and also under the *Privacy Act 1988*, subject to the Exclusions that apply.

The strongest position to better protect privacy is under the *Australian Constitution*. However, unlike its many Western peers, the *Australian Constitution* makes no mention of the protection of privacy in a bill of rights. The position of the federal government is stated to be that the International Covenant on Civil and Political Rights (ICCPR) and existing legislation, such as the *Privacy Act 1988* and the *TIA Act 1979*, adequately protect privacy. Australia agreed to be bound by and to respect the *ICCPR*, by ratifying the *ICCPR* in 1980 (Stratton 2013; *CACA* 1900 s 51(xxix)); DFAT 2018; *Kioa* (1985) 159 CLR 550; *Tasmanian Dam Case* (1983) 158 CLR 1; AHRC 2018; AHRC undated; Explanatory Memorandum, Privacy Bill 1988:

---

[1]See Sect. 5.1.2.2.4 in Chap. 5.
[2]See Sect. 5.1.2.2.4 in Chap. 5.

7 [16]).[3] The PJCHR uses Article 17 as a measure for Australian law, and in the context of the Agencies accessing and using information or documents collected from the Telco (PJCHR 2016, 18, 25 [2.48]).

The Australian Human Rights Commission (AHRC) monitors how human rights are implemented (*AHRC Act 1986* (Cth) ss 3(1) (definition of 'Covenant'), 10A, 11, 46C (4)(a), Schedule 2; ICCPR Article 17).

6.2   Privacy in Relation to Personal Information

Personal information is defined as information about an individual in the *Privacy Act 1988*. The meaning of personal information is extended to include location information the Telco is required to retain—telecommunications data, or the 'information or documents related to the communication', that is required to be retained, is deemed to be personal information (*Privacy Act 1988* s 6(1); *TIA Act 1979* s 187LA). The term privacy is therefore used in the context of the definition of personal information in the *Privacy Act 1988* and section 180F of the *TIA Act 1979*. Privacy and the powers of the Agencies should be balanced to ensure adequate safeguards for the privacy rights of the individual, as demonstrated by the Privacy Tests.[4]

However, for 'telecommunications data' or 'information or documents' to be legally regarded as personal information, the information must be 'about' an individual who is reasonably identifiable or an individual who has been identified, making location information personally identifiable information (PII).

The current definition of 'personal information' is:

> ... information or an opinion about an identified individual, or an individual who is reasonably identifiable:
>
> (a) whether the information or opinion is true or not; and
> (b) whether the information or opinion is recorded in a material form or not.
>
> Note: Section 187LA of the *Telecommunications (Interception and Access) Act 1979* extends the meaning of personal information to cover information kept under Part 5-1A of that Act (in the *Privacy Act 1988* s 6(1)).

This depends on two things: the context and the circumstances. The Telco can link various pieces of information to identify the individual. However, if it is not practical to identify the person from linking the information, the information may not be personal information. The identifiability of the person, and therefore, the classification of whether the location information in question is personal information, is made subject to financial costs, practicality and the likelihood that the information

---

[3]The ICCPR was ratified on 08/13/1980.

[4]See Sect. 5.1.2 in Chap. 5.

will be linked in a manner that is able to identify the individual (Explanatory Memorandum 2012: 61, Item 36).

Under the Explanatory Memorandum of the Privacy Amendment Bill of 2012, examples of personal information included information about an individual's physical description, residence, place of work, business and business activities, employment, occupation, relationship to other persons, recreational interests and political, philosophical or religious beliefs (Explanatory Memorandum 2012: [33]). This type of information concerns or relates to an individual, establishing a connection between the individual and the information, making the information 'about' that individual (*Telstra decision* [98]-[99]). In reaching the conclusion that information about a person's job is personal information, the Administrative Appeals Tribunal (AAT) referred to the Explanatory Memorandum 2012 (*Telstra Corporation Limited case*, [97]; Office of the Attorney-General 2015: 30–31). The Explanatory Memorandum 2012 does not make or set the law but was used by the AAT as an extrinsic aid to interpret the law and find that information about a person's work is personal information. The Federal Court referred to this approach by the AAT and did not object to it (Parliament of Australia 2006; *AIA* s 15AB(1) (b) and (2)(e)).

Personal information may also qualify as sensitive information. Sensitive information includes information or an opinion about an individual's racial or ethnic origin; political opinions; membership of a political association; religious beliefs or affiliations; philosophical beliefs; sexual orientation or practices; or criminal record; health information about an individual; or biometric information; that is also personal information (*Privacy Commissioner court case* [41]; *Privacy Act 1988* (Cth) s 6(1) (definition of 'sensitive information')). There is potential to build a detailed picture of a person's activities, relationships and behaviours under the telecommunications data retention scheme. This was not the case before, and so the disclosure of 'telecommunications data' should be limited to investigations of serious offences and security threats (Evidence to PJCIS 2015: 46–47 (Pilgrim)). If the collection is not limited to serious offences, additional safeguards should be introduced. The Parliamentary Joint Committee on Intelligence and Security (PJCIS) accepted that location records are also sensitive, as did the Attorney-General's Department (AGD) (PJCIS, *Advisory Report* 2015: 97 [3.92]; AGD, Submission No 27, *Inquiry* 2015, 29 cited in PJCIS *Advisory Report* 2015, 93 [3.79]). Yet, despite this, personal information may be collected under the less stringent rules of the *CAC Determination 2018*. The Agencies may collect and use personal information and sensitive information after applying the Privacy Tests (*Privacy Act 1988* Schedule 1, APP 6.1; AG's Guidelines ss 6, 10, 11).

6.2.1 The Personal Nature of the Location Information That Is Required to Be Retained

The Exclusions were introduced to reduce the volume of location information the Telco is required to retain. However, the Exclusions generally do not protect privacy adequately. One of the Exclusions are that the Telco is not required to retain personal information prior to, during and after a voice or SMS communication (PJCIS, Advisory Report 2015: 97 81 [3.33], [fn 31]). The PJCIS accepted that the detail and frequency of the location records that are required to be retained are significantly reduced by the Exclusions (PJCIS, Advisory Report 2015: 97 [3.92], [3.79]). The Privacy Commissioner however warned about the personal and sensitive nature of personal information—even if the Exclusions are applied. The location information retained at the start and at the end of the voice or SMS communication may still reveal '. . . information about the behaviours of individuals at a level approaching the equivalent effect of real time location tracking.' (OAIC, Submission No 92: 2015, 41 Appendix B [5]). This information may be historical location information, but it is collected without suspicion based, on reasonable grounds, unlike for prospective location information, where suspicion based on reasonable grounds is required for the AFP to collect the location information (*TIA Act 1979* s 178(2); *CAC Determination 2018*). This is especially so given the technological advances made with satellite enabled 5G location precision that is able to reveal locations within a 3–5 m radius (Koivisto et al. 2017; NGMN 2015; 5G PPP undated; 3GPP 2017; La Trobe University 2019).

Privacy protections are subject to the discretion and interests of the Agencies and the Telco, and the effectiveness of the Exclusions may be placed in significant doubt. Given this, privacy is not adequately protected under the *CAC Determination 2018*. This is so because despite the Exclusions—substantial location information that reveals personal information about the individual can still be retained and disclosed under less stringent requirements (OAIC Submission No 92, 2015: 41 Appendix B [5]; Telstra, Submission No 112, 2015: 4 [8]). The Telco has the discretion to retain more location information, and has the legal duty to disclose the location information in its possession, whether the Telco is required to retain the metadata or not, both under section 280 of the *Telecommunications Act 1997* and under the *CAC Determination 2018*, even if that location information is not required to be retained (Telstra, Submission No 112, 2015: 5[8]; *TIA Act 1979* s 187C; *TA 1997* ss 275A, 276, 280, 313(3), (4); 3131(7); *TIA Act 1979* ss 174(1), 175(1), 176(1), 177(2), 178 (1), 179(1), 180(1)).

6.2.1.1 The Potential Impact on Tech-Savvy Young Australians

In analysing the usage patterns for mobile communications in relation to the Exclusions to only record and store location information at the start and at the end of a Voice, SMS, email, chat, forum, social media communication demonstrates that the Exclusions are ineffective. Australians and residents are tracked, and their locations are stored most of the times, and there is no meaningful limit that the Exclusions have on preserving the privacy of any person using mobile communications, given its popularity. Ninety-two per cent of Australians aged 18–24 accessed the internet three or more times a day. On the other hand, only 43% of those aged 65 and over, used the internet three or more times a day. The mobile phone is also the most frequently used device to access the internet. For three or more times a day, seven days a week, and over various internet devices the location information and other metadata are collected and stored. This is true for 92% of young people (ACMA 2018, p. 58).

6.2.1.2   The Potential Impact on Journalists

Location information reveals personal information about an individual and his or her relationships easily and without much effort required. This is demonstrated with the example of Mr Will Ockenden (Mayer et al. 2016; Ockenden 2016).

Mr Ockenden was an Australian Broadcasting Corporation (ABC) reporter who requested and obtained his location information from a Telco. The location information that revealed the personal information about Mr Ockenden was location information the Telco accepted was personal information and disclosed to him. It may be assumed that the location information disclosed was only location information that was collected at the start and at the end of the communication, practically applying the Exclusions. The location information was for the period: 23 September 2014 to 2 April 2015. The location information of Mr Ockenden was captured 12,100 times in six months, roughly at a rate of 67 times a day or 3 times an hour. Mr Ockenden then released his location information to the public and invited the public to tell him what the location information revealed. After over 300 responses, the public made the following observations about him:

a. he worked for the ABC in the neighbourhood called Ultimo;
b. he lived in Manly, Sydney. The street addresses were wrong, but close;
c. he plays golf in Manly, and spends most of his weekends in Manly;
d. he travelled via bus and ferry on routes, guessed by looking at the departure times of the different modes;
e. he got off a bus on a specific time on a given day;
f. he was stuck in traffic on a specific day on the Spit Bridge in Manly, and he was travelling to Hawkesbury at lunchtime for the Australia Day weekend;
g. he moved to the Redfern neighbourhood (the day he moved, his mobile phone stopped communicating with cell towers in Manly);
h. he was in Hobart for Christmas;
i. he made domestic flights, the flight numbers and departure times were corroborated by Google;
j. his top ten contacts and their identities, but guessed correctly with some help from Mr Ockenden;

  k. he called his parents, because he did not text them; and

  l. he went on a flight to Victoria, but they could not correctly guess what the trip was for

Mr Ockenden replied that the feedback was mostly accurate and frightening (Ockenden 2016).

6.2.1.3   The Mapbox Platform

Mr Ockenden used the Mapbox software Platform to analyse his location information. Mapbox is a location data platform for mobile and web applications, a stepping stone to add location features, which include maps, search and navigation. The platform allows for the visualisation of location information on a map. Using the Mapbox Platform helps to analyse the location information, potentially making the person 'reasonably identifiable' (Mapbox 2018; Ockenden 2016).

    Any person can purchase and use this platform and create a map, making the analytics solution easily available to the general public, the Agencies and public bodies collecting location information under section 280 of the *TIA Act 1979*, to use for analysing the locations of their targets. The platform was available from USD499 per month for a commercial licence and for USD0.50 for 1000 web map views. The software is affordable and easy to obtain and is able to reveal locations, personal information of the individual (Mapbox 2018; Ockenden 2016).

6.3   The Debate About Certain Types of Location Information as Personal Information

The question whether a certain type of information is personal is in part a factual question. The identifiability of the individual is dependent on the potential for matching and linking the various pieces of information to the individual (*Privacy Commissioner court case* [63]; *WL case* [52]; OAIC 2013: 21). The question whether a certain type of information or document is personal information under the *Privacy Act 1988* (Cth) is also assessed against the legal status of the location information. The location information is divided into various legal categories, which indicates the value or significance of that type of location information, which in turn hints at whether the location information may be 'about' the individual and therefore be personal. To analyse whether the relevant location information is personal, the various categories location information is placed under, must be studied.

6.3.1   Finding the Meaning of the Words: 'About an Individual'

In the *Privacy Commissioner court case*, the very narrow issue of statutory interpretation was what the words 'about an individual' meant, as applied in the *Privacy Act 1988* (Cth) prior to 12 March 2014 (2 [4], [41]). The Privacy Commissioner argued the phrase 'about an individual' should be disregarded:

> The Privacy Commissioner submitted that if there is information from which an individual's identity could reasonably be ascertained, and that information is held by the organisation, then it will always be the case that the information is about the individual (ts 59). In other words, the words "about an individual" would "do no work" and have no substantive operation (ts 59) (*Privacy Commissioner case* 15 [62]).

The Federal Court of Australia (FCA) rejected the argument of the Privacy Commissioner, stating that the words 'about an individual' cannot be ignored because it implies that the individual must be the subject of the information in question (*Privacy Commissioner case* [62], [63]). The FCA formulated the privacy test to determine whether the information in question is personal, as follows:

> The concept of "personal information" to which an organisation must provide an individual with access is very broad. It encompasses untrue information which is not recorded in any material form. It is, however, constrained by the requirements that:
>
> (i)   it must be held by the organisation;
> (ii) it must be "about" the individual who requested access; and
> (iii) it must be about an individual whose identity is apparent, or can reasonably be ascertained, from the information or opinion (*Privacy Commissioner court case* [60]).

The FCA accepted that the information can be about various things, stating: 'Information and opinions can have multiple subject matters' (*Privacy Commissioner court case* [63]). If a single piece of information that starts out by not being about a person, may end up being about a person when it is combined with other separate pieces of information. If separate pieces of location information is combined and with other extra information, any of the three categories of location information may end up being personal information. The FCA stated that, based on the facts of every case, it must at first be determined whether every single item of information or the combined pieces of information requested from the Telco is about the individual. Secondly, once having determined that the information is about an individual, in order to determine whether the identity of the person is reasonably ascertainable, one must undertake an evaluative conclusion (*Privacy Commissioner court case* [63]).

The FCA cited the Deputy President in *Telstra decision*:

> The Deputy President considered the dictionary definition of "about" as meaning "concerning or relating to someone or something; on the subject of them or it" ([97]). She gave examples of numerous matters from the Explanatory Memorandum which accompanied the Privacy Bill 1988 (Cth) which concerned or related to an individual, and were therefore "about" the individual (eg physical description, residence, place of work, business

activities, employment, occupation, investments and property holdings, relationships to others, recreational interests, political, philosophical or religious beliefs) (11 [41]).

The location information retained for billing purposes related to Mr. Will Ockden's residence, place of work, business activities, employment, occupation, relationships and recreational activities. The Agencies are allowed to access these types of personal information in terms of sections 10.4 and 13 of the AG's Guidelines, section 180F of the *TIA Act 1979* and the Australian Privacy Principle (APP) 3 in the *Privacy Act 1988*, but subject to the Privacy Tests.

The FCA was criticised for its decision not to recognise the 'telecommunications data' under question as personal information, and thereby creating an outdated data privacy framework '. . . that ignores the working reality of contemporary information infrastructures and processing' (Goldenfein 2017). The 'telecommunications data' is still being made subject to the being 'about' the person, as opposed to identifying that various types of data can be linked and indirectly be about the persons (Goldenfein 2017). I do agree that this is a higher onus to bear. Location information that is voluntarily retained and voluntarily disclosed to the Agencies, is not deemed to be personal, and must therefore first be about the individual, to qualify as personal information. Goldenfein also claims that this makes the Australian system antiquated. This may not be an accurate characterization of the decision and the intention of the FCA's decision. The important and progressive principle of the FCAs decision is that the FCA stated aggregated information may be about an individual, even if a single piece may not be about an individual. In this manner the court clearly identifies that the various types of data can be linked and indirectly be about the persons. If the separate pieces are combined, the information may be about an individual:

> The words "about an individual" direct attention to the need for the individual to be a subject matter of the information or opinion. This requirement might not be difficult to satisfy. Information and opinions can have multiple subject matters. Further, on the assumption that the information refers to the totality of the information requested, then even if a single piece of information is not "about an individual" it might be about the individual when combined with other information. *However, in every case it is necessary to consider whether each item of personal information requested, individually or in combination with other items, is about an individual.* This will require an evaluative conclusion, depending upon the facts of any individual case, just as a determination of whether the identity can reasonably be ascertained will require an evaluative conclusion (emphasis added) (Privacy Commissioner case 16 [63]).

The test requires that the information be 'about' the individual—the person must be the subject of the information. However, on the whole, the FCA essentially differentiates between an apparent case of identity and a case where the identity may not be apparent. The FCA developed a three-legged test to determine if information is personal information, ensuring that at the second stage of the inquiry indirect relations are catered for, which indirect relations the FCA recognises. This second stage of the inquiry allows for the rich modern field of data-matching and Big Location Data (BLD) analytics, where, if the information is combined with other information, it becomes about the individual and therefore personal information.

Location information just by itself and with no linkage to a habit, trait, religious belief, or political view, true or not, it is reasonably challenging or impossible to identify who the information is about. This is quite a modern legal view of the FCA that can be used to assess various types and classes of location information to determine, if it is personal information, which the Agencies must handle accordingly. This personal information test of the FCA is applied and analysed below.

6.3.2   Categorising the Types of Location Information as Personal Information

Based on the Exclusions the pool of location information can be divided into two broad categories.

These are the location information:

a. the Telco is not required to retain prior to, during and after the communication— the Telco is only required to retain the location information generated at the start and at the end of a communication; and
b. the Telco is not required to retain the Cell-ID of the neighbouring cell—the Telco is required to only retain the location information for the Cell-ID of the cell tower the mobile device used to make or receive the communication at the start and at the end of the communication.

These two categories can be studied separately to decide whether any given example of location information is legally personal information. The Telco may still voluntarily retain and disclose the two types of location information described above (ETSI 2017a: 9-10 [4.6]; *TIA Act 1979* ss 187A (1), 187AA (1) item 6). Also, the Agencies have the power to issue authorisations and notifications under the *CAC Determination 2018* to request all types of location information, despite the Exclusions. Based on the Exclusions, the types of location information can be divided further into the following three categories:

c. **Metadata that is Mandatory to Retain:** Location information retained at the start and end of the voice or SMS communication, which is the location information generally used for billing purposes and linked to the identity of the individual;
d. **Metadata that is Voluntary to Retain:** The location information retained prior to, during and after the voice or SMS communication; and
e. **Metadata that is Voluntary to Retain:** Location information that did not handle the voice call or SMS communication, such as the neighbouring Cell-ID and the latitude and altitude of the mobile device generated from the neighbouring cell.

The Sections below discusses whether each of these three categories are and should be classified as personal information using the test developed by the FCA in 2017. This is important because, based on whether the type of location information is classified as personal information, the Agencies will decide whether to apply the 'Privacy Tests'. This in turn indicates the level of privacy protection, and thus the basis for assessing whether there is an adequate balance between the powers of the Agencies and privacy. For example, the Privacy Tests will apply to the location information the Telco is legally required to retain. The Privacy Tests may not be legally required to apply to the location information retained voluntarily for commercial, network maintenance or cybersecurity purposes; or location information disclosed to other public bodies and non-law enforcement agencies such as city councils, under section 280 of *TA 1997*.

6.3.3   Metadata That Is Mandatory to Retain: Location Information Retained at the Start and End of the Voice or SMS Communication

Location information retained at the start and at the end of the voice or SMS communication is the location information generally used for billing purposes and is linked to the identity of the individual (Telstra, *Privacy* (2016)). This was the type of location information the Telco agreed to disclose to Messrs Ockenden and Grubb in the *Telstra decision* because the Telco accepted that the location information retained at the start and end of the voice or SMS communication is 'about the individual' and is personal information (*Telstra decision* 4 [5. (1)], Exhibit C, Exhibit JC-1 in fn. 5).

If the location information is used to make a call and that location information is used to issue an invoice to the customer and can show the estimated location where the call started and the estimated location where the call ended, then it is highly likely that this class of location information relates to the person, is 'about' the individual and is thus personal information. This can also be safely concluded given that location information can be personal information if the location information is related to a communication to which the individual is a party:

(1) The *Privacy Act 1988* applies in relation to a service provider, as if the service provider were an organisation within the meaning of that Act, to the extent that the activities of the service provider relate to retained data.

(2) Information that is kept under this Part, or information that is in a document kept under this Part is taken, for the purposes of the Privacy Act 1988, to be personal information about an individual if the information relates to:

(a) the individual; or a communication to which the individual is a party (*TIA Act 1979* s187LA).

This class of location information can be about the individual because this class of location information is retained when the person makes or receives a call or SMS and when the call or SMS is terminated (*Telstra decision* 4). The communication is one to which the person is a party, and there can be little dispute that this class of location information is about the person. Given the precedent set by *Telstra decision* to disclose the location information used for billing, it is unlikely that any Telco would argue that location information used for billing is not personal information. This was the reason why this class of location information was not an issue in the *Privacy Commissioner court case*, and as such, the FCA did not have to rule on it on appeal (*Privacy Commissioner court case* 16–17 [65]). The type of location information that was at issue in the *Telstra decision* was: 'Cell tower location information beyond the cell tower location information that Telstra retains for billing purposes . . .' (*Telstra decision* 8 [9.]). This latter type of location information was not disclosed to Mr Grubb. The location information retained prior to, during and after the voice or SMS communication and the retained location information that did not handle the voice call or SMS communication may be location information that is not used for billing purposes and not be linked to the identity of the individual in the billing database. It was on these facts that Telstra did not disclose the cell tower location information beyond the cell tower location information that Telstra retains for billing purposes to Mr Grubb (*Telstra decision* 8 [9.]). This latter class of location information, which is generally not used for billing, is legally analysed below, as to whether that type of location information can legally be classified as personal information.

6.3.3.1   Most Location Information That Is Required to Be Retained Is Deemed to Be Personal Information

The term 'retained data' is information the Telco is or has been required to keep under the metadata retention scheme. Retained data is deemed to be personal information (*TIA Act 1979* ss 187AA, 5(1)). Location information that is not required to be retained is not 'retained data', but is metadata voluntarily retained. The question is whether the personal information voluntarily retained before or during a communication is also personal information.

Not All Retained Location Information Is Personal Information

According to the AGD, although the information that is required to be retained is likely to be personal information, the fact that the Telco is required to retain the telecommunications data and is retaining this information does not automatically mean the information is personal information. Under the standard definition of personal information, what constitutes personal information will vary, depending on whether an individual can be identified or is reasonably identifiable in the particular circumstances. As a result, not all information held by service providers may fall within the standard definition of personal information (Revised Explanatory Memorandum 2015: 66 [360]). Even if the information is voluntarily retained, it may not qualify as personal information, also because it is voluntarily retained does not mean it is not personal information. The FCAs 2017 test must be applied to make a determination.

Section 187LA of the *TIA Act 1979* makes it clear that retained telecommunications data will be deemed to be personal information about the individual only if it meets one of two conditions: (i) either the location information relates to the individual; or (ii) the location information relates to a communication to which the individual is a party (Supplementary Explanatory Memorandum 2014, [116.]). If the location information is used for billing purposes, it relates to the individual. If the location information is retained at the start and at the end of the communication and the location information is collected from the location server, stored in a database and then disclosed over what is referred to as the Handover Interface B (H1-B) interface (SEDNode) to the Agencies, the location information may relate to the communication (ETSI 2017a: 15 [4.1]). If the location information retained with every call or SMS reveals that the mobile device that is registered in the name of the individual is regularly spotted near the ABC, as demonstrated by Mr. Ockenden's location information, the latitude and velocity of the mobile device and the ID of the cell tower may relate to Mr Ockenden.

It is likely that all location information stored at the start and at the end of a voice call or SMS is likely to be considered as personal information. As such, the Agencies would be required to apply the 'Privacy Tests' when collecting the location information. If the location information is generated in the IP-mediated 4G and 5G networks, when Mr. Ockenden did not make a voice or SMS communication or when his parents did not call him, and the Telco has this Cell-ID in its possession, the location information may not be considered personal information, and as such the Privacy Tests may not be applied when collecting this Cell-ID. This scenario is critically analysed below.

6.3.4   Metadata That Is Retained Voluntarily: Location Information Retained Prior to, During and After the Voice or SMS Communication

The bigger challenge for privacy is the location information that is not used for billing purposes. This is the location information that may be voluntarily retained by the Telco and used for network maintenance or other commercial interests such as Geofence data—to identify a listed device entering or exiting an area (Munson and Gupta 2002). The GeoFence data may include location information used for billing but may also include the location information voluntarily retained prior to, during and after a communication. This location information may be linked to a pseudonym that is not an International Mobile Subscriber Identity (IMSI). Using the IMSI would identify the person, and in that instance the location information voluntarily retained prior to, during and after a communication may be personal information. If the IMSI and the billing account identifiers such as name and account number are replaced by a pseudonym to de-identify the person from the location information voluntarily retained prior to, during and after a communication, the latter information may still be personal information (OAIC 2015: 61; Explanatory Memorandum 2012: 60). The fact that the mobile device can be listed to be detected for GeoFence events means the individual can be identifiable, which would make the location information personal information under the definition of personal information, even if the Exclusions were applied.

The location information voluntarily retained prior to, during and after a communication, and the location information retained at the start and end of a communication by the Telco and used for services such as a GeoFence event (or something similar, like identifying shoppers in a mall to enable tracking their movements and the items of clothing they look at) may be personal information, even with a pseudonym.

The Agencies still have the power to issue an authorisation and notification under the *CAC Determination 2018* to request access to both classes of location information:

a. the location information voluntarily retained prior to, during and after a communication, and
b. the location information required to be retained at the start and end of a communication (ETSI 2017a: 9–10 [4.6]; *TIA Act 1979* ss 187A (1), 187AA (1) item 6).

The question whether the telecommunications data is personal information depends on the facts of a given case (*Privacy Commissioner case*, [63]). The relationship between data linking, data matching and personal information is apparently not adequately considered in Australia (Goldenfein 2017). If we speculate using the GeoFence example above where pseudonyms may replace the IMSI to de-identify the person, the IMSI may also be replaced to re-identify the person. The use of de-identification and re-identification techniques means the person is identifiable. If the location information voluntarily retained, despite the Exclusions, such as the Cell-ID when Mr Ockenden's parents did not call him or when he did not make a call or sent an SMS, is linked to other data, such as the shopping habits or to identify the nature and needs of customers to improve customer satisfaction, the broad range of location information used for this purpose can be linked to a person regardless of the use of pseudonyms or other types of de-identification techniques (Sarkar 2015). In all these instances the Cell-ID would be personal information. It would be unfair to state that because no call was made the Cell-ID is not personal information and the Cell-ID can continue to be used for other commercial interests, which can be linked to the individual, such as using the GeoFence technology.

Telstra indicated that its billing system is separate from the network elements (the location servers) that collect and exchange the location information. On this basis Telstra argued that the information that is not used for billing is not location information that is about the individual. Telstra indicated that the network elements are distributed widely, and the information cannot be aggregated reasonably to identify the person; in fact, Telstra hardly ever did this (*Telstra decision* [48], 26 [61. (2)(d)]; 44–45 [112]). However, even if Telstra did not factually aggregate location information that is not used for billing purposes and that is not used to deliver the voice or SMS communication to the individual, this information may still potentially be used for other services such as GeoFence. This information, albeit de-identified, is still linked to the mobile device that may later be linked to identify a person. In the latter instance, location information not used for billing purposes and not used to deliver the voice or SMS communication to the individual can still be personal information.

The location information retained prior to, during and after the voice or SMS communication is not required to be retained, and it is not clear if section 187LA of the *TIA Act 1979* would apply because the provision directly refers to 'retained data' but not to telecommunications data that may be voluntarily retained. For this class of location information only the definition of personal information under the *Privacy Act 1988* is relevant. The location information retained prior to, during and after the voice or SMS communication can be analysed in three sub-classes:

a. The location information retained during the voice or SMS communication;
b. The location information retained prior to the voice or SMS communication; and
c. The location information retained after the voice or SMS communication.

These classes of location information are discussed below.

6.3.4.1   Metadata That Is Retained Voluntarily: The Location Information Retained During the Voice or SMS Communication

The location information retained during the voice or SMS communication includes, for example, when the mobile device changes its location as it moves from point A to point D. The altitude, latitude, velocity and ID of the mobile device while the person is making or receiving a phone call, or an SMS is related to the persons receiving and making these communications. The Telco may retain the location information, such as samples of Cell-IDs, at regular times during the voice call at points B and C, to see how the mobile device has changed locations (ETSI 2017a: 9-10 [4.6]). If the location information is retained to keep track of the device, it may be said that the location information is about the mobile device and how it changes its location. The location information recorded at the cell towers from points A, B, C and D, may all hand over the connection from one cell to the next, and if these location data points are used for billing or linked to the identifier of the mobile device, the location information may qualify as personal information. The location changes may be made independent from the voice call that the mobile device is connected to. The changing Cell-IDs may be retained when the call is being forwarded, after the call has already started and is in progress (ETSI 2017a: 9-10 [4.6k]). The question whether this class of location information is personal information, is based on the facts of the case. If the particular Telco retains samples of these Cell-IDs and can link the Cell-IDs to the identity of the mobile device, such as its serial number (the International Mobile Station Equipment Identity or IMEI, or short), or the IMSI, and thus in turn the individual, the Cell-IDs would be personally identifiable and thus be personal information. Another Telco may not have the capability and as such the data may not be personal information. The location changes are required to be traced thus requiring retention of the Cell-IDs—for interception purposes, for example (ETSI 2017a: 9-10 [4.6]). One of the key reasons for the retention of Cell-IDs would be to obtain interception warrants and tracking the mobile device during the conversation ((ETSI 2017a: 9-10 [4.6]). The Cell-IDs can likely be retained because European Telecommunications Standards Institute Technical Specification (ETSI TS) 102 656 which outlines the 'Requirements of Law Enforcement Agencies for handling Retained Data and Lawful Interception', supports the retention of the Cell-ID during a call (ETSI 2017a: 9-10 [4.6]).

If the Telco opted to store sample Cell-IDs, then the sample Cell-IDs would be personal information. If the Telco discloses the sample Cell-IDs to the Agencies, a stronger case can be made that such disclosure is made because of the use of the sample Cell-IDs for the purposes and functions of the Agencies, the sample Cell-IDs would make the individual identifiable and thus the sample Cell-IDs become personal information. Telstra indicated that it did not disclose location information it did not use for billing to the Agencies *(Telstra decision*, 8 [9]). Under those unique facts, as far as Telstra is concerned, Telstra did not have Mr Grubb's personal information as far as it concerned non-billing data. The Administrative Appeals Tribunal (AAT) could then simply just have concluded that if however, Telstra could and did link and aggregate the location information not used for billing to other information, then in that hypothetical case the location information, even if the data was not used for billing, would be personal information.

It is possible that when it comes to types of location information that may be voluntarily retained the question whether the location information is personal information, because it depends on the facts of a case, may be different between the various Telco. Unless the *TIA Act 1979* prescribes the circumstances under which the various types of location information that may be voluntarily retained are deemed to be personal information when retained and used for commercial or law enforcement and security functions and purposes under the *TIA Act 1979*, the uncertainty will remain. This uncertainty allows the less restricted use of the location information under the assumption that it is non-personal information, as opposed to treating it like it is personal information and then applying the Privacy Tests to the types of location information that are voluntarily retained and possibly voluntarily disclosed to the Agencies.

6.3.4.2 Metadata That Is Retained Voluntarily: Location Information Retained Prior to a Voice or SMS Communication, and Location Information Retained After a Voice or SMS Communication

The location information retained prior to a voice or SMS communication and the location information retained after a voice or SMS communication are distanced from the voice or SMS communication that is taking place. The first question is whether the location information is distanced from the individual, in that the location information is not related to the individual and is not about the individual. The individual would not be apparent from this location information because the location information is not generated to deliver the call or the SMS the individual is receiving or making. In that sense there is a missing connection between this location information and the individual's communication. Looking at how the mobile device is tracked, this includes the regular connections to the cell tower when no call is made is and therefore no call is charged. There is no direct connection to the individual and any voice or SMS communication. The location information generated prior to and after a communication, and when no voice call or SMS is made, is primarily about the tracking of the device in the IP-mediated 4G and 5G networks. This type of location information may however be used for commercial purposes such as the SAS® Customer Intelligence and SAS® Master Data Management modules, where (SAS Institute Inc. 2018). The identifiers such as the telephone number or IMSI may be replaced with a pseudonym. In that instance where the pseudonym is used, the algorithm that generates the pseudonym can identify or re-identify the IMSI, the IMEI or telephone number, making this type of location information potentially personal information. Also, if this class of location information is used for other purposes such as checking the quality of the service for the mobile phone of an individual, the use of the services and tracking the phone for this purpose, this class of location information could be personal information.

The second question is: whether, if the location information is combined with other information such as the location information generated at the start and at the end, or with the IMSI, IMEI, or the telephone number, the information then becomes personal information because the identity of the individual is reasonably identifiable when the location information is combined with other information. This question is answered in the affirmative, contrary to the decision of *Telstra decision*, but consistent with the view of the *Privacy Commissioner case*. According to the *Telstra decision*, any other application of the location information generated does not alter the primary purpose and functioning of the technology, even if the location information is matched with other external information and reveals habits about the person, the residence of the person or details about the work-related activities of the person, such as Mr. Ockenden. Johnston (2017) argued that viewing the 'telecommunications data' in question in the *Telstra decision* in this way was a narrow and binary formulation. The information cannot be just about one thing (Johnston 2017, p. 83). The *Privacy Commissioner case* planted the seed for the idea that the metadata may not just be about the primary purpose of the location information—the primary purpose of delivering communications or tracking the device in the network. If the facts can demonstrate that the location information was matched, and the identity of the person was revealed or is reasonably ascertainable, by the location information that tracked the mobile device, whether it delivered the voice call or whether there was no voice communication to deliver, the location information can also at the same time be about the individual. Unlike the AAT, the FCA accepted that the information can be about various things: 'Information and opinions can have multiple subject matters' (*Privacy Commissioner court case* 16 [63]).

A single piece of information that starts out by not being about a person may end up being about a person when it is combined with other separate pieces of information. If the pool of location information is combined with extra information, any of the three categories of location information may end up being personal information. The *Privacy Commissioner case* stated that, based on the facts of every case, at first it must be determined whether every single item of information or the combined pieces of information requested from the Telco are about the individual. Secondly once having determined that the information is about an individual, in order to determine whether the identity of the person is reasonably ascertainable one must undertake an evaluative conclusion. The FCA, stated that aggregated information may be about an individual, even if a single piece may not be about an individual (*Privacy Commissioner court case* 16 [63]). The FCA differentiates between a case of identity that is obvious from the information, and a case where the identity may not be apparent. I agree with Johnston (2017) and argue that the AAT took a very technologically driven narrow interpretation. Location information is inherently designed to be about tracking the mobile device in the IP-mediated 4G and 5G networks, with the view of delivering the communication (the location information contained in a message) to the mobile device or the location server or the SEDNode portal from where the location information is downloaded and given to the Agencies (iiNET 2015; ETSI 2017d: 58 [5.2.3]). However, location information may be applied to a myriad of other purposes, and as such the location information forms various relationships that end up being about the individual, such as Mr Ockenden. The primary design and purpose of location information remains, but that does not exclude other relationships. The location information may start out being about the delivery of the voice and SMS communication to the recipient, as it is exchanged via the network elements, such as the location server, but a new relationship is formed with the individual, at the secondary level. The location information now serves a secondary purpose, but still an important purpose, that requires greater privacy protection, under stricter rules.

6.4 The Use of Big Data Analytics Software

Maurushat et al. (2015) stated, given the promises of improved policing and intelligence by Big Data analytics (BD), safeguards will be required. These include de-anonymisation and passing regulations about when re-identification may be required. Maurushat (2016) described the perceived advantages, risk and challenges of BD, and its uses for being able to predict and investigate criminal and intelligence incidents. Chan and Moses (2017) made the clarion call to better understand BD analytics technology, its challenges, its use and influence, its governance and its regulation in an ethical manner (Smith et al. 2017). Bennett and de Koker (2017) and de Koker et al. (2018) stated BD algorithmic decision-making is inherently opaque but argued that for social acceptance of the data-driven decision-making powers of the Agencies the powers must be clear, and be subjected to open public debate, ensuring a certain level of public 'translucency' to using algorithms to process data and then taking decisions based on such automated processes. Casanovas Romeu et al. (2017) raised the complexity between law and BD, arguing that for the effective regulation of BD, legal tools, used in combination with semantic ones, would be required.

6.4.1   The Definition of Big Location Data

Big data is generally accepted to be about the ability to combine various types of data and to analyse it (Boyd and Crawford 2012). Big data is about how big data sets are, referred to as the 'volume'; how they are processed at high speeds, referred to as 'velocity'; and how diverse the data is, referred to as 'variety' (Gandomi and Haider 2015). The data is collected from various sources and analysed with the aim of finding answers to problems (SAS Institute Inc. 2018).

It would appear that the 'use' of Big Location Data (BLD) analytics is allowed by the law, in terms of the meaning of the word 'use'. Uses include the aggregation, summarising, ingesting into an analysis platform, obtaining results and using those results in an investigative process for law enforcement (OAIC 2015: 28–29).[5] BLD analysis is when location information is integrated with other types of information. This may be referred to as 'data matching'.[6] These external sources are diverse and include information from social networks such as Twitter and Facebook (Open Source Intelligence or OSINT); from other public agencies such as the tax office; from criminal records of the state police; from road traffic records; from social security records; and from social welfare records (Minister for Justice 2016; D2D CRC, *Integrated Law Enforcement* (2018)). The records are aggregated and linked to identify the individual and identify other unknown aspects of the individual's behaviour and actions. This aggregation can be done in the manner described by the FCA in the *Privacy Commissioner case*.

The collection, aggregation and use of the location information needs to be 'in connection with', 'reasonably necessary' and 'directly related' to the activities of the Agencies which are in turn considered as directly related to the functions and purposes of the Agencies (*Privacy Act 1988* Schedule 1, APPs 3.1, 3.4). The behaviours of the person detected through BLD can be considered an activity that is related to the function of investigating any offence or to determine if a person is relevant to security. The aggregated data can be analysed to search for changes in the individual's behaviour and to see if the person behaves differently from what is known. In the latter instance, conclusions can be made about whether the person is acting suspiciously—that is, different from the known profile and may now start to pose a security or criminal risk, that may warrant the interception of the contents of their communications. A profile of the individual can be created and be matched to

---

[5]The word 'use' is not defined in the *TIA Act 1979*, nor in the *Privacy Act 1988*.

[6]Data matching is defined as '. . . bringing together of at least two data sets that contain personal information, and that come from different sources, and the comparison of those data sets with the intention of producing a match.' See: OAIC (2014).

other persons to identify overlaps. The profiles are queried, and recommendations are made about how to treat the individual. The person's activities are profiled and analysed on an ongoing basis, and this can be done without the person being involved in an offence—not being under suspicion of having committed or committing an offence. The person can be ranked and rated, based on how much of a threat the person may pose to security and public safety (D2D CRC 2018).

6.4.2   The Australian Criminal Intelligence Model and Associated Management Strategy

The 'Australian Criminal Intelligence Model and Associated Management Strategy' addresses the intersecting domains of national security, serious and organised crime, policing and community safety. The Agencies define criminal intelligence as: '... insights and understanding obtained through analysis of available information and data on complex offending patterns, serious organised crime groups or syndicates and individuals involved in various types of criminal activities' (Commonwealth of Australian 2012, 2017) This strategy lies at the heart of accessing and using BLD analysis. The differentiating factor introduced by the location information retention and disclosure scheme is granularity. This arises from the volume of location information generated and required to be stored for two years, coupled with the capability to match the data and link it to an identifiable individual.

Under its Enterprise Transformation, the ASIO 2020 goal, ASIO is undergoing a digital transformation by adopting Big Data analysis technology to transform its investigations and inquiries. This strategy was adopted at the recommendation of former Telstra CEO, David Thodey. ASIO is looking to '...change [its] business model to capitalise on the benefits of augmented decision-making and data science; establish a strong, digitally enabled culture; reform ... human resources practices; establish strategic partnerships with industry, academia and government; and strengthen innovation within the Organisation. In line with the review's recommendations, during this reporting period we commenced preparations for a major transformation to ensure ASIO remains fit for purpose in an increasingly complex security and operating environment' (ASIO 2019a, b). To be prepared for the future, ASIO plans to '...take advantage of big data, artificial intelligence, and machine learning, among a handful of other emerging technologies' (Barbaschow September 6, 2019).

6.4.3 The Secondary Use of Location Information in Other Investigations, Inquiries and Activities to Enforce the Law

The Privacy Tests that are meant to protect privacy and limit the powers of the Agencies work increasingly fall short.

6.4.3.1 Transferring Evidence from One Investigation to the Next Without Fully Applying the Privacy Tests

Location information obtained under one investigation can be used, where relevant, as evidence in other criminal trials. In *the Zhi court case*, information was obtained by intercepting two telephone services. The warrants were lawfully issued. This was so because the warrant could be issued if the contents intercepted can assist in connection with the investigation of a serious offence, if the person against whom the warrant is issued is involved in the offence or another person is involved in an offence. Three warrants were issued, but two of the warrants did not involve Zhi Qiang Han (*TIA Act 1979* s 46; *R v Zhi* 120 [4]). The offence in question was the supply of prohibited drugs. Zhi Qiang Han was not suspected of having committed the offence and was not charged. The third warrant was issued in respect of Zhi Qiang Han for the investigation of an offence about demanding money with the intention to steal. The issue on appeal was whether the information obtained from the intercepted communications from the two warrants about drug use, was lawfully obtained and was admissible in respect of the trial about demanding money (*R v Zhi* [5]-[6]; *DMT Act 1985* s 25).

Again, the interception warrants did not concern Zhi Qiang Han as he was not involved in the investigation of those serious offences. The legal exemption is that the lawfully intercepted information may be used for a prosecution of an offence, punishable for a minimum 3-year imprisonment. The offence in question carried a maximum 10-year imprisonment term. The New South Wales Court of Criminal Appeal (NSWCCA) unanimously decided to allow the use of the intercepted material in the second trial against Zhi Qiang Han although he was not part of the original interception warrant, and no Privacy Tests were applied when the content was intercepted because he was not named in the interception warrant ([1], [6], [12], [21]; *TIA Act 1979* s 74(1)). The *Zhi court case* sets the precedent that intercepted information can be used in respect of a secondary person, even if no privacy safeguards were applied in respect of the secondary person because no warrant was issued in respect of the secondary person. The privacy implications of this precedent, if it were to be applied to location information, are grave.

6.4.3.2   The Location Information May Be Shared for Secondary Investigations, Inquiries and Activities to Enforce the Law

The original location information collected from the Telco may be disclosed and used for other investigations, other inquiries, other offences and other persons, in addition to the original investigation, the original inquiry, the original offence and the original persons, in respect of whom the location information was originally collected. As a general rule, an employee of the Agencies or the Telco who reveals that an authorisation or notification has been issued under the *CAC Determination 2018* to collect location information, or who uses the authorisation or notification may be imprisoned for two years. However, the employee of the Agencies or the Telco, may reveal that an authorisation or notification has been issued under the *CAC Determination 2018* to collect location information or use the authorisation or notification, if it is 'reasonably necessary' to enable ASIO to perform its functions or if it is to enforce the criminal law (*TIA Act 1979* ss 181, 181A (1)-(6); 181B (3), (6); 182A, 182B). ASIO and the AFP are therefore allowed to collect, use and share location information to enforce the criminal law in respect of other offences and in respect of other persons other than the original reason and other than the original person in respect of whom the authorisation and notification under the *CAC Determination 2018* was requested and issued. If the secondary disclosure and use is reasonably necessary to enforce the criminal law, then the secondary use and secondary disclosure of the location information is allowed (*TIA Act 1979* ss 181, 181A (3), (6), 181B (3), (6); 182A, 182B).

6.4.3.3   The 'Connection Test' and the 'Reasonably Necessary Tests' and Big Location Data Analytics

In terms of the Connection Test and the Reasonably Necessary or Directly Related Tests, the personal information collected about person A may be used to investigate and inquire into the actions of person B. However, the Privacy Tests is not applied in respect of person B. As illustrated by Mr Ockenden's location information and personal information, the location information collected and analysed about person A can reveal personal information about person B, as illustrated by the *Zhi court case*. Person B was not the original target of the location information that was collected, but the location information of person A can be used in an investigation about person B, without having to apply for an authorisation that requires the Privacy Tests—Connection Test and the Reasonably Necessary or Directly Related Tests to be applied in respect of person B. This is justified on the basis that the location information is used 'in connection with' the performance of the functions of ASIO or is directly related to or reasonably necessary for the law enforcement activities and purposes of the AFP. The expressions 'in connection with'; 'reasonably necessary' in Australian Privacy Principle (APP) 3.1 and APP 3.4; and the 'directly related' in APP 3.1 and APP 3.4; are an indication of the broad discretion of the powers of the

Agencies and how unlimited the access to and the use of the location information is, legally classified as metadata, as subscriber data, and not as the contents of a communication. The secondary investigation, the secondary inquiry, the secondary offence and the secondary person were never anticipated and so no Privacy Tests are applied in respect of the secondary investigation, secondary inquiry, secondary offence or secondary person.

There is no limit to the use and re-use and disclosure and re-disclosure of the location information. This re-use and continued sharing are a broad power both the AFP and ASIO possess. There is no telling against what other person the location information may be used. The Agencies do not require re-authorisation of the location information if the purpose for which the location information was collected changes. The effect of the Connection Test is that the scope of use of the location information is undefined and unlimited. The permitted continued re-use and sharing of the location information under the 'in connection with' principle undermines the privacy safeguards. Based on how the *Gant* and *Samsonidis court cases* interpreted the term 'in connection with' and relating that interpretation to the Connection Test and the Reasonably Necessary or Directly Related Tests, it can be said that the Privacy Tests under the *CAC Determination 2018* practically only applies in respect of the original investigation, the original inquiry, the original offence, and the individual that is the original target of the inquiry or investigation. If the Privacy Tests are applied prior to collecting the location information, then the privacy assessment is not undertaken in respect of the facts of the secondary investigation, the secondary inquiry and the secondary person. By the time the secondary investigation and inquiry commences, the location information has already been collected. In the circumstances, the privacy safeguards are not applied if the location information already collected is shared and re-used for the secondary investigations, secondary inquiries and secondary individuals. The Connection Test and the Reasonably Necessary or Directly Related Tests practically exempts the Agencies from applying the Privacy Tests in respect of the secondary investigation, the secondary inquiry and in respect of the secondary person. This means the Agencies practically only need to issue authorisations and notifications under the *CAC Determination 2018,* in respect of the primary investigation, the primary inquiry, the primary individual and the primary offence. The Agencies may lawfully forego the Privacy Tests, in respect of the secondary investigation, the secondary inquiry and the secondary person. The Privacy Tests are effectively only required for, applicable to and limited to the primary investigation, the primary inquiry, the primary individual and the primary offence. This means the AFP does not need to issue an authorisation and notification under the *CAC Determination 2018* to the Telco for the location information for the secondary investigation, the secondary inquiry and in respect of the secondary person because the investigation or inquiry is 'reasonably necessary' to enforce the criminal law and 'reasonably necessary' to investigate an offence.

6.4.3.4   The Secondary Use of Historical and Prospective Location Information Versus Serious and Minor Offences

The AFP must suspect that the individual is involved in a serious offence, based on reasonable grounds, as the test, to conduct an investigation and to collect and use the prospective location information (*TIA Act 1979* ss 6A, 6B). The *CAC Determination 2018* requires that, when the AFP is collecting the historical location information, the AFP must be satisfied, on 'reasonable grounds', that any interference with the privacy of *any person or persons* that may result from the disclosure or use is 'justifiable and proportionate', having regard to the gravity the conduct and the seriousness of the offence in question (*CAC Determination 2018* ss 8–12). Historical location information may be collected for non-serious offences as well (*CAC Determination 2018* ss 10–12). It is only prospective location information that may be collected for serious offences, and the word 'investigation' that requires suspicion is only used in the *CAC Determination 2018* in respect of serious offences. In respect of minor offences, the AFP is doing, what may be referred to as what is 'reasonably necessary for the enforcement of the criminal law,' instead of being referred to as an investigation and therefore no specific reference to 'investigation' and no reference to requiring suspicion of an offence based on reasonable grounds.

If the historical location information is collected and used for the secondary reasonably necessary enforcement of the criminal law, it means the AFP is not required to conduct the Privacy Tests as set out in the revised section 180F of the *TIA Act 1979*. If the prospective location information is collected and used for the secondary investigation the AFP must still have suspicion that the individual is involved in a serious offence, based on 'reasonable grounds', as a test to conduct an 'investigation' and to collect and use the prospective location information (*CAC Determination 2018* ss 10–12). However, since the location information has already been collected from the Telco, and the AFP does not need to issue an authorisation and notification under the *CAC Determination 2018,* the re-use and sharing of the location information, for the purposes of the secondary investigation, the AFP is not required to apply the privacy safeguards to the new set of facts, the secondary offence, and the secondary individual. The reasoning is that the AFP would be using and sharing the location information for the purposes of enforcing the criminal law and the location information has already been lawfully obtained under the APP 3.5 Lawful and Fair Means Test. The privacy safeguards applied in terms of the primary investigation, primary offence and the primary individual are considered acceptable to re-use and share the same location information for a different offence, a different individual and for a different set of facts. Privacy interference and the privacy impact assessment is based on the material and the facts of every case. The privacy impact assessment is unique to an offence and the relevant individual whose movements are being scrutinised. Using the Privacy Tests passed for the one offence and the one individual in respect of another offence and another individual does not seem to be a proper balance of the privacy interests of the individual being investigated under the secondary offence. In the circumstances, the privacy interests of the secondary individual are not appropriately considered but are instead undermined. It is unfair to the second individual to effectively say that because a privacy impact analysis was already done in respect of the location information, and even though that privacy impact had nothing to do with the secondary individual, the location information can be used without applying the Privacy Tests specifically in respect of this secondary individual. In these circumstances, the investigation, the inquiry and law enforcement function undermine the criminal justice system. The Privacy Tests should be applied in respect of every individual, and the gap in the law that practically prevents the application of the Privacy Tests should be corrected. Added to this, the person is unable to challenge the secondary use of the location information. The secondary individual's protections as provided for in section 180F of the *TIA Act 1979* are practically denied, because the Privacy Tests are not applied judicially and not even by the Agencies in respect of the secondary individual at the time the location information is collected. The message this sends is that the privacy is not equally protected for all individuals. This is not fair to the secondary individual; whose privacy deserves protection just as much as the primary target. Privacy would be better protected if the Privacy Tests are also applied in respect of the secondary individual, independent of the primary target.

6.4.3.5 Secondary Use of Location Information and Big Location Data Analytics

The Connection Test and the Reasonably Necessary or Directly Related Tests, raises questions when applied to the broad functions of the Agencies. If an Agency plans to build a BLD storage and analytics database to use for future investigations, would this qualify as directly or indirectly related to the functions, and would the collection of all the location information generated within any given period be reasonably necessary for populating the database? The answer is yes. The initial development and the continued use or BLD analytics of this broad storage database or platform, by the Agencies, may qualify as relevant, useful and as incidental and conducive to the Agencies performing their broad law enforcement functions and activities. The purpose and functions of ASIO include the broad power to '. . . undertake inquiries to determine whether a particular subject or activity is relevant to security; to investigate subjects and activities relevant to security' (AG's Guidelines s 6). In terms of the 'in connection with', the 'reasonably necessary' or the 'directly related' principles, the broad powers of the Agencies to build a BLD analytics platform would be lawful, and without judicial oversight and the accompanying scrutiny of its impact on privacy. The location information collection powers of the Agencies may be too broad in scope and not be sufficiently limited. The threshold is low because almost any function or activity can be included in this 'directly related or reasonably necessary' basket, justifying the collection and storage and the use of the location information for an activity such as BLD analytics.

The *CAC Determination 2018* is clear that some context of the criminal offence being investigated or inquired into or the criminal law being enforced must be connected to the power to access and use location information (*TIA Act 1979* s 180F). The intention is that regard should be had to the type of offence, to the type of person, and the type of impact on *individual privacy*. The 'in connection with', 'reasonably necessary' and 'directly related' principles do away with this very intention. These principles allow the Agencies the power to act without those facts and circumstances, and thereby impact the privacy of the secondary person. The interference with privacy is indirectly 'endorsed' or 'condoned' by the 'in connection with', 'reasonably necessary' or 'directly related' principles—the law allows for the Agencies not to respect the privacy safeguards by granting the Agencies the discretion not to issue authorisations and notifications under the *CAC Determination 2018* and the Privacy Tests in respect of the secondary investigation, secondary inquiry, secondary offence and the secondary individual (*Privacy Act 1988* (Cth) Schedule 1, APPs 3.1, 3.4). The Agencies can continue using the location information that was already obtained for a different law enforcement purpose and activity. By allowing the re-use of location information for secondary activities and in respect of secondary persons without specifically requiring re-authorisation of the re-use for these secondary activities that were not originally anticipated and intended, the privacy of the secondary individual is negatively impacted and afforded no protection.

The *CAC Determination 2018* requires that the Telco be given information regarding the likely relevance and usefulness of the information and documents, and the reasons why the disclosure is sought. If the reason changes, how is the use of the location information for a secondary reason a proper protection of privacy? The proper reasons can be stated in the authorisation, but the location information can then be used for potentially improper reasons or alternative reasons even if they are related to the broad activities of the Agencies. This creates a gap for possible misuse of the location information. Also, how would '. . .anything incidental or conducive to the performance of the functions' (*AFP Act 1979* s 8(1)(c)) be dealt with in the circumstances of BLD analytics that would reveal personal information of all persons somehow connected to the primary individual, as was the case with Mr. Ockenden's location information?

6.4.3.6 Analysing the Location Information to See Connections

Under the 'in connection with', 'reasonably necessary' and 'directly related' principles, the continued use or data mining—the analysis of the BLD database to seek relations and new connections, in terms of the words used by the *Samsonidis court case*—would excuse the Agencies from having to first think about and assess the likely relevance and usefulness of the location information before analysing it. The Agencies may continue to conduct pre-emptive analysis and speculative data matching because they are able to circumvent the Privacy Tests under these circumstances, just to see how useful or useless the information may be.

6.4.4 Law Enforcement Activities Are Not Specifically Required to Be Based on the Reasonably Necessary or Directly Related Standards

Under the Connection Test and the Reasonably Necessary or Directly Related Tests, 'in connection with', 'reasonably necessary' and 'directly related' principles, the activities related to the functions of the Agencies are not questioned; they are simply accepted as reasonable. The important question is, how is the BLD storage and analytics database used to create profiles of individuals, and how would it be used for speculative data matching when a person is not involved in an offence but where the person is still 'relevant to security'? Does the creation and use of the BLD storage database, as an activity, adequately protect privacy if it is an activity exercised without prior judicial oversight but left to the sole discretion of the Agencies?

The broadness of the functions and activities of the AFP undermine the protection of privacy by the 'Connection Test' and the 'Reasonably Necessary or Directly Related Tests' and the 'reasonable grounds' and 'reasonable belief' standards. In the *CAC Determination 2018* and section 180F of the *TIA Act 1979,* the requirement is that the authorised officer approving the collection of location information (both prospective and historic) must be satisfied on 'reasonable grounds' that any inter-ference with the privacy of *any person or persons* that may result from the disclosure or use is 'justifiable and proportionate' having regard to the gravity of any conduct in relation to which the authorisation is sought. The facts the AFP will use to issue the authorisation and notification under the *CAC Determination 2018* need to be suffi-cient to persuade the AFP that the collection of the location information is 'reason-ably necessary' or 'directly related' to its functions or activities, as per the *George court case* (4 [8]).[7] If the secondary individual and secondary offence is not part of the materials used to assess the privacy impact, how adequately and fairly is the privacy of the individual protected and if the location information collected can then be used for other facts and another individual that was not part of the original analysis? Should the use of the location information not be limited to the facts and circumstances under which they were originally collected and approved? If the facts change, should the collection of the location information not be approved separately for that specific secondary purpose, even if it is broadly still a law enforcement purpose, function or activity? Is this not a better process of protecting individual privacy?

---

[7]The 'APP3.1 Reasonably Necessary or Directly Related Personal Information Test' refers to 'reasonable belief'. Similarly, the facts the AFP will use to issue the authorisation and notification under the *CAC Determination 2018* need to be sufficient to persuade the AFP that the collection of the LI is 'reasonably necessary' or 'directly related' to its functions or activities. The assumption is that the AFP must still comply with the 'reasonable belief' standard when it issues an authorisation and notification under the *CAC Determination 2018* to collect location information. To clarify this, the *CAC Determination 2018* may need to make a cross-reference to APP 3.1.

The terms 'reasonable grounds' and 'reasonable belief' seem like strong standards to protect privacy—the AFP must act on the facts. The weakness lies with what the enforcement related activities and functions of the AFP are. The key function of the AFP is policing. Police services are defined to include all '. . . services by way of the prevention of crime and the protection of persons from injury or death, and property from damage, whether arising from criminal acts or otherwise' (*AFP Act 1979* s 4(1) (definition of 'police service'). If the location information is remotely linked to any of those services, the AFP may collect the location information irrespective of the underlying motivation for the collection of the location information—be it political or racial. The activities may relate to actions needed to perform the functions of the Agencies. The activities of conducting an inquiry, an investigation and detecting a criminal activity seem above board. One activity that monitors the movements of individuals and that is not discussed much publicly is the collection of location information and use of BLD software analysis to obtain personal information about the individual as part of the investigation, inquiry and detection of the criminal activity. The functions and activities of the AFP requires the AFP to assist to deliver on key strategic priorities, such as intelligence gathering and developing databases of intelligence (*AFP Act 1979 s* 8; Minister for Justice 2016; Keenan 2014).

The test is not whether the function or activity, such as the BLD platform and software analyses, are based on 'reasonable grounds', 'reasonable belief' and is 'reasonably necessary'. In other words, do the crime statistics, the nature of emerging crimes, the rate of crime, justify the operational law enforcement activities of the AFP? The typical question would be: Has crime, based on a statistical and scientific evidence base, as opposed to polling data, become worse that BLD software analysis is required and used to potentially analyse location information of persons not suspected of an offence? The activities and functions of ASIO are accepted as is and not placed under public scrutiny. As long as the facts are enough to show that it is to carry out the task of building a BLD storage and analytics database, to investigate murders and theft using the same database, in terms of the key strategic activities, the collection of the location information would be 'reasonably necessary' or be 'directly related' to the activity of developing the BLD storage database. How the Agencies go about operationally, is not questioned and not properly inspected, and what impact this capability has in future for society in general, regarding potential misuse and the safeguards to prevent such potential misuse.

Considering the revealing nature of location information, using mobile cell phones that use satellite tracking technology, such as GPS, that tracks movement and the movements are recorded at the start and end of every communication, and 4G and 5G small cells that are more precise than traditional cell towers, the law is tilted in favour of the Agencies (Germano 2010; Battersby 2012; Nohrborg 2017; ACMA 2016; ETSI 2017c: 20 [3.1]). The so-called 'coarse' location estimates are more precise than before (ETSI 2017b: 49 [8.3.1], 12 [4.1]). To better protect privacy, search warrants for content are issued under stricter conditions than notices to collect location information, despite location information leaking the sensitive information of the individual. This discriminatory treatment of precise location information to contents of a communication, that are equally sensitive, has no rational connection to the aim of public safety. Search warrants are also issued for sensitive information, but under stricter conditions for the same purpose to ensure public safety.

A Judge may impose stricter conditions on the types of information that may be seized, and any material wrongly seized may be challenged openly. In this digital age, where the mobile device is a location tracker and reduces the search radius and keeps the location information available for longer periods, it is commendable that the Agencies should also need a measure of 'reasonable belief', based on the facts of a case, to collect the location information. However, the 'Connection Test' and the 'Reasonably Necessary or Directly Related Tests' are too broad, so much so that requests for a mass collection of the location information of every single mobile phone or of communities, or sub-groups thereof, would be justifiable to build a BLD storage database. The reports of 'African gangs' invading houses in Melbourne's West can be used to justify the mass collection of location information during the nights the reported incidents occurred (Hutchinson et al. 2018). This would include location information of every single person that was in the area at the time and analysing their location information to identify them, and to rule others out, but only after they have been identified and their location information records have been retained and can be used for other AFP law enforcement related activities. But the person is first ruled in, just to be ruled out—based on not being involved in an offence. The suspects and the innocent person's location information would be justified for collection, as the activity is to police the neighbourhood and to rule out which persons are residents and which visitors may be the suspects. Creating a BLD storage database would be 'reasonably necessary' and 'directly related' to the policing function and the activity of developing the database for analysis. The privacy of the residents and the suspects would be impacted, and the authorisation and notification under the *CAC Determination 2018* would not have been approved by a Judge or magistrate. Given that the persons are unknown at the time of the collection and the persons may not have made or receive communications at the time of the alleged criminal activities, the location information may not be regarded as personal information and the Privacy Tests may not need to be applied. The Agencies can then continue to use this location information for any other secondary investigation, secondary inquiry, secondary individual and secondary offence that is not related to investigating the 'African gangs' in Melbourne's West. This data can be kept and used in respect of any of the persons, including the residents, for any other investigation or inquiry. Throughout this whole process not one Judge would have approved the collection, use and the analysis of the location information. This is not an adequate protection of privacy.

6.4.4.1 Poor Governance Under the Attorney-General's Guidelines, the CAC Determination 2018 and the Ministerial Guidelines

Even if the Privacy Tests were applied, no restrictions are placed in the Ministerial Guidelines, the *CAC Determination 2018* or the *TIA Act 1979* that would give the public confidence that such an automated BLD storage and analytics database may not be put into operation, and if so what the publicly available governance measures would be to ensure the location information would not be misused or result in biases influencing the AFP's activities. There may be internal governance documents that are not available publicly that serve as checks and balances (Evidence to PJCIS (Edward) cited in PJCIS, *Advisory Report* 2015: 54 [2.43]). Even if the location information is not misused, just the fact that the location information can potentially be collected at such a scale to identify all persons and work out their actions, the question is if the public would expect and accept that from the AFP for their 'safety', or perhaps that level of activity may need prior judicial approval? Would the public expect that an independent third party such as the judiciary is informed of how the database is used? Would the public not expect that the use of the database be independently audited? The public would expect independent third-party authorisation to collect the location information and to use the location information, and for that activity to be audited externally. There is no telling what other unexpected personal information may be revealed and how the AFP officers may use the information in ways where any misuse may not be easy to detect. If the BLD analysis shows that a resident that is a friend of an AFP officer, family member or lover may be having an affair, there is no way of preventing that information from being shared. It would be hard to trace back to the officer. The external oversight bodies may not become aware of it, or may but only months after the fact, when they conduct their inspections. The Judge or magistrate may not prevent it either, but the Judge or magistrate may demand that the AFP demonstrate how such unexpected revelations may be minimised and how to impose clear restrictions on further use and sharing and possibly deleting the information, based on the facts at hand. These restrictions can be written into the warrant, and if the warrant is open to challenge the actions of the AFP may be reviewed. The Judge could also request information about the cell tower sites, to determine if they are femtocells and issue instructions that limit the collection of the location information to a more defined time, based on the incident reports, and identified cell towers and limit the radius of location information that can potentially be collected.

A Judge can review what location information in respect of a person may be 'reasonably necessary' and only allow the disclosure of such a restricted set of location information. The Judge may call in the Telco as a witness to verify the position of the cell towers and use witness accounts to work out the collection radius. These possible restrictions are left to the discretion of the AFP and are not sufficiently limited by the Privacy Tests, the Connection Test, the Reasonably Necessary or Directly Related Tests, the 'reasonable grounds and the 'reasonable belief' standards.

In the *George court case*, it was stated that a magistrate must be satisfied that, based on the material provided, there are reasonable grounds for suspicion and belief (5 [11]). In the absence of an external third party, there is no one else that must be satisfied, except for the senior member of staff in the AFP that is approving the authorisation and notification under the *CAC Determination 2018*, for location information that is personal. The AFP determines the scope of its law enforcement activities, and solely determines the types of information that is required to carry out those activities. The AFP will not decide on a law enforcement activity that undermines its own activity by imposing stricter rules that make it difficult to obtain that information. The AFP has an inherent interest that the law enforcement activity it created, such as the BLD analytics project, is successful and to ensure that the monetary investments were not futile. The AFP alone sets the limits of its law enforcement activities to use BLD and no magistrate or Judge is asked to question the scope of the activity, for which the location information is collected. Although the 'reasonable grounds' and 'reasonable belief' are objective standards, the fact that the final decision rests on the AFP alone leaves the privacy protection to the subjective state of mind of the AFP with no external review possible. The AFP alone decides what facts it will use in the authorisation and the notification under the *CAC Determination 2018* such that it considers sufficient to collect the location information. A Judge or magistrate could ask for further information to substantiate the application. The AFP could cherry-pick the information that advances the investigation and omit material facts, from the authorisation and notification that is submitted to a senior official that potentially undermines the investigation, to obtain approval for the authorisation and notification. The senior officer could also allow or cooperate with the omission of material facts, which may reduce the amount of location information collected or that may be collected in the first place.

Location information may be collected for an activity that is directly related to the functions of the AFP, although this does not qualify as a 'specific purpose'. The location information may be collected for offences and non-offences and these activities are not sufficiently specified, except for the reference to investigations of serious and minor offences. The location information may be collected to develop a BLD storage database, and that would be a lawful purpose. It is not clearly restricted, and no clear public rules are outlined in the *TIA Act 1979*, the *CAC Determination 2018*, the Ministerial Guidelines or the AG's Guidelines, on how such a resource would be governed from an ethical and legal standpoint to prevent misuse and address instances of misuse.

The 'reasonably necessary' standard is an objective standard but is weakened by the fact that it is subject to the activities of the AFP and these activities can range from using the location information to predict future crime and of a given ethnic, religious or political group. The AG's Guidelines and the Ministerial Direction of the AFP do not sufficiently restrict such activities or the governance measures that would apply to using the location information for such purposes. Such use of the location information that poses potential discriminatory and racial biases would be justified as lawful because it is reasonably necessary to use against persons that may be posing future criminal threats. Any person may potentially commit a future crime and therefore all persons pose a threat to the general public. This reasoning would justify the mass collection and use of the automated BLD storage and analytics database. The automated BLD storage and analytics database can for example have a functionality whereby automated alerts are created, when certain individuals approach a certain area and the police officers can be dispatched to the area. The GeoFence software allows for this type of functionality (Sarkar 2015; Namiot 2013; SAS Institute Inc. 2017). The person can then be sending a notification that the AFP is aware of his or her movements, to discourage the person from entering the area where the AFP may think the person is likely to commit a future minor offence, without needing suspicion of an offence (*TIA Act 1979* ss 6A, 6B). Such a functionality may hypothetically be used, as part of bail conditions, such that the person always carries their mobile device, so they are tracked and sent automated messages if they are about to breach bail conditions. The AFP currently has the broad power to undertake all these activities and justify these tracking programs.

These automated prediction programs are neither expensive nor difficult to develop as commercial protocols, and examples already exist that can be adapted and reverse engineered for law enforcement activities (Sarkar 2015; Namiot 2013; SAS Institute Inc. 2017; *TIA Act 1979* ss 6A, 6B; *CAC Determination 2018*).

6.4.4.2 Functions of ASIO Are Wide and Broad, and the Attorney-General's Guidelines Are Permissive Rather Than Limiting

ASIO may use location information for speculative data matching (Evidence to PJCIS 2015: 40 (Thom). ASIO may '. . . undertake inquiries to determine whether a particular subject or activity is relevant to security' (AG's Guidelines s 6).

ASIO must determine if a person is of security interests and may pose a risk in future (AG's Guidelines s 6.1). This allows for speculation.

Prior to the 2007 AG's Guidelines, there was a prohibition on 'speculative data-matching', a stricter requirement, but which has since been removed:

> Prior to the 2007 Attorney-General guidelines, there was a prohibition on what was called speculative data-matching, I think, which would appear to have been a stricter requirement in the previous guidelines and was changed in 2007. That was before my time in this position, so I am not completely on top of that (Evidence to PJCIS, 2015: 4, 40 (Thom).

This is a broad power ASIO possess. However, ASIO states the accountability and the many oversight mechanisms that have withstood the test of time include ministerial accountability, parliamentary review and independent oversight, and rigorous internal policies and controls. These are the system of checks and balances. According to ASIO, these measures are ignored in public debates (Evidence to PJCIS 2014: 5–6 (Hartland)). These measures do 'consider individual rights, such as privacy, proportionality and minimising intrusion as well as the collective community right to feel safe and secure' (AGD, Submission No 27, *Inquiry* 2015: 11 [1.2.]). The AG's Guidelines are held up as the governance tool that will ensure the appropriate type of metadata is disclosed to the Agencies, in the absence of other publicly available governance instruments. The AGD informed the PJCIS the Agencies are only permitted to access telecommunications data on a case-by-case basis and to the extent that it is necessary to do so, as part of a legitimate investigation (Evidence to PJCIS 2014: 2 (Jones). ASIO provides timely advice on threats to the security of Australia, the Australian people and Australian interests (AG's Guidelines s 3). Any means used by ASIO for obtaining information must be proportionate to the gravity of the threat posed and the probability of its occurrence (Evidence PJCIS 2014: 5-6 (Jones). However, the AG's Guidelines are permissive rather than restrictive.

6.4.4.3   Trawling Through the Location Information

ASIO is adamant it is not trawling through data it collects (Evidence to PJCIS 2014: 19 (Hartland). ASIO refuted allegations of mass surveillance levelled, stating that ASIO does not engage in large-scale mass gathering of communications data. ASIO addressed fears of misuse and assured the PJCIS the location information is only used to perform its functions. ASIO claimed, during the PJCIS hearings about the introduction of the telecommunications data retention scheme, that it lacks the resources, the need or inclination for mass surveillance (PJCIS, *Advisory Report* 2015: 53). ASIO stated:

> The other thing I might add is that I know commentary is often made about us trawling through data for security purposes. We can only ever legislatively look for material, seek data, when we believe there is a nexus to security. *We do not have the resources, ability, time, energy or inclination to be trawling.* These are selective. We are looking at individuals of security concern. The concern expressed by some in the public—that we monitor communications of all Australians and that we are seeking to do that and that this would provide that — is erroneous (emphasis added) (Evidence to PJCIS 2014: 19 (Hartland).

The quote above implies ASIO may not possess BLD analytics-like capability. ASIO may only analyse location information using BLD analytics or otherwise when ASIO believes that there is a nexus or connection to security. However, fast forward to 2019 and ASIO is looking to incorporate BD analytics into its operational activities (ASIO 2019a, b). The metadata retention framework was approved on the basis of ASIOs claim that it lacks the resources or inclination for mass surveillance. Given that ASIO is looking to obtain this capability it may be time to review and reset the metadata retention and disclosure scheme. The assumption was that the Connection Test would not be applied in a BD analytics environment based on machine learning and powered by artificial intelligence (AI).

The AGD informed the PJCIS the Agencies are only permitted to access telecommunications data on a case-by-case basis and to the extent that it is necessary to do so as part of a legitimate investigation (Evidence to PJCIS 2014: 2 (Jones). However, an investigation can be targeted at an identified or identifiable person or group of persons, and even persons that are unknown. An incident may be investigated for which no person has yet been identified or is identifiable (AG's Guidelines s 6). The authorisation and notification process set out in the *CAC Determination 2018* is well suited for accessing location information in respect of unnamed persons, because it does not require a person to be named when the location information is requested—the Agencies can simply detail the location information they seek (*CAC Determination 2018* ss 8–12). Telecommunications data obtained from the Telco helps with the identification of the target of the investigation.

In keeping with the phrase 'in connection with', ASIO does not only exercise surveillance based on persons known to be of interest. ASIO also exercise surveillance and request location information from the Telco to determine if the person could be a suspect. ASIO may therefore look at more than just individuals that have already been identified as a security concern. The access and use of the location information is not required to be only targeted at an identified subject, or an identified group of persons (AG's Guidelines s 6). Unlike the requirements for warrants, where a person must be named, under the *CAC Determination 2018* no person is required to be identified beforehand (*TIA Act 1979* ss 9, 9A, 183; *CAC Determination 2018* ss 8–12).

This allows the Agencies greater discretion to collect location information in respect of unnamed persons, to analyse the location information with the aim of identifying a suspect for the first time (AG's Guidelines s 6.1).

The AG's Guidelines do not prohibit the analysis of the location information using electronic and automated data matching techniques, and to determine whether a particular subject or activity is relevant to security (AG's Guidelines s 6). Another criticism of ASIO is the denial that there is no measure of trawling, whether BLD analytics is used to analyse the telecommunications data or not and even if it is analysed manually. There is some measure of trawling that is inherent to the role of ASIO. It may not be as wide as some may believe, but it is inherent. The surveillance is not always targeted, and it cannot be targeted, because some persons and activities may not be known to the Agencies or may not appear suspicious, but if analysed further may reveal more suspicious behaviour. Even if ASIO may not intentionally trawl through the location information, the AG's Guidelines do not explicitly have a guideline governing trawling. Speculative data matching is a tool for trawling.

6.4.4.4   No Legal Requirement for ASIO to Delete Information That Is No Longer Required for National Security

Once the data is analysed and stored, it appears there is no legal requirement for ASIO to delete information that is no longer required for national security. This is despite there being provisions that allow for the destruction of the data after five years if the data is not of security interest, as per the 2012 Agreement with the National Archives of Australia. Personal information not required by the government agency should not be retained by a government agency. The Inspector-General of Intelligence and Security (IGIS) undertook to address this matter as a project for that year. The project would ask the question: "at what stage do they decide whether they [the data] are not of security interest and when do they dispose of them?"

(Evidence to PJCIS 2015: 37–39 (Thom)). IGIS, as the oversight body did not know the amount of information ASIO retains, claiming that that information is classified (Evidence to PJCIS 2015: 37–39 (Thom); IGIS 2019, Submission 36).

For this reason, it was recommended that the AG's Guidelines be reviewed to address the issue of whether ASIO may collect and maintain a comprehensive body of reference material to contextualise intelligence derived from inquiries and investigations and maintain a broad electronic and automated analytics database against which information obtained in relation to a specific inquiry can be checked and assessed (Evidence to PJCIS 2015: 38 (Thom); IGIS 2019, Submission 36).

6.5 Conclusion

The *TIA Act 1979* assumes location information retained by the Telco is personal information. This position somewhat strengthens the protection of privacy. However, the problem arises with location information that is not required to be retained. In the latter instance, location information can be 'about an individual' when linked with other information that identifies the person, based on the facts at hand. The use of automated big data analytics software, based on machine learning and artificial intelligence, to analyse location information to reveal a profile about the individual is unprecedented and a game changer in that it gives the Agencies the ability to analyse location information in an automated manner and draw conclusions. The longer period of retention allows for granularity that provides greater insight and intelligence about the individual and may reveal the identity of the individual. The use of automated analytics is indirectly supported by the AG's Guidelines and the intelligence strategies. The use of automated analytics is more invasive than examining location information manually. The security and law enforcement strategies of the Agencies enable the use of BLD machine learning and AI analytics to identify personal information about the person, but with few restrictions to minimise the impact on privacy and prevent other discriminatory practices that may arise. The activities that are related to the purposes and functions of the Agencies, such as developing a BLD storage platform appear not to be tested whether such an activity is based on reasonable grounds, whether the inquiry or investigation itself that uses the BLD is justifiable and is perhaps not politically motivated or racially biased, and if so, how to ensure it is reasonably justifiable. The privacy safeguards do not test the acceptability of the activities of the Agencies. As long as the activities of the Agencies are not questioned, but instead accepted as safe and sound, privacy is not able to be adequately protected. In the latter instance, privacy protection is subjected to the broad discretion of the Agencies, which remains unquestioned by a third independent party.

The Agencies can use the 'in connection with', the 'reasonably necessary' and the 'directly related' principles to bypass the Privacy Tests, without a third independent party questioning the soundness of the security and law enforcement activities of the Agencies.

This is an indication that the law enforcement interests unfairly outweigh those of privacy. This flexibility in the law is an indication of how privacy is not sufficiently protected. If privacy where to be sufficiently protected, the rules would be harder and tougher, to collect location information from the Telco, to ensure that there is as less discretion under the broad powers of the Agencies. Also, whenever the location information is re-used in respect of the secondary individuals, the privacy of the secondary individual is not protected under section 180F under the *TIA Act 1979*, and specifically under the *CAC Determination 2015* and *CAC Determination 2018*. It is under these sorts of circumstances that the Agencies can claim that they abide by the law and that collecting the telecommunications data is less intrusive. If no name is listed in the authorisation requesting the location information from the Telco, and no person is apparent, the telecommunications data is not about the person—the person is not apparent, the person is not reasonably ascertainable, because it takes an effort to identify the person. In this instance the metadata is not personal information, despite being deemed to be personal information. In that instance the Privacy Tests need not be applied. The stage at which the person is identified is not transparent and is not able to be challenged. The limits to the powers of the Agencies are ineffective to properly protect location information as personal information and thereby fail to adequately protect privacy. Privacy is further impacted by the fact the location information collected for one investigation may be used for another investigation, and in respect of another individual, but no Privacy Tests are required to be applied in terms of the second individual. Even after the privacy safeguards were improved in 2015 by the various tests, because of the unlimited scope of the Agencies purposes, functions and related operational activities, privacy is poorly protected. To protect privacy better, the question should instead be whether the activities for which location information is stored by the Telco and collected, accessed and used by the Agencies should be 'with judicial oversight' in the first place. In this manner privacy is better protected instead of privacy being left to the discretion of the Agencies, who decide on the activities related to their functions based on their public safety interests and strategic directions issued by the executive branch of government.

References

3GPP (2017) 5G; Study on Scenarios and Requirements for Next Generation Access Technologies (3GPP TR 38.913 version 14.2.0 Release 14) 2017-05

5G PPP (undated) 5G Vision. https://5g-ppp.eu/wp-content/uploads/2015/02/2G-Vision-Brochure-v1.pdf. Accessed 27 Aug 2019

ACMA (2016). http://www.acma.gov.au/Industry/Spectrum/Radiocomms-licensing/Apparatuslicences/apparatus-licensing-arrangements-for-femtocells. Accessed 4 Aug 2017

ACMA (2018) Communications report 2017–18

Acts Interpretation Act 1901 (Cth)

Acts Interpretation Act 1901 (Cth) (*AIA 1901*)

AHRC (2018) Human Rights Explained: Fact sheet 7: Australia and Human Rights Treaties. https://www.humanrights.gov.au/human-rights-explained-fact-sheet-7australia-and-human-rightstreaties. Accessed 28 Aug 2019

ASIO (2014) Submission No 12.1 to the Parliamentary Joint Committee on Intelligence and Security, Parliament of Australia, Inquiry into the Telecommunications (Interception and Access) Amendment (Data Retention) Bill 2014

ASIO (2019a) Director General's Review. https://www.asio.gov.au/AR2018-01.html. Accessed 18 Sept 2019

ASIO (2019b) Management and Accountability. https://www.asio.gov.au/AR2018-05.html. Accessed 18 Sept 2019

Attorney-General's Department (2016) Attorney-General's Guidelines in relation to the performance by the Australian Security Intelligence Organisation of its function of obtaining, correlating, evaluating and communicating intelligence relevant to security (including politically motivated violence) 2016', 2016 (the Attorney-General's [AG's] Guidelines)

Attorney-General's Department (AGD) (2015) Submission No 27 to the Parliamentary Joint Committee on Intelligence and Security, Inquiry into the Telecommunications (Interception and Access) Amendment (Data Retention) Bill 2014, 16 January 2015

Australia & New Zealand Bank v Ryan (1968) 88 WN (Pt l) (NSW) 368

Australian Broadcasting Corporation (ABC) v Lenah Game Meats Pty Ltd [2001] HCA 63

Australian Federal Police Act 1979 (Cth) (*AFP Act 1979*)

Australian Human Rights Commission (AHRC) (undated) What are human rights? https://www.humanrights.gov.au/about/what-are-human-rights. Accessed 28 Aug 2019

Australian Human Rights Commission Act 1986 (Cth) (*AHRC Act 1986*)

Australian Privacy Commissioner (APC) (2015) Submission No 92 to the Parliamentary Joint Committee on Intelligence and Security, Parliament of Australia, Inquiry into the Telecommunications (Interception and Access) Amendment (Data Retention) Bill 2014, January 2015

Barbaschow A (2019, September 6) Terrorism, espionage, and cyber: ASIO's omne trium perfectum. https://www.zdnet.com/article/terrorism-espionage-and-cyber-asios-omne-trium-perfectum/. Accessed 18 Sept 2019

Barclays Bank v Taylor [1989] 1 WLR 1066

Battersby L (2012, July 6) Telstra offers signal boost – at a price. The Sydney Morning Herald. http://www.smh.com.au/business/telstra-offers-signal-boost%2D%2Dat-a-price-20120706-2115f.html. Accessed 29 Aug 2019

Bennett ML, de Koker L (2017) Open secrets: balancing operational secrecy and transparency in the collection and use of data for national security and law enforcement agencies. Melb Univ Law Rev 41(2):530. http://classic.austlii.edu.au/au/journals/MelbULawRw/2017/32.html

Boyd B, Crawford K (2012) Critical questions for big data: provocations for a cultural, technological and scholarly phenomenon. Inf Commun Soc 15:662

Casanovas Romeu P, de Koker L, Mendelson D, Watts D (2017) Regulation of big data: perspectives on strategy, policy, law, and privacy. Health Technol:335–349

Chan J, Moses LB (2017) Making sense of big data for security. Br J Criminol 57(2):299–319

Christoj v Barclays Bank [2000] 1 WLR 937

Comcare v Banerji [2019] HCA 23 (7 August 2019) (the *Comcare court case*)

Commonwealth of Australia Constitution Act *1900 (Cth) (CACA 1900)*

Commonwealth of Australia (2012) Australian Criminal Intelligence Management Strategy 2012–15. http://www.aph.gov.au/DocumentStore.ashx?id=1c12c52d-439c-492e-acc9-e90c4ba50ee3. Accessed 28 Aug 2019

Commonwealth of Australian (2017) Australian Criminal Intelligence Management Strategy 2017–20. https://www.afp.gov.au/sites/default/files/PDF/ACIM-strategy-2017-20.pdf. Accessed 28 Aug 2019

Commonwealth v Tasmania (Tasmanian Dam Case) *(1983) 158 CLR 1*

Communications Access Coordinator's (CAC) Telecommunications (Interception and Access) (Requirements for Authorisations, Notifications and Revocations) Determination 2015 (Cth) (at 9 October 2015) (CAC Determination 2015)

D2D CRC (2018) Integrated Law Enforcement. https://www.d2dcrc.com.au/rd-programs/ integratedlaw-enforcement/. Accessed 4 Jan 2018

de Koker L, Chan J, Mendelson D, Bennett Moses L, Maurushat A, Vaile D, Gaffney, Sadler G, Grierson P, Cater D (June 2018) Australia Report. Big Data Technology and National Security. Comparative International Perspectives on Strategy, Policy and Law. Law and Policy Program. Data to Decisions Cooperative Research Centre. https://uploads-ssl.webflow.com/ 5cd23e823ab9b1f01f815a54/5cff12f563db55c367e6c7ca_Big%20Data%20Technology% 20and%20National%20Security%2C%20Comparative%20International%20Perspectives% 20on%20Strategy%2C%20Policy%20and%20Law%20-%20AUSTRALIA%20REPORT.pdf

Department of Foreign Affairs and Trade (DFAT) (2018) Treaties Last Updated 08/30/2010. http:// www.info.dfat.gov.au/Info/Treaties/Treaties.nsf/AllDocIDs/ 8B8C6AF11AFB4971CA256B6E0075FE1E. Accessed 28 Aug 2019

Drugs Misuse and Trafficking Act 1985 (NSW) (DMT)

European Telecommunications Standards Institute (ETSI) (2017a) Lawful Interception (LI); Retained Data; Requirements of Law Enforcement Agencies for handling Retained Data

European Telecommunications Standards Institute (ETSI) (2017b) LTE; Evolved Universal Terrestrial Radio Access Network (E-UTRAN); Stage 2 functional specification of User Equipment (UE) positioning in E-UTRAN (3GPP TS 36.305 version 14.2.0 Release 14)

European Telecommunications Standards Institute (ETSI) (2017c) LTE; Evolved Universal Terrestrial Radio Access (E-UTRA) and Evolved Universal Terrestrial Radio Access Network (E-UTRAN); Overall description; Stage 2

European Telecommunications Standards Institute (ETSI) (2017d) Digital cellular telecommunications system (Phase 2+) (GSM); Universal Mobile Telecommunications System (UMTS); LTE; Network architecture', 2017, (3GPP TS 23.002 version 14.1.0 Release 14) ETSI TS 123 002 V14.1.0 (2017-05)

Evidence to Parliamentary Joint Committee on Intelligence and Security (PJCIS), Parliament of Australia, Canberra, 29 January 2015, 38 (Vivienne Thom, Inspector-General of Intelligence and Security, Office of the Inspector-General of Intelligence and Security)

Evidence to Parliamentary Joint Committee on Intelligence and Security, Parliament of Australia, Canberra, 17 December 2014, 19 (Kerri Hartland, Acting Director-General, ASIO)

Evidence to Parliamentary Joint Committee on Intelligence and Security, Parliament of Australia, Canberra, 17 December 2014, 2 (Katherine Ellen Jones, Deputy Secretary, National Security and Criminal Justice Group, Attorney-General's Department)

Evidence to Parliamentary Joint Committee on Intelligence and Security, Parliament of Australia, Canberra, 29 January 2015, 46–47 (Timothy Pilgrim, Australian Privacy Commissioner, Office of the Australian Information Commissioner)

Evidence to Parliamentary Joint Committee on Intelligence and Security, Parliament of Australia, Canberra, 30 January 2015, 65 (Lewis Duncan Edward, Director-General of Security, Australian Security Intelligence Organisation) cited in Parliamentary Joint Committee on Intelligence and Security, Parliament of Australia, *Advisory Report on the Telecommunications (Interception and Access) Amendment (Data Retention) Bill 2014* (Cth) *2015*

Explanatory Memorandum, *Privacy Bill 1988 (Cth) 7 [16]*

Explanatory Memorandum, Privacy Amendment (Enhancing Privacy Protection) Bill 2012 (Cth)

Federal Commissioner of Taxation v Australia & New Zealand Banking Group (1979) 143 CLR 499

Gandomi A, Haider M (2015) Beyond the hype: big data concepts, methods, and analytics. Int J Inf Manage 35:137

George v. Rockett (1990) 170 CLR 104 20 June 1990 (the *George case*)

Germano G (2010) The Impact of Femtocells on Next Generation LTE Mobile Networks. PowerPoint Presentation at the FemtoForum, 2010, 1–30. ftp://www.3gpp.org/Information/

presentations/presentations_2010/2010_05_Moscow/Femto_Forum_Germano.pdf. Accessed 28 Aug 2019

Goldenfein J (2017, January 19) Australia's privacy laws gutted in court ruling on what is 'personal information'. The Conversation. https://theconversation.com/australias-privacy-laws-gutted-incourt-ruling-on-what-is-personal-information-71486. Accessed 28 Aug 2019

Human & Constitutional Rights Resource Page (2018). http://www.hrcr.org/safrica/privacy/austr_law.html. Accessed 28 Aug 2019

Hutchinson S, Ferguson R, Urban R (2018, January 6) African Gangs Reign of Fear in Melbourne's West. The Australian. https://www.theaustralian.com.au/nationalaffairs/state-politics/african-gangs-reign-of-fear-in-melbournes-west/newsstory/deb78713fb90f132c8df28b2b163fd24. Accessed 4 Apr 2018

iiNET (2015) Law enforcement agencies contact. https://www.iinet.net.au/about/legal/law.html. Accessed 8 July 2017

Inspector-General of Intelligence and Security (IGIS) (2019) Submission 36 to the Parliamentary Joint Committee on Intelligence and Security. Review of the mandatory data retention regime, July 2019

Johnston A (2017) Privacy law: data, metadata and personal information: a landmark ruling from the federal court. Law Soc NSW J (LSJ) 83. https://search.informit.com.au/documentSummary;dn=672220148307678;res=IELAPA. Accessed 28 Aug 2019

Keenan M (12 May 2014) Ministerial Direction Australian Federal Police. https://www.afp.gov.au/about-us/governance-and-accountability/ministerial-direction. Accessed 28 Aug 2019

Kioa v West *(1985) 159 CLR 550*

Koivisto A, Hakkarainen M, Costa M, Kela P, Leppanen K, Valkama M (2017) High-efficiency device positioning and location-aware communications in dense 5G networks. IEEE Commun Mag 55(8):188–195. https://doi.org/10.1109/MCOM.2017.1600655

La Trobe University (2019) Submission 10 to the PJCIS, Review of the mandatory data retention regime, July 2019

Laster (1989) Breaches of confidence and of privacy by misuse of confidential information. Otago Law Rev 7:31, 424

Loyd v Freshjeld (1826) 2 Car & P 325; 172 ER 147

Mapbox (2018) A Mapping Platform Powered by The Best Data in The World. https://www.mapbox.com/about/maps/. Accessed 28 Aug 2019

Maurushat A (2016) BD use by law enforcement and intelligence in the national security space: perceived benefits, risks and challenges. Media Arts Law Rev 21(3):1–27

Maurushat A, Benett-Moses L, Vaile D (2015) Using 'Big' Metadata for Criminal Intelligence: Understanding Limitations and Appropriate Safeguards. ICAIL '15, Jun 08–12, 2015, San Diego, CA, USA. ACM 978-1-4503-3522-5/15/06. https://doi.org/10.1145/2746090.2746110

Mayer J, Mutchler P, Mitchell JC (2016) Evaluating the privacy properties of telephone metadata. Proc Natl Acad Sci U S A 113(20):5536–5541

Minister for Justice (Cth) (Media Release, 15 June 2016) Investing in innovation for our law enforcement elite

Munson JP, Gupta VK (2002) Location-based notification as a general-purpose service. (Paper presented at the Proceedings of the 2nd international workshop on Mobile commerce, Atlanta, Georgia, USA, 28 September 2002)

Namiot D (2013) GeoFence services. Int J Open Inf Technol 1(9):30–33

Next Generation Mobile Networks Ltd (NGMN) (2015) 5G white paper. https://www.ngmn.org/uploads/media/NGMN5GWhitePaperV10.pdf. Accessed 27 Aug 2019

Nohrborg M (2017) LTE 3GPP. http://www.3gpp.org/technologies/keywordsacronyms/98-lte. Accessed 28 Aug 2019

Ockenden W (2016, August 16) How your phone tracks your every move. ABC. http://www.abc.net.au/news/2015-08-16/metadata-retention-privacy-phone-willockenden/6694152. Accessed 28 Aug 2019

Office of the Attorney-General (2015) Report 1 of the Data Retention Implementation Working Group (IWG), 30–31. http://www.aph.gov.au/DocumentStore.ashx?id=f261eba5-534c-4627-906c-a1bdd142b394. Accessed 28 Aug 2019

Office of the Australian Information Commissioner (OAIC) (2013) Australian Privacy Principles and National Privacy Principles – Comparison Guide. https://apo.org.au/node/33783. Accessed 28 Aug 2019

Office of the Australian Information Commissioner (OAIC) (2014) Guidelines on Data Matching in Australian Government Administration. https://www.oaic.gov.au/privacy/guidance-and-advice/guidelines-on-data-matching-in-australian-government-administration/. Accessed 28 Aug 2019

Office of the Australian Information Commissioner (OAIC) (2015) Australian Privacy Principles Guidelines Chapter B: Key concepts, Version 1.2 ed., Vol. B

Parliament of Australia (2006) Was there an EM?: Explanatory Memoranda and Explanatory Statements in the Commonwealth Parliament. https://www.aph.gov.au/About_Parliament/Parliamentary_Departments/Parliamentary_Library/Browse_by_Topic/law/explanmem/wasthereanEM. Accessed 28 Aug 2019

Parliamentary Joint Committee on Intelligence and Security (PJCIS), Parliament of Australia, Advisory Report on the Telecommunications (Interception and Access) Amendment (Data Retention) Bill 2014 (Cth) 2015

PJCHR, Human rights scrutiny report Thirty-fifth report of the 44th Parliament (25 February 2016)

Privacy Act 1988 (Cth)

Privacy Commissioner v Telstra Corporation Limited [2017] FCAFC 4 (*Privacy Commissioner court case*)

R v Zhi Qiang Han [2011] NSWCCA 120 (the *Zhi court case*)

Revised Explanatory Memorandum, Telecommunications (Interception and Access) Amendment (Data Retention) Bill 2015 (Cth), 2015

Robertson v Canadian Imperial Bank of Commerce [1994] 1 WLR 1493

Samsonidis v Commissioner, Australian Federal Police [2007] FCAFC 159 (5 October 2007) (the *Samsonidis court case*)

Sarkar N (2015) Using analytics and automation to create personalised customer journeys. Presentation at the SAS Forum, Sydney, Australia, May 7. https://www.sas.com/en_au/events/sasforum/2015/sas-executive-forum.html#speakers. Accessed 6 Feb 2016

SAS Institute Inc. (2017) SAS Master Data Management. https://www.sas.com/en_au/learn/software/customer-intelligence-360/tutorials/upload-data.html. Accessed 7 Aug 2017

SAS Institute Inc. (2018) What is big data? https://www.sas.com/en_au/insights/big-data/what-isbig-data.html. Accessed 7 Aug 2017

Smith GJD, Moses LB, Chan J (2017) The challenges of doing criminology in the big data era: towards a digital and data-driven approach. Br J Criminol 57(2):259–274

Stratton J (2013) Library Council of New South Wales, Hot Topics 85, Human Rights, Chapter 4c: Implementing treaties in Australian law. https://legalanswers.sl.nsw.gov.au/hot-topics-human-rights. Accessed 28 Aug 2019

Supplementary Explanatory Memorandum, Telecommunications (Interception and Access Amendment (Data Retention) Bill 2014

Taylor (2000) Why is there no common law right of privacy? Monash Univ Law Rev 26:240–241

Telecommunications (Interception and Access) Act 1979 (Cth) (*TIA Act 1979*)

Telecommunications (Interceptions and Access) (Requirements for Authorisations, Notifications and Revocations) Determination 2018 (Cth) (at 20 November 2018) (*CAC Determination 2018*)

Telstra (2015) Submission No 112 to the Parliamentary Joint Committee on Intelligence and Security, Inquiry into the Telecommunications (Interception and Access) Amendment (Data Retention) Bill 2014, January 2015

Telstra (2019) Privacy. https://www.telstra.com.au/privacy/customer-access. Accessed 20 Aug 2019

Telstra Corporation Limited and Privacy Commissioner [2015] AATA 991 (18 December 2015) (*Telstra decision*)

Tournier v National Provincial & Union Bank of England [1924] 1 KB 461

Victoria Park Racing and Recreation Grounds Co Ltd v Taylor (1937) 58 CLR 479

Watts D, Casanovas P (2019) Privacy and Data Protection in Australia: a critical overview. https://www.d2dcrc.com.au/article-content/privacy-and-data-protection-in-australia-a-critical-overview-extended-abstract

Winterton Constructions v Hambros (1992) 39 FCR 97, 114-15

WL v La Trobe University (General) [2005] VCAT 2592

Chapter 7
Oversight Exercised Over the Powers of the Agencies

7.1 A Schematic Outline of the Metadata Retention and Disclosure Framework

In order to critically analyse how effective oversight over the powers of the Agencies are, it is necessary to understand how the metadata retention and disclosure framework is structured. The outline is presented in Fig. 7.1 below:

The Telco may retain metadata, either under the legal requirement or voluntarily. The types of metadata include location information. There is no external oversight from the Commonwealth Ombudsman, the Inspector-General of Intelligence (IGIS) or the courts (except in respect of journalists) before the location information is collected from the Telco and used by the Agencies. The oversight is conducted after the location information has already been disclosed to, collected and then used by the Agencies. There is also no prior oversight by IGIS, the Commonwealth Ombudsman or the judiciary over the metadata disclosed under section 280 of the *TA 1997,* to other public bodies.

7.2 What Oversight Means

In the context of this framework, oversight refers to the reviews, inspections, authorisations to collect location information under the *CAC Determination 2015* and the *CAC Determination 2018*, and approvals for warrants carried out by bodies such as the members of the Administrative Appeals Tribunal (AAT) and the Judges issuing warrants. Oversight may take place before or after the location information has already been collected. Other authorities relevant to these practices are IGIS, the Commonwealth Ombudsman, the Communications Access Co-ordinator (CAC) in the Home Affairs Department.

© Springer Nature Switzerland AG 2020
S. Shanapinda, *Advance Metadata Fair*, Law, Governance and Technology Series
44, https://doi.org/10.1007/978-3-030-50255-3_7

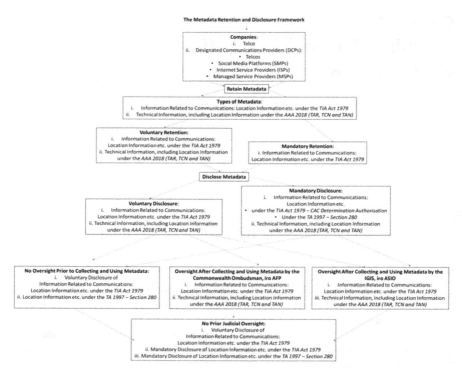

Fig. 7.1 The Metadata Retention and Disclosure Framework

7.3   The Inspector-General of Intelligence and Security and ASIO

ASIO conducts internal checks on the exercise of its powers, but not all the governance documents are publicly available. IGIS is the external oversight body that investigates, and issues reports regarding the access to and use of location information by ASIO in accordance with the Attorney-General's (AG's) Guidelines. The inspections of IGIS are the checks and balances in respect of ASIO's use of location information in relation to its powers (Evidence 2014, 17 (Hartland); Evidence 2015, 65 (Edward) cited in PJCIS, 2015, p. 54 [2.43]; IGIS 2019, Submission 36: 6). IGIS inspects whether there is compliance with the law, and the propriety of particular activities of ASIO. Its role also extends to inspecting the effectiveness and appropriateness of the internal procedures of ASIO relating to the legality or propriety of the activities of ASIO (*IGIS Act* s 8(1)(a) (i), (ii), (iii), (iv); IGIS 2015, p. 21). On a case-by-case basis, samples of records are inspected. IGIS inspects whether the power exercised by ASIO to collect location information via a telecommunications data authorisation issued under the *CAC Determination 2018* is proportionate, as set out in the AG's Guidelines (AGD 2016; Evidence to PJCIS

2015, p. 41 (Thom). The limits in the AG's Guidelines are more permissive than they are restrictive, making these limits potentially ineffective.

The AG's Guidelines were first issued in 2007. The metadata retention scheme was adopted in 2015, but the AG's Guidelines have not been updated since then. As such, IGIS requested that the AG's Guidelines be reviewed and re-issued as a matter of priority, given the continuous technological advances in the volume and the personal nature of the telecommunications data collected and processed which has disproportionately increased the powers of ASIO, compared to before: 'ASIO has gained access to a range of intrusive powers, and has exercised these powers in a changing security and technological environment' (IGIS 2019, Submission 36: 6, 12 [5.4]).

7.3.1   Oversight Over TARs, TANs and TCNs: Notification Obligations

IGIS was granted new oversight powers over ASIO with the introduction of the *Telecommunications and Other Legislation Amendment (Assistance and Access) Act 2018 (AAA 2018)*. IGIS must be informed when a Technical Assistance Request (TAR), Technical Assistance Notice (TAN) and Technical Capability Notice (TCN) has been issued, varied, revoked, extended. The Designated Communications Provider (DCP) must be informed that it has the right to complain to IGIS. The DCP may request that an assessment about whether the proposed TCN be carried out be given. The assessment report must be submitted to IGIS (*AAA 2018* ss 317HAB(1), 317JA(15), 317(6), 317MAA(3), 317MAB(1), 317MA(IE), 317Q(12), 317R(5), 317TAB(1), 317(ID), 317WA(6)(d), 317X(6), 317YA(6)(d), 317Z(3)).

7.3.2   Inspection Outcomes

IGIS identified no issues of concern during the 2014–2015 financial year. IGIS highlighted a requirement for improved record keeping and documenting of decisions in relation to investigations. IGIS was satisfied that the AG's Guidelines were followed IGIS reported that the prospective data authorisations it reviewed confirmed that ASIO 'has regard' to the AG's Guidelines. IGIS reported that ASIO only made requests to access data in order to perform its functions. ASIO states IGIS has no concerns over its collection and use of historic and prospective metadata. ASIO indicated to the PJCIS that it abides by the law. IGIS informed the Parliamentary Joint Committee on Intelligence and Security (PJCIS), there is a high rate of compliance. IGIS did not identify any concerns in relation to ASIO exercising its powers. IGIS reported ASIO did not exhibit a systemic problem (IGIS 2015, pp. 19–21, 24; Evidence to PJCIS (Hartland) 2014; Evidence to PJCIS (Edward) 2015; Svantesson 2012, pp. 270–271; PJCIS 2015, p. 54 [2.158]; IGIS 2017, p. 18).

The 2017 Independent Intelligence Review considered the oversight arrangements as rigorous and independent. This, despite the powers being concentrated in the arms of the executive and thereby providing independent assurance about the legality and propriety of the intelligence operations:

> In our view, it strikes an appropriate balance between the need for intelligence agencies to function with confidentiality, to be operationally effective (subject to checks and balances applied by legislation and responsible Ministers) and the requirement for robust accountability in a democratic society (Commonwealth of Australia 2017, pp. 8–9, 111 [7.4], 117 [7.22]).

The Agencies were commended for the prevailing culture of compliance (Svantesson 2012). IGIS agreed:

> Our inspections of ASIO's access to prospective telecommunications data and historical telecommunications data showed that the prospective data authorisations were authorised at the appropriate level, were undertaken in connection with ASIO's functions and demonstrated regard for the Attorney-General's Guidelines (the Guidelines)' (IGIS 2018, p. 22).

However, given how broad the legal powers are, it is easy for ASIO to comply with the low compliance standards.

7.3.3   Issues Raised by the Inspections and Reviews

In *2015* IGIS reported on errors in a small number of cases to comply with the internal approval policy to collect historical telecommunications data. The errors included not recording the approval of requests, and requests not being approved at the appropriate level. ASIO has undertaken to remind its staff of the relevant internal approval requirements (IGIS 2015, pp. 24–25).

IGIS also raised concerns about why ASIO did not use less intrusive methods to collect telecommunications data. The requests for prospective data used ambiguous wording. They did not adequately explain why less intrusive methods for obtaining the information had not been used or were not regarded as appropriate in the case at hand. ASIO explained the context, and IGIS was satisfied that it was consistent with the AG's Guidelines. ASIO undertook to remind staff of the need to clearly document whether less intrusive methods were considered, and to explain whether and how the less intrusive techniques may not be effective under the circumstances. ASIO could explain the use, and the use was in line with the AG's Guidelines (IGIS 2015, pp. 24–25).

Due to an error in the interception system of a Telco, ASIO received SMS content. This was contrary to the prospective data authorisation. The error was due to the Telco making changes to its system. ASIO was not aware of the changes, and no testing was done prior to the implementation. The error was detected in less than 2 days. ASIO access logs showed that no personnel member had access to the content. The internal governance measures of ASIO include access logs, which are used to trace access to, and the use of the information collected from the Telco (IGIS 2015, pp. 24–25).

There were a few concerns: 'IGIS staff identified a small number of instances in which ASIO retained metadata, or telecommunications interception data that was not relevant to security' (IGIS 2018, p. 22). It is not clear how IGIS addressed this issue, because ASIO is restricted to only collect and use metadata relevant to security.

7.3.3.1   Oversight and Big Location Data

The 2017 Independent Intelligence Review recommended a review of the intelligence laws, based on the principle that the laws should be easily understood and clearly state the activities that are permitted. The review recommended to assess the collection, sharing and use of bulk data in a flexible way that is balanced with appropriate privacy protections (Intelligence Review 2017, p. 92 [6.13]–[6.14]). The review was completed in December 2019, but the public document will only be made available sometime in 2020 (AGD 2019).

7.4   The Commonwealth Ombudsman and the AFP

The Commonwealth Ombudsman was granted new oversight powers over the AFP with the introduction of the location information retention obligations in October 2015 (*DRA 2015* Schedule 3). The oversight '. . . serves to provide an important level of public accountability and scrutiny of agency practices by virtue of the Ombudsman public reporting regime . . .' (Revised Explanatory Memorandum 2015, p. 111 [678]–[679]). The Commonwealth Ombudsman must inspect retained records of authorisations and notifications and issue a report. The AFP must keep records about whether the authorisations to collect location information were properly made. The records must also include whether the officer approving the collection of the location information took into account the 'Privacy Tests' and 'Reasonably Necessary or Directly Related Tests', and other relevant considerations (*Telecommunications (Interception and Access) Act 1979* (Cth) s 186A). In this way the Commonwealth Ombudsman is required to assess and state in its reports whether the AFP complied with the 'reasonably necessary', 'justifiable and proportionate' and 'reasonable grounds' standards; and hopefully shed light on what these standards mean in a practical sense. The Commonwealth Ombudsman conducts compliance audits in respect of the AFP. The records are inspected to assess compliance with the legal requirements (*TIA Act 1979* s 180F; Commonwealth Ombudsman 2015, p. 8).

7.4.1   Oversight Over TARs, TANs and TCNs: Notification Obligations

The Commonwealth Ombudsman was also granted new oversight powers over the AFP with the introduction of the *AAA 2018*. The Commonwealth Ombudsman may inspect the records of the AFP for compliance. The report is submitted to the Minister of Home Affairs, who must table the report, or a redacted version to each House of the Parliament. The AFP must notify the Commonwealth Ombudsman within 7 days after having issued or having extended the original TAR, TAN when the TAR or TAN has been amended, revoked or extended.

The Attorney-General must also inform the Commonwealth Ombudsman about the TCN that has been issued, when the period is extended, the notice is revoked and when the notice is amended. The DCP may request that an assessment about whether the proposed TCN be carried out be given. The assessment report must be submitted to the Commonwealth Ombudsman (*AAA 2018* s 317ZRB(3), (6), (7)); 317ZRB, 83 (4), 186B(1A), 55(2B)), 317TAB(2), 317TA(IE), 317X(7), 317Z(4)), 317HAB(4), 317JA(18), 317JB(9), 317MAB(2), 317MA(1F), 317Q(13), 317R(6)). 317WA(1), (6)(e)(ii), 317YA(6)(e)).

7.4.2   Inspection Outcomes

Despite the 'strong compliance culture', the Commonwealth Ombudsman's inspection reports identified a number of compliance concerns. These included: non-adherence to journalist information warrant provisions; authorisations that were improperly made; inability to sufficiently demonstrate required privacy considerations; access to unauthorised telecommunications data; statistical issues; and poor record-keeping.

- In April 2017, the AFP accessed the telecommunications data of a journalist without obtaining the required Journalist Information Warrant (JIW). This was contrary to the legal requirements. This issue remained unaddressed till the 2018–2019 reporting period (Commonwealth Ombudsman 2018, p. 2).
- Privacy was appropriately considered in general terms. What remained a concern was that agencies were unable to demonstrate that the authorised officers met the required privacy considerations. Also, the offences listed in the authorisations and notifications of the *CAC Determination 2015* did not match the applications made to senior officers to request that they authorise the Telco to disclose the metadata (Commonwealth Ombudsman 2018, p. 10). In other words, it was not clear how the officers demonstrated how they met the 'Privacy Tests' in practical terms, at an operational level.
- During March and October 2015 period, AFP officers that did not have the power to authorise the disclosure of metadata did in fact authorise the disclosure of

metadata, affecting at least 3249 records. This was contrary to the law. A total of 240 authorisations affected ongoing investigations and inquiries. By April 2018 the metadata was not fully quarantined. The Commonwealth Ombudsman considered this breach as a large-scale issue of non-compliance (AFP 2019; Commonwealth Ombudsman 2018, pp. 10–11; *AAA 2018* s 5AB(1A)).

- A significant number of historic telecommunications data authorisations, the telecommunications data obtained by the agencies was either outside the date range specified on the authorisation or was dated after the Telco was notified of the authorisation. The Telco provided telecommunications data the agencies had not requested (Commonwealth Ombudsman 2018, pp. 13, 15).
- Not all authorisations for metadata were made by all the Agencies in writing, especially in urgent cases. The Commonwealth Ombudsman described these verbal authorisations as a 'standardised process' (Commonwealth Ombudsman 2018, pp. 16–17). The Telco did not decline the verbal requests. This, despite the legal requirement the authorisation and notification under the *CAC Determination 2018* must be in writing or in an electronic format and must be signed by the authorised officer. There is therefore no legal framework for verbal authorisations. This complicates the inspections, as there are no records to inspect. The verbal request do not seem recorded either as voice recordings to keep an audit trail. The Commonwealth Ombudsman is therefore unable to determine whether the Privacy Tests have been applied (Commonwealth Ombudsman 2018, p. 16). Under APP 3.1 AFP is required to obtain metadata by Lawful and Fair Means. It would appear as it if this test was not complied with. Any such authorisations should be seen as unprocedural and procedural justice would not have been extended to the persons whose metadata was collected. At worst, these acts are tantamount to being unlawful and breaching the individual's privacy. The law does not indicate how the relevant agencies exercising this conduct would be disciplined and held accountable. The effect is that the agencies act with almost no accountability. This puts the evidentiary use of the metadata in question simply because the evidence used to lay any charges were not collected in the required procedural fashion.
- During the 2016–2017 period, some agencies that did not routinely keep records indicating when notifications occurred. Some records were lost. In three cases the agencies were unable to demonstrate that all telecommunications data obtained had been properly authorised. The forms of the authorisations, revocations and notifications used to collect the metadata did not meet the requirements of the *CAC Determination 2015* (Commonwealth Ombudsman 2018, pp. 19, 21).
- The Telco has also kept sending information to the agencies after the authorisations have been revoked and are no longer valid (Commonwealth Ombudsman Submission 20 2019, p. 7). The Commonwealth Ombudsman did not specify in its reporting whether these agencies specifically included the AFP but neither specified who these bodies were. It is assumed that these agencies may include the AFP as well.

7.5   The Extent of Compliance Standard

The duty of the Commonwealth Ombudsman is to inspect the records to determine the 'extent' of the AFP's compliance. This may be referred to as the 'extent of compliance' standard. The Commonwealth Ombudsman reported the AFP had a 'strong compliance culture' (*DRA 2015* s 186B; Commonwealth Ombudsman 2017, p. 23).

The 'extent of compliance' standard undermines the privacy safeguards introduced in 2015. It is not clear what a 'high rate of compliance' means (*DRA 2015* s 186B; PJCIS 2015). The Agencies either comply with the law or they are noncompliant. Wording such as the 'extent of compliance' and a 'high rate of compliance' are indicative of a degree of tolerance for non-compliance, and the exact threshold of this tolerance is uncertain.

The access may be lawful but given the broad and non-transparent powers, their breadth and the almost complete absence of effective restrictions make it easy for the Agencies to comply with the broad powers in the laws. As stated by IGIS: 'Consequently, the risk of non-compliance with statutory requirements is low' (IGIS 2019, Submission 36: 6).

These broad powers are illustrated by there being no restriction on the use of Big Location Data (BLD) analytics; on the use of location information collected for primary investigations to be used for secondary investigations and secondary individuals in respect of whom privacy assessments were not conducted; or on the use of location information collected for investigations being used for non-investigations, just to enforce the criminal law and to carry out unspecified 'activities' related to their functions, if 'reasonably necessary' as opposed to being 'necessary'. The 'extent of compliance' standard implies a level of condoning non-compliant activities of the Agencies. It does not set a 'zero-tolerance' level to any non-compliance but implies that a certain level of non-compliance may be acceptable and tolerated. This is indicative of 'light touch' regulation, as opposed to sending a message of the expectation of strict compliance. As such, little to no disciplinary or accountability measures may be taken in respect of the non-compliance outcomes described above.

7.6   Oversight Exercised Is Based on Complaints Submitted

The inspection powers of IGIS are subject to complaints received, and requests from the AG and from the Prime Minister. The Commonwealth Ombudsman may exercise oversight in its sole discretion. The Commonwealth Ombudsman investigates the conduct and the practices of the AFP, including complaints about serious misconduct. The DCP may complain to the Commonwealth Ombudsman about the TAR. The AFP must inform the DCP about its right to lodge complaints (*IGIS Act* ss 8(1) (a), 9–12; *DRA 2015* s 186J; Commonwealth Ombudsman 2015, p. 8; *AAA 2018* s 317MAA(4)(b)(i)).

7.7   The Right to be Forgotten

Law enforcement agencies are also not required to store the records of the authorisations for the metadata collected from the Telco for designated periods (Commonwealth Ombudsman Submission 20 2019, pp. 4–5). This means the oversight body may not be able to inspect these records to determine if the law was complied with.

On the other hand, the Agencies are not required to destroy the metadata they collected (Commonwealth Ombudsman Submission 20 2019, pp. 4–5; IGIS Submission 36 2019, p. 13 [5.5]). This means the metadata is either retained indefinitely or may continue to be used for other inquiries. It also means that the information is destroyed at any time and at the sole discretion of the Agencies. In such a case, if no records are kept until the oversight body reviews it, the information may be destroyed to hide anything the Agencies do not want the oversight bodies to inspect and report on. This allows for an opportunity of misuse. The Commonwealth Ombudsman is visible assess whether privacy was duly considered, whether only the required information was collected and used and not more information than was necessary, whether the information collected was authorised or not, or whether the contents of a communication were also collected or not. There is therefore no oversight over the destruction of the information. This creates a gap in the oversight procedures, where misuse can take place, creating a blind spot.

Another oversight gap is that the Commonwealth Ombudsman has no oversight over the information collected under other laws, such as under section 280 of the *Telecommunications Act 1997* and the *Migration Act 1958*. As such, the Commonwealth Ombudsman is unable to oversee the collection of unnecessary metadata, as reported by Telstra, under section 280. The information may be used without inspecting whether these laws have been complied with, and not addressing any instances of misuse (Commonwealth Ombudsman Submission 20 2019, p. 7).

7.8   The Conflict of Interest Between Privacy and Law Enforcement

The role of the Agencies as both sole guardians of privacy and as adjudicators over privacy interference, with no independent adjudicator, creates a conflict of interest that undermines the post-2015 privacy safeguards. The protection of privacy is a limit placed on the powers of the Agencies to access and use location information. The law deems retained location information to be personal information. The individual can access their personal information (*TIA Act 1979* s 187LA; *Privacy Act 1988* s 6(1), Schedule 1, APP 6). The *TIA Act 1979*, the *ASIO Act 1979*, the AG's Guidelines, and the Ministerial Direction issued by the Minister of Justice allow the Agencies access to location information, but under less stringent requirements than access to the contents of a communication (*TA 1997* s 275A, 276, 280; *TIA Act 1979* s 187A (1), 187AA (1) items 1–6; *CAC Determination 2018*; AG's Guidelines ss 10, 11; Ministerial Direction 2014, p. 3).

The Agencies are required to consider privacy when they request access to the location information and must use the least intrusive method of collecting the location information (*TIA Act 1979* s 180F; AG's Guidelines ss 10.4, 11). The circumstances under which the collection of the location information may be considered as less invasive are not spelt out. The Agencies have great discretion. The Agencies alone decide if the operational tactics they use will be more invasive or less invasive, with no external prior approval or review of the activities directly related to their functions, or tactics carried out 'in connection with' their functions. The public is asked to trust that the Agencies will take the harder option, the option that is in favour of preserving privacy, rather than a more convenient but more intrusive one. Where efficiency, agility and the speedy conclusion of an investigation is of prime importance, faced with the choice it is difficult to see how the Agencies would rather choose to opt for the more difficult option.

The Agencies may access location information generated and stored over any period. Location information collected for a month would often be more revealing than the location information gathered for a week. In that case, would the Agencies be expected to request the location information generated over a week or the location information generated over a month? The Agencies must make a statement that any interference with privacy is justifiable and proportionate, considering the likely relevance and usefulness of the location information requested (*CAC Determination 2018* ss 10–12). The Agencies are asked to make statements but these statements are not made under oath, and can simply be copied and pasted (AFP 2015, pp. 74–103; *CAC Determination 2018* ss 8–12).[1] The Agencies are not specifically asked to practically demonstrate the likely relevance and usefulness of the information based on the facts at hand for the *CAC Determination 2018*. The Commonwealth Ombudsman reported it is unable to verify how law enforcement agencies practically demonstrate how they determine and apply the requirements, such as those stemming from the Privacy Tests under the *CAC Determination 2015* (Commonwealth Ombudsman 2018, p. 10). If specifically asked to consider and demonstrate the usefulness of the location information, as opposed to simply stating that the location information will be useful, privacy would be better protected. The Agencies could be required to demonstrate that, for example, in the example of Mr Ockenden's location information, the location information generated between 23 and 26 December 2014 is likely to indicate Mr Ockenden was in Tasmania when a phone call was made from his parent's landline number to Mr X, in which Mr X is suspected of revealing secret government information that was leaked in a newspaper article (Ockenden 2016). The location information will be useful to showing that Mr Ockenden may have been the person that made the call to Mr X, who can be assumed to be his

---

[1]The Historical Call Charge Records (CCR) Request form is made in terms of ss 178A (2) and 179 (2) of *TIA Act 1979*, and The Historical Subscriber Request forms made in terms of ss 178A (2) and 179(2) of *TIA Act 1979*.

source for the story. A statement required to be drafted like this is linked to the particular facts and shows how useful the location information is, as opposed to the option of making a non-specific formal statement from a template. The usefulness of the nature and amount of location information collected could thus be properly demonstrated to a third party. The third party could be an Administrative Appeals Tribunal (AAT) member or a Judge who has a security clearance. In the absence of more specific, strict and independent privacy parameters that would require the Agencies to more closely justify and limit the quantity of location information collected it is doubtful whether the Agencies collect only the location information that is reasonably necessary. The Agencies are put in a predicament by this potential conflict between privacy interests and operational convenience and may be reluctant to slow down an investigation by collecting less location information if they can collect more. The bodies that are entrusted with balancing privacy interests and law enforcement interest are the Agencies themselves, the entities that seek the personal information and are granted powers to access it under less stringent requirements. No Judge or AAT member is involved to make an independent assessment of whether privacy may have been breached when the location information was accessed, based on the volume of location information collected over a given period in a given case. Under a domestic preservation notice covering content, only the communications stored for the period between the date the notice is issued and the day after the notice is served on the Telco, or the communications that will be generated for the 29 days after the notice is served on the Telco, may be collected (*TIA Act 1979* s 107H). No such limit exists under the authorisation and notification issued under the *CAC Determination 2018* for historical location information. The AFP is simply asked to list the details of the information to be disclosed (*CAC Determination 2018* ss 10–12). The Agencies are therefore allowed access to location information that is personal and revealing, unlike the situation for content where the Agencies are required to obtain a warrant and then only after the Judge or the Attorney-General is satisfied that the disclosure is reasonably necessary (*CAC Determination 2018* ss 8–12).

There is no practical and independent indication of the quantity of location information that may be considered 'reasonably necessary' or 'justifiable and proportionate' considering the seriousness of the offence, the likely relevance and usefulness, and the reason for the disclosure vis-à-vis the privacy of the individual (*CAC Determination 2018* ss 8–12). Given that the quantities may be difficult or impractical to prescribe, the sole judgment of the Agencies is what is relied on, trusting that the Agencies will apply the facts properly and only collect the quantity of location information that is justified on 'reasonable grounds'. Given the conflict between privacy and law enforcement, it is likely the Agencies may often collect more location information than is based on 'reasonable grounds', or what the Agencies in their sole judgment consider is 'reasonably necessary' and based on 'reasonable grounds'.

The Agencies continue to collect location information under less stringent requirements than are appropriate, even after location information was deemed to be personal information by the *TIA Act 1979* (s 187LA). While the privacy safeguards became tougher for the AFP under section 180F of the *TIA Act 1979* no such changes with stricter requirements were introduced for ASIO. Location information reveals personal information (Mayer et al. 2016; Ockenden 2016). The location information is disclosed to both the AFP and ASIO under less stringent requirements by issuing an authorisation and notification under the *CAC Determination 2018*, even with the introduction of section 180F of the *TIA Act 1979*, without any third party independently verifying the application for location information and either granting or denying that application.

The contents of an e-mail message or SMS communication may only be disclosed under a Part 2–2 warrant issued by a judge. The Judge must be satisfied that by accessing those stored communications, the access would likely assist the investigation of a serious contravention in which the person is involved. No prior warrant is required for its location information, and the Agencies need not demonstrate to the Telco or any third independent party that the location information would likely assist with the investigation of a contravention of an offence, serious or otherwise; the AFP can simply make a statement that the AFP is satisfied that any interference with privacy is justifiable and proportionate, considering the likely relevance and usefulness of the location information. The AFP may solely in its subjective judgment make the determination that it is satisfied that the location information is reasonably necessary, and no third party verifies that conclusion independently or is required to also be satisfied that the quantity of location information collected would be reasonably necessary and not be excessive (*TIA Act 1979* ss 116(1)(d)(i), 178(3), 179(3), 180(4); *CAC Determination 2018* ss 10–12).

The question is whether, after the reports by the Commonwealth Ombudsman, based on the AFPs own level of compliance, the AFP can continue to be trusted to self-certify the collection and use of personal information.

7.9 Oversight Occurs After the Fact

External oversight occurs after the Agencies have already issued the authorisation and notification under the *CAC Determination 2018* and collected and used the location information in the primary and secondary investigation, inquiry or activity to enforce the criminal law; and potentially in respect of another individual and not only the initial individual in respect of whom the privacy impact assessment was made when the authorisation and notification was issued (*TIA Act 1979* s 186A; Evidence to PJCIS (Thom) 2015, p. 41). The Commonwealth Ombudsman and IGIS are public oversight bodies that are part of the executive arm of government and not part of the judicial branch (Hardy and Williams 2014; Williams 2016; Shanapinda, S.: Advance metadata fair: The retention and disclosure of location information as metadata for law enforcement and national security, and the impact on privacy—An Australian story. Dissertation, UNSW Sydney (2018, pp. 178, 364–365)).

The oversight is not conducted in advance, at the time of collection of the personal information by the independent judiciary (*TIA Act 1979* s 186A; Evidence to PJCIS 2015, p. 41 (Thom).

The oversight bodies carry out their inspections after the location information has been collected, whereas for personal information such as voice and SMS communications, a Judge, Administrative Appeals Tribunal (AAT) member or the AG verifies the privacy impacts beforehand. Privacy is impacted at the time the location information is collected. As a result, the privacy impact for location information should be also assessed, at the time of an application under the principles in the *CAC Determination 2018*, by an independent third party.

The collection of the location information is what starts to impact the privacy of the individual. The impact continues as the location information is analysed and connected to other information, and more personal information is revealed. IGIS inspections are unable to make an assessment on privacy impacts at the crucial time, before or at the time of location information collection. The internal authorisation process for the location information is done by ASIO itself at the crucial time, and this has been criticized for being a 'self-certification process' (Evidence to PJCIS 2015, p. 31 (Leonard).

The oversight bodies do not conduct prior approvals or prior inspections of the authorisations and notifications under the *CAC Determination 2018*, to verify from an independent perspective like that of a Judge, AAT member or magistrate, that the collection and use of the location information was justifiable and proportionate, and reasonably necessary. The interference with privacy is best inspected prior to the collection or at worst, at the time of collection, rather than after the fact. If the oversight bodies later determine that privacy of certain location information was not justifiably interfered with, it is not clear what the appropriate remedies may be, if any. The belated inspections of IGIS may not be the most appropriate tool to protect privacy in this context. This is demonstrated by the reports of non-compliance, and the inaction taken to instil accountability. The non-compliance, although not systemic, is downplayed as minor or as simple human error, that can be fixed with education. However, there has been little indication of public accountability by not addressing the non-compliance—it has been met with public silence so far.

7.10 Oversight Concentrated in the Executive Branch of Government

The *ex post facto* oversight role and the power to exercise security and law enforcement functions are concentrated in the hands of the executive arm of government (Hardy and Williams 2014). The AFP and ASIO both report to the same Minister of Home Affairs (AFP, undated). The surveillance powers are now concentrated in the hands of the Minister of Home Affairs (ASIO, undated).

The Communications Access Coordinator (CAC), which is located in the same organisation as the Minister of Home Affairs, sets the limits to the exercise of the AFP and ASIO powers in terms of the *CAC Determination 2018* and the AG's Guidelines. The limits are to consider the privacy of the individual and only collect location information and other metadata that is justifiable and proportional to the exercise of the powers of the Agencies. These powers are however broad, as indicated by terms such as 'security', 'person of interest', 'in connection with' and 'investigation'.

7.11   The Telco Is Not Inspected Like the Agencies Are, to Verify If They Disclose Only Information That Is Reasonably Necessary

The Telco is not inspected like the Agencies are, to verify whether the Telco discloses only location information that is reasonably necessary to enforce the criminal law, and that they are not disclosing more location information than is reasonably necessary: 'IGIS does not oversee these private sector service providers or the data retained by them' (IGIS 2019, Submission 36: 3). This, despite the fact that the Telco discloses more information than is authorised to be disclosed—'. . . a carrier erroneously provide[d] information relating to a service other than the service specified in the ASIO authorisation' (IGIS 2019, Submission 36: 3–4). The information was quarantined and not used. Telstra also confirmed that other public bodies collect more information than is necessary (Telstra Submission 35 2019, p. 2). Given the broad scope of the *CAC Determination 2018* request that allows the Agencies to list the details of the location information they seek, no one except the Agencies know where the lines are practically drawn by the 'reasonably necessary' principle, and how the 'reasonably necessary' principle would be applied (*CAC Determination 2018* ss 10–12).

The Telco is only required to retain location information at the start and at the end of the call (*TIA Act 1979* ss 187A (1), 187AA (1) item 6). Should the principle be that the Telco should not disclose the location information during the call? Or is this left to the discretion of the Telco, or should the *CAC Determination 2018* be amended to state that the Agencies are not permitted to request the location information retained during and after the call? Or should the question about the disclosure of voluntarily retained location information that is in excess of what is required to be retained, not be addressed under a warrant issued by a judicial officer?

Telstra indicated to the AAT that it only discloses the identity of the cell that handled the communication. Telstra is still required by law to disclose this information if the Agencies request for it, even if it is information not used to provide the communications service the mobile device is connected to (*TA 1997* ss 275A, 276, 280, 313(3), 313(4), 313(7); *TIA Act 1979* ss 174–184). The *CAC Determination 2018* does not specifically prohibit or restrict the Agencies from requesting the identity of the neighbouring cell that did not connect the mobile phone, a cell other than the one with the strongest signal, and that is not used for billing purposes. This was described as 'mobile cell location information beyond the mobile cell location information that Telstra retains for billing purposes' (*Telstra decision* 21 [50.(3)]).

The Telco is required to comply strictly with the authorisation and notification. There is no provision that the Telco may refuse or ask for a review of the application. However, under the TAN, TCN and TAR, the DCP may lodge a dispute and complain to the Commonwealth Ombudsman. These two frameworks may need to be aligned. The Telco is not required to apply the Privacy Tests or the 'Reasonably Necessary or Directly Related Tests' and is not able to act as a gatekeeper for the privacy of its customer (*AAA 2018* s 317MAA; *TA 1997* s 313(3), (7); *CAC Determination 2018* ss 8–12).

7.12   Confidentiality and the Difficulty to Challenge the Activities of the Agencies

The Telco is prohibited to inform the person of the location information collected about them, even if they were to ask (*TIA Act 1979* ss 181A (1), (2), (4), (5); 181 (B1), (2), (4), (5); 182A (1), (2)). In replying to the PJCIS' comment that journalists are not informed about the application for a JIW, the Attorney-General replied that a person under investigation may destroy evidence if informed and frustrate the investigation (PJCHR 2016). However, there is little or no opportunity for an individual to become aware that the location information may have been misused. There is little or no opportunity for an individual to know that only location information that was reasonably necessary was collected. Telstra reported other bodies are collecting more metadata than is necessary (Telstra Submission 35 2019, p. 2). The Commonwealth Ombudsman raised similar concerns in 2019, stating: 'Under the mandatory data retention scheme, an agency's actions are covert, so a person is typically unaware that an agency has accessed their telecommunications data. As a result, it is unlikely that the Office will receive a complaint about an agency's actions to access telecommunications data under the scheme' (Commonwealth Ombudsman Submission 20 2019, p. 8).[2] Moreover, the Commonwealth Ombudsman has no oversight over metadata collected under section 280 of the *Telecommunications Act 1997*.

Not many complaints have been lodged with the Commonwealth Ombudsman. The Human Rights Law Centre (HRLC) therefore recommended that persons be informed that their information has been collected so they are able to exercise their rights to lay complaints, as was decided in court cases in the EU (HRLC 2019, Submission 19). For the person to lodge a complaint they would need be aware of the privacy breach. The collection of the location information is a confidential process

---

[2]See Sect. 5.1.2.2 in Chap. 5.

(*CAC Determination 2018* ss 8–9; TIA Act 1979 s 108(1)). The individual is not informed of the location information requests and disclosures. The affected individual would find it challenging to collect copies of the authorisations and notifications to challenge the Agencies and whether and how they met the Privacy Tests. It is significant that the oversight bodies conduct their investigations based on complaints (*IGIS Act 1986* ss 10, 11, 12). However, obtaining the information necessary to identify a possible breach and to make a credible and specific complaint is practically almost impossible. IGIS confirms that no complaints have been lodged and none may be lodged given that persons who are subject to the inquiries are not aware their data is collected and used, and the operations are covert (IGIS 2019, Submission 36: 9). ASIO is exempt from the *Freedom of Information Act 1982* (Cth), which means a person is not able to request from ASIO the location information collected about them (*CAC Determination 2018* ss 8–9; *TIA Act 1979* s 108(1); NAU 2018). The Telco is not allowed to give a copy to the individual. The individual is not aware of the inquiry or investigation into their movements. This governance scheme therefore lacks significant safeguards to protect the privacy of the individual.

7.13   Pre-Warrant Checks Are Not Inspected, and Undermine Privacy

The Telco conducts 'pre-checks'. Pre-checks are not a procedure provided for under the *CAC Determination 2018* (Evidence to PJCIS 2015, p. 17 (Hughes). The oversight bodies are not able to pick up on the pre-checks because no record about a pre-warrant check is created of an authorisation or notification under the *CAC Determination 2018*. This loophole is exploited by the Agencies and the Telco complies with such request. The only procedure provided is that if the Agencies requires any location information for its functions, even if it is to check whether a telephone number is active, the authorisation and notification under the *CAC Determination 2018* must be completed. This procedure is one that protects the privacy of the individual. If this procedure is bypassed, the privacy of the individual is not protected. The Agencies do not apply the Privacy Tests and the Reasonably Necessary or Directly Related Test, when making pre-warrant checks. The use of a pre-warrant check is not inspected by the oversight bodies, and this is another factor that undermines privacy.

7.14   No Oversight Conducted Over Location Information Used Against Secondary Individuals

Oversight is not conducted in respect of location information that is re-used and shared for secondary investigations and secondary inquiries and in relation to secondary individuals. An authorisation or notification is not required to be issued by the Agencies for secondary inquiries, secondary investigations and secondary individuals for other offences, in terms of the 'Connection Test', the 'in connection with' principle and the 'Reasonably Necessary or Directly Related Tests' (*TIA Act 1979* ss 174(2), 175(3), 176(4)). Any inspection conducted is primarily focussed on the primary individual in relation to the primary offence and not the secondary individual.

7.15   ASIO Has a Low Threshold to Meet to Access Telecommunications Data

IGIS continues to be concerned about the low threshold ASIO has to access data: 'The legislative threshold that ASIO is required to meet for access to the data is low; it is that the request is "in connection with" the performance by ASIO of its functions' (*TIA Act 1979* ss 175(3), 176(3); IGIS 2015, p. 24; IGIS Submission 36 2019, p. 6 [3.1]).

The Agencies are also not prevented from accessing location information in respect of investigating minor offences (OAIC Submission No 92 2015, p. 21). It is easy to comply with threshold under the Connection Test. ASIO's compliance with this low legal threshold is, perhaps not surprisingly high (*TIA Act 1979* s 174 (2), 175(3), 176(4); Evidence to PJCIS (Thom) 2015, pp. 37–39).

In relation to telecommunications data authorisations, the inspections examine:

a. whether the authorisation was approved at the appropriate level, noting that approval for prospective data authorisations must be at a higher level than historical data authorisations;
b. whether the collection of that information is related to ASIO's functions; and
c. whether there was compliance with the AG's Guidelines, in particular whether the activity was proportionate to the gravity of the threat, and whether there was sufficient justification for not using less intrusive methods to obtain the data (PJCIS *Advisory Report* 2015: 273).

The AGD disagreed, arguing that: '"Reasonably necessary" is not a low threshold' (Revised Explanatory Memorandum 2015, p. 17 [96]). Domestic preservation notices may only be applied for in cases of a serious offence (*TIA Act 1979* s 107J (1)). ASIO is not required to provide short particulars of offences in the authorisations and notifications under the *CAC Determination 2018* to collect the location information (*CAC Determination 2018* ss 8–9). This allows ASIO the flexibility that ASIO need not be investigating an offence, and therefore need not always have a suspicion of an offence on reasonable grounds, to collect historical location information for minor and serious offences. The Agencies are not required to have a suspicion of an offence based on reasonable grounds to access historical location information, whether it is a minor or serious offence (*CAC Determination 2018* ss 8–12; *TIA Act 1979* ss 107J (1), 178(2)). The ability to access location information for all types of investigations and not just serious offences, and in terms of the *CAC Determination 2018*, is a low threshold because only a simple link, connection or relationship needs to be shown to the functions of ASIO for ASIO to collect the location information.

The oversight bodies check that procedures have been complied with. The oversight bodies do not have the legal power to question the operational activities of the Agencies. The oversight bodies cannot question if the speculative data-matching was justified in the circumstances and based on the facts that the collection of the location information was based on. The oversight bodies simply check that the correct person approved the authorisation and notification, and that the location information was used for a function or activity of the Agencies under the law.

It may seem that because the Agencies comply with the law and have a culture of compliance, and are certified as such by the oversight bodies, then privacy must be adequately protected. The Privacy Tests and Reasonably Necessary or Directly Related Tests are premised on the idea that the collection and use of the location information must be in connection with or directly related to the activities of the Agencies—these activities are not themselves inspected, at an operational level, to verify if they are based on good faith and on reasonable grounds. An activity such as developing a mass storage location information database, which would not be prohibited. The Big Location Data (BLD) storage and analytics database would be in compliance with the AG's Guidelines and the functions and activities of the Agencies but may disclose more information than is relevant and needed for an investigation. The inspections of the Agencies are based on the assumption that the activities of the Agencies are sound and acceptable, instead of allowing the oversight bodies to check that the location information is used for activities that are not only lawful, but that for instance, the political or religious biases of officers are practically kept at bay and do not influence their actions. The officers can be asked to make declarations about their personal beliefs and prejudices and be recused from the collection of location information where it may be suspected that their personal beliefs and information collected may conflict. If these personal biases are kept hidden, the current framework does not allow for an opportunity to identify such problems. In the circumstances, the Agencies would still be complying with the law. IGIS continues to report that given the low threshold and the broad powers, compliance will unsurprisingly be high (IGIS 2019, Submission 36: 8; IGIS 2018, p. 22; IGIS 2017, p. 18).

The Agencies can develop any type of activity that has a law enforcement component to it, and it would be justifiable, (perhaps unintentional) even if the impact of the activity may be the discriminatory treatment of a sector of society (Chan and Moses 2017; Smith et al. 2017). The database may identify a certain neighbourhood as a high crime rate area based on the location information of residents collected and analysed. This community may then be impacted by high law enforcement activity in the neighbourhood and come to feel like they are being singled out by the Agencies. In all these examples, the oversight bodies would still certify that the Agencies are abiding by the law and are compliant when there was a problem with how the location information is used that resulted in, for instance, improper discriminatory practices, such as racial profiling.

7.16   The Use of Less Intrusive Methods to Access Telecommunications Data

In respect of ASIO, the threshold remains the same, irrespective of whether it is existing or prospective location information that is sought to be disclosed. The external oversight is based on a low threshold. This low threshold is the 'Connection Test' ASIO must comply with. With regards to authorising and disclosing existing information, there is no limitation as to the seriousness of the offence. The threshold set by the AG's Guidelines is considered higher, and compliance with this threshold is also high:

> In addition to the T(IA) test, ASIO must also comply with guidelines made by the Attorney-General. These guidelines set a slightly higher standard that require that ASIO investigative activities should be undertaken using as little intrusion into individual privacy as is possible and that wherever possible the least intrusive techniques of information collection should be used before more intrusive techniques. Compliance with this requirement is also high, although I note that access to telecommunications data has historically been considered to be a less intrusive investigative technique by ASIO (Evidence to PJCIS, Thom 2015, p. 8).

Clear guidelines should be made distinguishing whether it is considered less intrusive to access and use historical or prospective location information. The *CAC Determination 2018*, a legislative instrument, does not specifically require ASIO to '... to clearly document whether less intrusive methods have been considered and explain if they are not likely to be effective in a particular case' (IGIS 2015, pp. 24–25) and neither do the AG's Guideline in Guideline 10.4. It may be best that such a legislative instrument should require ASIO to '... to clearly document whether less intrusive methods have been considered and explain if they are not likely to be effective in a particular case' regarding location information (IGIS 2015, pp. 24–25).

The wording used by ASIO to authorise the disclosure of prospective data was found to be ambiguous. It did not explain in clear terms why less intrusive methods of obtaining prospective location information were not followed or were considered inappropriate in the circumstances. IGIS stated: 'The ASIO Guidelines do not provide any guidance on what particular techniques are considered more intrusive than others' (IGIS 2019, Submission 36:7).

It may be argued that it would be less privacy intrusive to collect historical location information than to collect prospective location information. Prospective location information is about future movements of the mobile device and the individual. Historical location information is also about past movements of the mobile device and of the individual. The key difference is that prospective location information is near real-time, as opposed to historical location information, which may generally be days, weeks or months older. With prospective location information, the movements of the individual may be tracked in minutes or hours.

Under what circumstances, as explained by ASIO to IGIS, was the more intrusive method used and justified? The answer to this question is perhaps a confidential one. Past case studies could be used by ASIO and the AG's Department to help develop practical guidelines in this regard, if that has not been done already, to help to guide the discretion of the Agencies and help limit their discretion, based on past facts that were considered acceptable and less intrusive.

7.16.1 Equally Personal or Less Intrusive?

The content of a voice, SMS communication and location information can all reveal personal information (OAIC Submission No 92 to the PJCIS 2015, p. 41 Appendix B [5.]; Telstra, Submission No 112 to the PJCIS 2015, p. 4 [8]). ASIO informed the PJCIS that requesting historical communication data is often one of the most useful as well as one of the least intrusive methods of establishing those matters of fact, and that ASIO does not collect the maximum amount of available location information (Evidence to PJCIS (Edward) 2015).

The act of collecting location information is intrusive in and of itself. The access and use of location information is not necessarily less intrusive than collecting the contents of a communication. The use of the location information by analysing it to reveal personal information is another way in which privacy is interfered with. The interference of privacy by collecting location information and the analysis of the location information afterwards, and any continued use, should be assessed for what it is—revealing of personal information at every step. In comparing it with content, content is also revealing of personal information.

The collection of location information that was generated for a day is less intrusive than location information of a week. The more location information was collected, and over time, and various pieces are put together, the more personal information it reveals. Given the confidential nature of the investigations of ASIO, there is no way of verifying that the minimum or the maximum amount of location information was collected. ASIO sets its own limits and makes the sole subjective decision of the volume of location information it considers reasonably necessary in the circumstances. ASIO is entitled to collect the maximum volume, even if chooses not to, as no incremental or maximum levels are set. ASIO could collect the maximum available location information and would still be compliant with the law and this would be considered less intrusive because location information is legally classified as telecommunications data. That is because the *CAC Determination 2018* allows ASIO to detail the volume, as it considers reasonably necessary 'in connection with' its functions. The open source and affordable software such as Mapbox platform are easy to use and easily reveals personal information (Ockenden 2016; Mapbox 2018). Collecting location information appears less intrusive than intercepting a voice call or an SMS for its content. However, location information can easily be analysed to reveal the movements of persons, to corroborate intercepted communications, or for use to apply for an interception warrant. This makes location information an indirect tool that aids interception and other warrants. This use signifies how vital location information is; it is not the least intrusive measure. Having the key to the door cannot be considered least intrusive because the key grants unfettered access into the house, which one would not have without the key. Location information is that key that unlocks inquiries, investigations, and law enforcement activities that are related to the functions and purposes of the Agencies. The interception warrant on many occasions would depend on the Agencies collecting location identifiers, such as the International Mobile Subscriber Identity (IMSI) (ETSI 2016, p. 145), and location information. In the absence of the location information these warrants may not be granted. The role of location information should not be downplayed as insignificant, and access to it as being least intrusive. Location information is valuable as it is the foundation to unlock other investigatory tools on which warrants heavily rely (Evidence to PJCIS (Hartland) 2014).

7.17   Conclusion

The role of the external oversight bodies entails inspecting compliance with relevant laws and Ministerial Guidelines after the location information has already been collected and after privacy may have already been impacted. The role of the external oversight bodies is 'light touch' regulation, with a low threshold that is allowed by a self-certification process for access to and the use of the location information. Under these circumstances, privacy is not well protected. To instil public confidence in the oversight role of IGIS, IGIS itself suggested the following ways in which oversight may be strengthened: that when an authorisation is issued, the reasons for the decision be stated; that ASIO be required to report its access of data under section 280; that it be considered whether data no longer relevant should be destroyed; and that public reporting and mechanisms to report to the AG be considered in respect of Journalist Information Warrants.

References

AFP (2015) Processing of prospective data authorisations. 74–103

AGD (2019) Comprehensive review of the legal framework governing the National Intelligence Community. https://www.ag.gov.au/national-security/consultations/comprehensive-review-legal-framework-governing-national-intelligence-community. Accessed 30 June 2020

Attorney-General's Department (AGDs) (2016) Attorney-General's Guidelines in relation to the performance by the Australian Security Intelligence Organisation of its function of obtaining, correlating, evaluating and communicating intelligence relevant to security (including politically motivated violence),' 2016 (Attorney-General's [AG's] Guidelines)

Australian Federal Police (AFP) (2019) Statement regarding unauthorised telecommunications data access in 2015', 26 July 2019. https://policenews.act.gov.au/news/media-releases/statement-regarding-unauthorised-telecommunications-data-access-2015. Accessed 29 Aug 2019

Chan J, Moses LB (2017) Making sense of big data for security. Br J Criminol 57(2):299–319

Commonwealth of Australia (2017) Independent Intelligence Review (June 2017)

Commonwealth Ombudsman (2015) Annual Report 2014–15

Commonwealth Ombudsman (2017) A report on the Commonwealth Ombudsman's monitoring of agency access to stored communications and telecommunications data under Chapters 3 and 4 of the Telecommunications (Interception and Access) Act 1979 For the period 1 July 2015 to 30 June 2016. Report by the Acting Commonwealth Ombudsman under s 186J of the Telecommunications (Interception and Access) Act 1979 March 2017

Commonwealth Ombudsman (2018) Report by the Commonwealth Ombudsman under s 186J of the Telecommunications (Interception and Access) Act 1979, November 2018. https://www.ombudsman.gov.au/__data/assets/pdf_file/0033/96747/201617-Chapter-4A-Annual-Report.pdf. Accessed 29 Aug 2019

Commonwealth Ombudsman (2019) Submission 20 to the Parliamentary Joint Committee on Intelligence and Security (PJCIS), *Review of the mandatory data retention regime*, July 2019

Communications Access Coordinator's (CAC) *Telecommunications (Interception and Access) (Requirements for Authorisations, Notifications and Revocations) Determination 2015* (Cth) (at 9 October 2015) (CAC Determination 2015)

European Telecommunications Standards Institute (ETSI) (2016) Digital cellular telecommunications system (Phase 2+) (GSM); Universal Mobile Telecommunications System (UMTS); LTE; Functional stage 2 description of Location Services (LCS). (3GPP TS 23.271 version 13.0.0 Release 13)

Evidence to Parliamentary Joint Committee on Intelligence and Security, Parliament of Australia, Canberra, 30 January 2015, 31 (Peter Leonard Guildford, Chairperson of the Media and Communications Committee, Business Law Section of the Law Council of Australia)

Evidence to Parliamentary Joint Committee on Intelligence and Security (PJCIS), Parliament of Australia, Canberra, 30 January 2015, 65 (Lewis Duncan Edward, Director-General of Security, Australian Security Intelligence Organisation) cited in Parliamentary Joint Committee on Intelligence and Security, Parliament of Australia, Advisory Report on the Telecommunications (Interception and Access) Amendment (Data Retention) Bill 2014 (Cth) 2015

Evidence to Parliamentary Joint Committee on Intelligence and Security, Parliament of Australia, Canberra, 17 December 2014, 17 (Kerri Hartland, Acting Director-General, ASIO)

Evidence to Parliamentary Joint Committee on Intelligence and Security, Parliament of Australia, Canberra, 29 January 2015, 17 (Kate Hughes, the Chief Risk Officer, Telstra)

Evidence to Parliamentary Joint Committee on Intelligence and Security, Parliament of Australia, Canberra, 29 January 2015, 41 (Vivienne Thom, Inspector-General of Intelligence and Security, Office of the Inspector-General of Intelligence and Security [IGIS])

Hardy K, Williams G (2014) National security reforms stage one: intelligence gathering and secrecy. Law Soc NSW J 6(November):68. https://search.informit.com.au/fullText;dn=20151952;res=AGISPT. Accessed 28 Aug 2019

https://assets.documentcloud.org/documents/3119594/AFP-Disclosure-Log.pdf. Accessed 29 Aug 2019

Human Rights Law Centre (HRLC) (2019) Submission 19 to the Parliamentary Joint Committee on Intelligence and Security, Review of the mandatory data retention regime, July 2019

IGIS (2017) Annual Report 2016–2017

IGIS (2018) Annual Report 2017–2018

Inspector-General of Intelligence and Security (IGIS) (2015) Annual Report 2014–2015

Inspector-General of Intelligence and Security (IGIS) (2019) Submission 36 to the Parliamentary Joint Committee on Intelligence and Security. Review of the mandatory data retention regime, July 2019

Inspector-General of Intelligence and Security Act 1986 (Cth) (IGIS Act)

Letter from the Attorney General, George Brandis to Hon Philip Ruddock MP, Chair of the PJCIS, 9 February 2016 cited in Parliamentary Joint Committee on Human Rights. Human rights scrutiny report. (25 February 2016)

Mapbox (2018) A Mapping Platform Powered by the Best Data in the World. https://www.mapbox.com/about/maps/. Accessed 28 Aug 2019

Mayer J, Mutchler P, Mitchell JC (2016) Evaluating the privacy properties of telephone metadata. Proc Natl Acad Sci USA 113(20):5536–5541

National Archives of Australia (NAU) (2018) Personal information in ASIO records – Fact sheet 53. http://www.naa.gov.au/collection/fact-sheets/fs53.aspx. Accessed 29 Aug 2019

Ockenden W (2016, August 16) How your phone tracks your every move' ABC News. http://www.abc.net.au/news/2015-08-16/metadata-retention-privacy-phone-will-ockenden/6694152. Accessed 29 Aug 2019

Office of Australian Information Commissioner (OAIC) (2015) Submission No 92 to the Parliamentary Joint Committee on Intelligence and Security, Inquiry into the Telecommunications (Interception and Access) Amendment (Data Retention) Bill 2014, January 2015

PJCHR, Human rights scrutiny report Thirty-fifth report of the 44th Parliament (25 February 2016)

Privacy Act 1988 (Cth)

Revised Explanatory Memorandum, Telecommunications (Interception and Access) Amendment (Data Retention) Bill 2015, (2015)

Smith GJD, Moses LB, Chan J (2017) The challenges of doing criminology in the big data era: towards a digital and data-driven approach. Br J Criminol 57(2):259–274

Svantesson DJB (2012) Systematic government access to private-sector data in Australia. Int Data Privacy Law 2(4):268–276

Telecommunications (Interception and Access) Act 1979 (Cth) (TIA Act 1979)

Telecommunications (Interception and Access) Amendment (Data Retention) Act 2015 (Cth) (DRA 2015)

Telecommunications Act 1997 (Cth) (TA 1997)

Telecommunications (Interceptions and Access) (Requirements for Authorisations, Notifications and Revocations) Determination 2018 (Cth) (at 20 November 2018) (CAC Determination 2018)

Telecommunications and Other Legislation Amendment (Assistance and Access) Act 2018 (Cth) (AAA 2018)

Telstra (2015) Submission No 112 to the Parliamentary Joint Committee on Intelligence and Security, Inquiry into the Telecommunications (Interception and Access) Amendment (Data Retention) Bill 2014, January 2015

Telstra (2019) Submission 35 to the PJCIS, Review of the mandatory data retention regime, July 2019

Telstra Corporation Limited and Privacy Commissioner [2015] AATA 991 (18 December 2015) (*Telstra decision*)

Williams G (2016) The legal assault on Australian democracy. QUT Law Rev 16(2):19–41

Chapter 8
Proposing the Judicial Location Information Warrant, to Better Protect Privacy

8.1 A Location Information Warrant Is Generally Required in the USA

The *Carpenter court case* took the fight over location information to the Supreme Court of the United States (SCOTUS). The case was about a series of robberies where no warrant based on probable cause was issued before investigators obtained the cell site location information. The location information was obtained based on 'reasonable grounds', with a believe that the information was relevant to an ongoing law enforcement investigation. The issue in the *Carpenter court* case was whether the warrantless search and seizure of historical cell phone records that reveal the location and movements of a cell phone user for over 127 days was allowed by the Fourth Amendment that protects privacy.

Technology companies submitted a brief explaining:

a. location tracking;
b. how the communications technology operates, by using smaller cells to reveal more precise locations;
c. how the telecommunications companies are used as one-stop shops by the law enforcement agencies to the extent that the agencies reduce the use of Global Positioning Tracking (GPS) tracking devices;[1]
d. how a software market was developed to analyse location information on behalf of the agencies;

---

[1] In Australia, in terms of 'Schedule 1—Australian Privacy Principles' and specifically 'Australian Privacy Principle 5—notification of the collection of personal information' in the *Privacy Act 1988* (Cth), the user must be informed if personal information is collected. In terms of 'Australian Privacy Principle 3.1—collection of solicited personal information', the Telco must only collect personal information if the information is reasonably necessary for or directly related to the Telco's functions. The Telco therefore collects all types of Location Information in the ordinary course of its business.

© Springer Nature Switzerland AG 2020
S. Shanapinda, *Advance Metadata Fair*, Law, Governance and Technology Series 44, https://doi.org/10.1007/978-3-030-50255-3_8

e. the personal nature of location information;
f. how the storage of location information by telecommunications companies are part of their ordinary business; and
g. the inherent nature of the telecommunications network to constantly transmit location information (Shanapinda, S.: Advance metadata fair: The retention and disclosure of location information as metadata for law enforcement and national security, and the impact on privacy – An Australian story. Dissertation, UNSW Sydney 2018: 178; *Carpenter court case* 2018; Technology Experts 2017; Technology Companies 2017; *Carpenter court case* 2016).

Australian common law also contains the 'reasonable grounds' principle, as interpreted in the *George court case* (1990: 4 [8]). The facts the AFP will use to issue the authorisation and notification under the *CAC Determination 2018* need to be sufficient to persuade the AFP that the collection of the location information is reasonably necessary or directly related to its functions or activities, as per the *George court case* (Shanapinda, S.: Advance metadata fair: The retention and disclosure of location information as metadata for law enforcement and national security, and the impact on privacy – An Australian story. Dissertation, UNSW Sydney (2018)). Despite the 'reasonable grounds' principle to collect the location information and based on the constitutional right to privacy under the Fourth Amendment, the *Carpenter court case* ruled that access to location information under the US' Stored Communications Act must generally be accompanied by a warrant issued under the probable cause standard, and not simply because the location information is reasonably necessary for an investigation and to enforce the criminal law. In considering these developments after the data retention scheme was passed, Australia may need to increase the standard by which the Agencies collect and use location information, by similarly requiring a judicial warrant.

8.2   Bulk Metadata Collection Violates Privacy in the EU

Directive 2006/24/EC[2] allowed for the retention and use of telecommunications data in the European Union (EU). The limit placed on this power was that such access must be necessary, appropriate and proportionate, within a democratic society for specific public order purposes. These purposes include: to safeguard national security, public security, the prevention, investigation, detection and prosecution of criminal offences. Whereas the EU adopted the principle of 'necessity and proportionality' to protect privacy, Australia adopted the 'justifiable and proportionate'

---

[2]Directive 2006/24/EC of the European Parliament and of the Council of 15 March 2006 on the retention of data generated or processed in connection with the provision of publicly available electronic communications services or of public communications networks and amending Directive 2002/58/EC.

principle; the 'reasonably necessary' standard (Directive 2006/24/EC, Recital 4, Articles 3, 4; *TIA Act 1979* s 180F; *CAC Determination 2018* ss 8–12).

Both the EU and Australia require that the collection of and the access to location information be proportionate to general public interest purposes. The key difference is that the EU standard requires necessity, a higher standard for the collection and use of location information considering that location information is crucial and that the EU agencies are not able to conduct investigations without it. The Australian standard requires the collection of location information to be justifiable. However, any activity collecting bulk location information may be justifiable for a wide range of law enforcement purposes, even if it has a discriminatory effect on minority groups. Directive 2006/24/EC allowed for the collection of a wide range of data from all types of communications. The *Digital Rights Ireland court case* ruled that access to the telecommunications data, was in bulk, and therefore violated the right to privacy under the EU Charter of Fundamental Rights, even though the collection of location information was based on the higher 'necessity' standard. In the EU, privacy must be protected at the higher standard—data may not be retained and accessed unless it is 'strictly necessary' (the *Digital Rights Ireland court case* 2014: [52], [56]).

In Australia, under the Exclusions, the Telco is only required to retain location information that is used to provide the communications service to the mobile device; and only retain location information at the start and at the end of a communication (*TIA Act 1979* ss 187AA (1) item 6; 187A (1)). The Exclusions to only store location information generated at the start and at the end of a communication, without a clear restriction not to store or collect location information prior to, during and after a communication, allows for the voluntary and discretionary collection of more location information than is necessary. Telstra reported public bodies do collect metadata more than is necessary (Telstra Submission 35, 2019: 2). Despite the Exclusions, revealing personal information may still be collected about the individual, that is more than necessary, but may be justifiable under the lower standards of 'justifiable and proportionate', the 'in connection with'[3] principle and the 'directly related'[4] principle (*TIA Act 1979* s 180F; *CAC Determination 2018* ss 10–12).

The use of Big Data (BD) analytics software, powered by machine learning and artificial intelligence (AI), may reveal more personal information about the individual and lead to misuse of the personal information collected. Another European Union (EU) protection is that EU legislation must lay down clear and precise rules governing the scope and application of the legislation. The EU court decided that given the data will be processed automatically, there is a significant risk that the data may be collected unlawfully, and it affects every persons communications, even the data of persons whose actions are not likely to be criminally serious—in other words, there is no link required between the data required to be retained and the public safety that is being protected (*Digital Rights court case* 2014: [54]-[55], [58]-[59]).

---

[3]See Sect. 5.2.3 in Chap. 5.
[4]See Sects. 5.1.2.3.1 in Chap. 5.

In Australia, under the Exclusions, the location information of every persons' communications must be collected at the start and end; and may be collected voluntarily by the Telco, prior to, during and after the communication. The location information may be collected of persons not suspected of being involved in serious criminal activities to see if they may have been involved in serious and or non-serious activities and to then apply for warrants. Under this general rule, the location information of any person may be collected and assessed to see if at some point they committed a crime, and this would also be for public safety. Equally, and hypothetically speaking, the activities of young people planning climate change protests and civil disobedience rallies may potentially be assessed, without a judicial warrant, to see what plans they have and in the national economic interest, considering the broad meaning of the term security. Given the mandatory bulk metadata retention and collection of unnamed persons, who are not suspected of serious criminal acts or threats to security, coupled with automated big location data processing potential, there is therefore not always a specific, clear and precise link required between the location information required to be retained and disclosed, to the public safety objective. The only link required is that the collection of location information be 'in connection with' the performance of the broad functions of ASIO or be reasonably necessary for or directly related to the broad functions and broad activities of the AFP, as opposed to being 'strictly necessary' (*TIA Act 1979* ss 175 (3), 176(3); 174(2), 175(3), 176(4); *Privacy Act 1988* Schedule 1 Part 2 3.1, 3.4 (d) (ii)). Under these principles, collecting and inquiring into the activities of climate change activist and 'African gangs' would be lawful, because the purpose is to enforce the broad functions, purposes and activities of the Agencies to enforce laws and safeguard the national interests, without clear and precise guidelines. Given the unclarity regarding the status of the AG's Guidelines and given how limited those guidelines are and that they allow for investigations and inquiries even in cases where there is no violent protests, and the example of the Federal Bureau of Investigations (FBI) guidelines in the United States (US), Australia may be in need of clear and precise public guidelines.

This discussion is an indication of the broad discretionary powers of the Agencies and how unlimited the access to and the use of location information is. Location information may be collected for minor offences and is not restricted to serious offences. There are no clear and precise rules have yet been publicly introduced in Australia governing the scope and application of the power to access and use location information. The limits imposed under the instruments such as the *TIA Act 1979* the *ASIO Act 1979*, the *AFP Act 1979*, the AG's Guidelines and the Ministerial Direction issued for the AFP, do not outline a clear scope for the use of BD analytics software but supports the use of automatic means to process location information, and such projects have already been rolled out on the basis that collection of Open Source Intelligence (OSINT) location information, from social networks, are for the public good and safety (Minister for Justice 2016). Under these circumstances, Australia did not overcome the privacy challenges such as those faced by the EU when it introduced the 'justifiable and proportionate' standard under section 180F of the *TIA Act 1979* and when it introduced the Exclusions (*CAC*

Determination 2018 ss 8–12). These measures do not adequately protect privacy. Under the common law, privacy is generally protected as a by-product of other interest that are protected, such as confidentiality clauses from contracts with banks, and privacy policies of the Telco and not under a Constitution containing a bill of human rights, as is contained under the Fourth Amendment in the US Constitution and the European Union (EU) Charter (Taylor 2000). These contracts and privacy policies of the Telco are set unilaterally by the Telco and skewed towards their commercial interests. As per the decision in the *Privacy Commissioner's court case* (2017), for information to be regarded as personal, the individual must first and foremost be the subject of the information—a higher onus to bear (2017: 15 [63]). Location information that is voluntarily retained and voluntarily disclosed to the Agencies, is not deemed to be personal, and must therefore first be about the individual, to qualify as personal information.[5]

8.3 Metadata Retention for Minor Offences Violates Fundamental Rights in the EU

Under section 1 of the Data Retention and Investigatory Powers Act (*DRIPA*), the telecommunications company may be required to retain relevant communications data. The data may be retained based on the standard that the data is necessary and proportionate. The retention notice issued, requiring the data retention, must describe the broad range of data and the period to be retained. The notice also covered historical and prospective data. The notice covered both serious and minor offences for purposes of national security, to prevent and detect crime, and in the interest of public safety (Regulation of Investigatory Powers Act 2000 (UK) cX, s 22 (2)(a)-(h)). The retained data could be disclosed under regulations or by a court order (*DRIPA* c X, s 1 (3), (6)(b)).

The standards and the purposes for which location information may be collected in Australia, and the process appear to be similar to that of the United Kingdom (UK). In Australia, an authorisation and notification are issued under the *CAC Determination 2018* to collect location information that is already retained.

In the *Watson court case*, the UK Court of Appeal decided that if the retained data is used for minor offences, *DRIPA* violates the Articles 8 and 9 of the EU's Charter of Fundamental Rights. As a result, when it comes to preventing, investigating, detecting and prosecuting criminal offences, if the purpose for collecting and using the retained data is not limited to serious crime, Section 1 of *DRIPA* goes against EU law. Instead, the retained data is collected in bulk and analysed using automated processing techniques, such as BD analytics software (*Watson court case* 3 [6.], 4 [6.2.e.1], 6 [13.], 9 [27]).

---

[5]See Sect. 6.3.1 in Chap. 6.

DRIPA also violates EU law if the collection and use of the retained data was not pre-approved by a court or an independent administrative authority in review proceedings (*Watson court case* 3 [6]; 6 [13]).

The court declined to decide whether the individual should be informed after the retained data has been collected as *DRIPA* did not make provision for such a notification (*Watson court case* 7 [20] – [21]).

Article 8 of the *European Convention on Human Rights* protects respect for the individual's correspondence.[6] Articles 7 and 8 of the *EU Charter* protects respect for the individual's communication and the protection of personal data concerning the individual. Australia has materially similar international obligations under Article 17 of the International Convention on Civil and Political Rights (ICCPR).

8.4   Analysis: Judicial Oversight Preferred as a Check on Executive Power

As represented by the court cases above and the relevant laws, the executive arms of all three US, UK and Australian governments appear intent on keeping the surveillance and investigatory power in the executive branch, shielded from judicial oversight. This is especially true with matters that relate to or are seen as posing threats national security. The Parts above discussed how the powers of law enforcement agencies have been successfully challenged in the courts in the EU, the UK and the USA. A common theme is the negative effect of a lack of judicial participation in the process of collecting and using telecommunications data. Australia can be a leader in the field of privacy and introduce meaningful judicial participation when disclosing location information to the Agencies by introducing changes in its primary legislation. The legal challenge is based on how revealing location information is technologically, and how severely this intrudes upon privacy protections contained in constitutional and international human rights charters. Legal challenges of this nature have not taken place in Australia, but the decision of the UK Appeals court declaring the law invalid due to judicial non-participation sends a strong signal that if democracies are serious about privacy protection, they should allow for prior administrative or judicial approval to the access and the use of telecommunications data, and not simply trust the sole judgment of the law enforcement agencies, as is the case in Australia. This seems to be the acceptable way the privacy of the individual may be legitimately interfered with in a democracy. Also, there must be clear guidelines to supervise the actions of the agencies.

---

[6]The *Convention for the Protection of Human Rights and Fundamental Freedoms,* opened for signature 4 November 1950, 213 UNTS 221 (entered into force 3 September 1953).

8.4.1 The 'Necessary and Proportionate' Standard Did Not Adequately Protect Privacy in the UK

Australian law, (the amendments to the *TIA Act 1979* and the *TA 1997* that introduced the data retention scheme), is influenced by the EU's 2006 Data Retention Directive (AGD 2014: 4 [A]). UK's *DRIPA* was based on the same 2006 Data Retention Directive (*DRIPA* Preamble).

The *Watson* decision was made despite the 'necessary and proportionate' standard being part of *DRIPA*. In Australia, the privacy standards are 'reasonably necessary', 'on reasonable grounds' and 'justifiable and proportionate' and the 'in connection with' principle under the section 180F Privacy Tests. The 'reasonably necessary' and 'justifiable and proportionate' standards are lower standards than the 'necessary and proportionate' standard (Selvadurai 2017; *TIA Act 1979* ss 177(1), 178(3), 179(3), 180(4), 180F; *Privacy Act 1988* Schedule 1 Part 2 s 3; *CAC Determination 2018* ss 8–12). The *Watson court case* clearly illustrates that without prior independent review to collect telecommunications data, privacy is not adequately protected. In those circumstances, the application of the 'necessary and proportionate' standard does not compensate for the lack of prior judicial approval and the use of the telecommunications data for minor offences. *DRIPA* and the EU Data Retention Directive 2006 could no longer be relied on as solid foundations for benchmarking after a European Court of Justice (ECJ) critical review of the Directive in 2014.

Australian law noted this and made changes in 2015, that strengthened the Privacy Tests. However, despite these positive changes aimed at strengthening privacy, privacy is still not adequately protected in Australia, compared to the UK, the EU and the USA. Selvadurai (2017) questioned whether the retention of telecommunications metadata is a necessary national security initiative or a disproportionate interference with personal privacy, by analysing the Australian framework in relation to the ECJ decision, given the similarities between the two scenarios. Selvadurai (2017) described the data as valuable to the Agencies, referring to the benefit of identification of associations between communicators, providing a precise digital profile and matching the data with data obtained from social media, to identify persons of interest (Selvadurai 2017, p. 36). Selvadurai (2017) described the scope of the *TIA Act 1979*, to analyse the effectiveness in calibrating the privacy and national security interests. Selvadurai (2017) concluded the post-2015 Australian framework that allows for access to telecommunications data, was drafted in a manner that sought to overcome the privacy challenges the EU faced (Selvadurai 2017, pp. 35–41). Selvadurai (2017, p. 36) referred to the EU Data Retention Directive that was invalidated by the ECJ, stating that, given this legal precedent, it is interesting that Australia requires the retention of specific kinds of telecommunications data. Australian courts on the other hand, endorsed the 'in connection with' principle and the 'reasonable grounds' principle in the *Samsonidis, Gant* and *George court cases*, where warrants were issued by a judicial officer or an administrative body. It would be interesting to see how an Australian court would rule on these standards where no prior judicial oversight took place, as in the *Watson court case*. In assessing whether the Australian location information retention and disclosure framework can really be said to have overcome the privacy challenges it is clear that privacy oversight challenges still remain. This is especially so given the 'justifiable and proportionate' principle, in combination with the 'in connection with' principle, the 'directly related' principle and the 'reasonable grounds' principle. This is so despite the privacy safeguards introduced in 2015. This situation is generally contrary to the claim by Selvadurai (2017) that the post-2015 Australian framework was drafted in a manner that overcame the privacy challenges the EU faced. The Australian framework may therefore require a judicial warrant system to fully overcome the privacy challenges that still exist.

8.4.2 Improving Human Rights in Australia

In the USA, the EU and the UK the legal challenges to the collection and use of location information are based on the Constitution and international human rights charters. While there is no equivalent constitutional protection in Australia, Australia is a signatory of the ICCPR that protects privacy under Article 17. The Parliamentary Joint Committee on Human Rights (PJCHR) uses Article 17 as a measure for Australian law (PJCHR 2016: 18, 25 [2.48]).

In the US and the UK, the *Watson* and *Carpenter court cases* successfully challenged the law, accusing it of not balancing privacy proportionately and not using a higher standard to access location information. The *Watson court case* is setting a precedent for a UK ally such as Australia, whose laws have similarly excluded prior judicial review of the notices and authorisations under the *CAC Determination 2018* to collect and use location information for law enforcement and security purposes. Access to retained data may possibly be challenged in Australia under the same principles as in the UK and the USA, but on legal grounds that are unique to Australia. These principles include:

a. the lack of independent judicial oversight, the use of the location information for non-serious offences and the bulk collection of the data—when compared to the UK; and
b. the use of the low standard of the location information being reasonably necessary for or directly related to the broad policing functions to collect the location information, as opposed to being based on a higher standard equivalent to probable cause or reasonable suspicion—when compared to the US.

In all instances, the common thread is that the challenges are based on requiring a higher standard and independent oversight to access data that is considered to be personal in nature and over which individuals have a right to privacy under their Constitutions, unlike in Australia. Australia however has no direct common law right to privacy, and no bill of rights in its Constitution for the protection of privacy under the Australian Constitution.

As UK laws were impacted by the *Watson court case*. The *Watson court case* sent a strong signal that pre-reviews of the access to retained data should be a basic measure of privacy protection. In response to the legal challenges the UK government consulted on and implemented the Communications Data Code of Practice in November 2018 (Home Office 2018), the Data Retention and Acquisition Regulations 2018 and established the Office for Communications Data Authorisations (OCDA) to consider requests for communications data from law enforcement and public authorities, and under the Investigatory Powers Act (IPA) 2016. The OCDA's role us summed up as follows:

> OCDA carries out the important function of safeguarding an individual's right to privacy under the Human Rights Act 1998. It makes independent decisions on whether to grant or refuse communications data requests, ensuring that all requests are lawful, necessary and proportionate (Crown 2019).

It is advisable for Australia to look into the future and introduce a location information warrant or generally a telecommunications data warrant regime as proposed below, without first having to resort to a court challenge, unlike its allies. If Australia continues to maintain its current retention and disclosure framework after the *Watson* and *Carpenter court cases*, from a judicial perspective, Australia may be isolating itself from two major jurisdictions with which it is allied.

Free speech and privacy are protected better under the American Constitution and case law, as personal rights, then privacy and free speech are protected under the privacy law of Australia, this despite America not having a comprehensive privacy law as Australia does. Privacy is generally protected as a by-product of other interest that are protected, such as confidentiality clauses from contracts (Taylor 2000).[7] Customers of the Telco are protected by privacy policies and standard terms and condition that contain clauses to protect the privacy of the customers, and under the *Privacy Act 1988*, subject to the exceptions that apply to the benefit of the Agencies (Vodafone 2019). Given that Australia does not have a common law privacy right that directly protects privacy but only does so indirectly, in this submission it is proposed that Parliament amend the *TIA Act 1979* to require judicial review of the authorisations and notifications prior to the collection and use of location information. Continuing the status quo places Australia, as a democracy, under a very peculiar position globally—location information may be collected and used for law enforcement and security without any prior judicial review and under a very low standard of the location information only having to be necessary for or directly related to policing and broad security purposes. In the UK, regarding the issue of law enforcement, this legal position would be a violation of privacy, as a human right, a

---

[7] Also see: Loyd v Freshjeld (1826) 2 Car & P 325; 172 ER 147; Tournier v National Provincial & Union Bank of England [1924] 1 KB 461; Australia & New Zealand Bank v Ryan (1968) 88 WN (Pt l) (NSW) 368; Federal Commissioner of Taxation v Australia & New Zealand Banking Group (1979) 143 CLR 499; Barclays Bank v Taylor [1989] 1 WLR 1066; Winterton Constructions v Hambros (1992) 39 FCR 97, 114-15; Robertson v Canadian Imperial Bank of Commerce [1994] 1 WLR 1493; Christoj v Barclays Bank [2000] 1 WLR 937; Laster (1989), p. 424.

right that Australians may not be able to directly claim under the Constitution. The *Privacy Act 1988* and the *TIA Act 1979* in section 180F protect privacy, but subject to the superior powers of the Agencies to collect personal information for broad law enforcement purposes, and without prior judicial review. Comparably, Australia's position cannot be said to be proportionate, given that the location information collected may be used without judicial involvement and for non-serious offences, given the sensitive information location information may disclose with the use of BD analytics software. Australia's poor privacy protection position is comparably at odds with the *EU Charter* and generally with human rights in the EU and the USA.

In its submission on the Data Retention Bill, the AGD stated that Australia would be violating its international obligations under the Budapest Cybercrime Convention, if Australian law were to limit access to historical metadata to only serious crimes (AGD Submission No 27, 2015: 44). In other words, to meet its international obligations, Australia must allow access to historical metadata for non-serious offences as well. As highlighted by the UK and US court decisions, the trend amongst Australia's allies is that, as far as the judiciary is concerned, international rights and constitutional rights require that access to historical metadata must only be accessed with a judicial warrant. If Australia amends the *DRA 2015*, requiring a judicial warrant to access location information and other metadata, then Australia would be complying with its international human rights obligations. Not doing so, may be a failure of Australia's international human rights obligations under the ICCPR. Article 17 requires that Australia protect the right to privacy. The international trend seems to be that privacy is best protected, in a democratic society, if a judicial warrant is required to access location information and other metadata.

8.4.3 Diagnosing the Australian Metadata Retention and Disclosure Framework

The Agencies claim that they cannot access the contents of communication, using the 'going-dark' argument—that the contents of a communication are encrypted as they are transported over the IP-mediated LTE network. The structure of surveillance laws has a traditional distinction between content and metadata. Given the development of modern IP-mediated communications technologies, with base stations that are nearer to each other and the coverage radius smaller in urban areas, the licensing and use of femtocells with a proximity radius of 3–4 m, and the popularity of smart phones with satellite positioning ability, the reliance on this traditional distinction works to the benefit of the Agencies and compromises privacy protections. The scales are thereby skewed in favour of the powers of the Agencies rather than adequately balancing the more revealing nature of modern-day mobile communications. The technological advancement in location precision allows for more personal and sensitive information to be revealed.

The classification of location information as metadata is what the Agencies rely on to access location information under less stringent requirements, and this undermines just how personal and sensitive location information can be. Location information is legally classified as information that relates to the affairs of a customer. This categorisation is in line with how the IP-mediated LTE network technically operates: location information relates to the affairs of the customer. However, location information is just as sensitive as the contents of a voice call. Despite the personal nature of location information, location information is ironically disclosed under less stringent requirements to the Agencies, than how content is disclosed. The legal obligation to retain location information, and to do this for 2 years, has effectively increased the volume of information the Agencies are likely to access and use. It guarantees continued access to location information. The Agencies are not likely to surrender this advantage, given how precise location information is becoming. The Agencies are more likely to prefer these existing power structures, which architecture compromises individual privacy more than may be fair.

The original motivation for passing the metadata retention laws was serious crime—it was terrorist crime. And no one would argue against that. The global trend to combat serious crime is a speedy response—additional bureaucracy to access potential evidence and to investigate. The public generally agrees that for serious crime the Agencies may have warrantless access to the location information. However, as time went on, and when the laws became clearer, it was clear that the retention regime did not only cover serious crime, but also covered non-serious crime as well. So, personal information and sensitive information—because of the advancement in technology—is used for less serious crime and by all types of public bodies and non-law enforcement agencies, such as local councils under section 280 of the *TA 1997* but without adequate governance guidelines to prevent potential misuse.

The Australian legal framework to collect and use location information may generally be described as follows:

a. it is a process of self-certification and there is no prior judicial oversight required to access the location information;
b. the location information is used for all types of offences, for broad inquiry and investigatory powers;
c. there is little chance to challenge the powers of the Agencies even after the collection of the location information, given the confidential nature of security investigations and inquiries;
d. the *ex post facto* oversight is done by bodies that are under the control and are part of the executive arm of government;
e. there is bulk collection and use of very revealing and personal location information, able to be used in machine learning and artificial intelligence software;
f. the location information may be used for any law enforcement and security activity which may be possible to justify as reasonably necessary to enforce the law and to protect the national security of Australia, despite the potential political biases and prejudices, although this is not known to have taken place; and

g. for Australia, the legal issue essentially comes down to whether the current legal framework, under these circumstances, can be said to fairly and adequately advance privacy protections or erode same

(Evidence, 2015, 31 (Peter Leonard Guildford; AG's Guidelines s 6.1; *AFP Act 1979* ss 4(1) (definition of 'police services'), 8(1) (bf)(ii), *TIA Act 1979* s 181).

The tracking cell towers; the software used to analyse and reveal personal information; the lack of sufficiently independent oversight before the collection and use of location information; the broad powers and discretion of the Agencies to use the location information—these all favour the powers of the Agencies unfairly. The privacy safeguards and the powers of the Agencies are therefore not well balanced (ETSI 2017: 44 [8.1.3.3.1]; APC, Submission No 92, 2015: 42 Appendix B [8]; *CAC Determination 2018* ss 8–12; *IGISA* 1986 s 8(1)(a)(iv); *DRA 2015*Schedule 3; Keenan 2014; *ASIO Act* s 4; Shanapinda, S.: Advance metadata fair: The retention and disclosure of location information as metadata for law enforcement and national security, and the impact on privacy – An Australian story. Dissertation, UNSW Sydney (2018)).

The metadata retention and disclosure framework may be improved, and a better balance may be struck with privacy under a judicial warrant process.

8.5   The Judicial Location Information Warrant Process

This section proposes stricter procedures and requirements to access and use location information by means of a Location Information Warrant (LIW).

The authorisation and notification process under the *CAC Determination 2018* can be described as a self-certification process that is supported by a low threshold, to use location information for the wide investigatory powers of the Agencies. The LIW process will encourage greater public trust and confidence if independent oversight bodies assess and pre-approve the applications for location information. It is crucial that the impact on the privacy of the individual and the proper level of appropriate restraint, is assessed in advance, by an independent third party. This independent third party should be sufficiently independent from the AGD, Minister of Home Affairs, IGIS, the Commonwealth Ombudsman, ASIO and the AFP (Evidence (Leonard) 2015; Evidence (Thom) 2015; *TIA Act 1979* ss 174 (2), 175 (3), 176(4)).

How to minimise the bureaucratic hurdles that may be created by these changes, can also be addressed.

8.5.1 *The Types of Location Information That Are Legally Personal Information*

The better means of protecting privacy is to state clearly in the *TIA Act 1979* and the *Privacy Act 1988* that location information is personal information, as a matter of law (as is already done, but on a narrower basis in section 187LA of the *TIA Act 1979*). Location information that is personal information should include, and be described as:

a. the velocity, altitude, latitude about a mobile telecommunications device and the identity of a base transceiver station (BTS) or commonly referred to as a cell tower);
b. whether a data point is accurate or estimated;
c. whether it is used for billing or not; and
d. whether generated prior to, at the start, during, at the end of, or after a telecommunications service; and
e. when linked with other information or data,

that is able to identify an individual and reveal personal information about the individual, whether aided by or not, the use of data analytics software.

Before collecting location information from the Telco, the Agencies should be required to obtain a LIW, after which the location information may be used. Similarly, before voluntarily disclosing location information to the Agencies, the Telco and the Social Media Platform company (SMP) must apply for a LIW. The LIW should be required even if no person is named, or no International Mobile Subscriber Identity (IMSI), account number or phone number is used to request the location information. Under these circumstances the LIW is a better protection for the privacy of the individual.

8.5.2 *The LIW Issuing Authority*

To strike an acceptable balance between the powers of the Agencies, public safety interests and privacy interests, and to minimise the conflict of these interests, an independent authority must be appointed to receive applications for a LIW. The independent third party could be: (i) a quasi-judicial body, with sufficient independence; and/or (ii) a court overseen by a Judge or magistrate, as an independent member of the judiciary—independent from the executive branch of government, but with a security clearance. The independent party would dilute the concentration of power in the hands of the AG and the Minister of Home Affairs and the Agencies. The third party would ensure predictability in the process.

8.5.3 Exceptions to Making the LIW Application

One must be mindful to avoid undermining the critical role of the Agencies and causing unnecessary delays to investigations. The Agencies, the Telco and the SMP would not be required to make applications for the LIW under the following circumstances:

a. If the time it will take to apply for the LIW, obtain the LIW and thereafter obtain the location information from the Telco would involve unreasonable delays that severely compromise or severely impede the investigation, inquiry or enforcement of the criminal law or safeguarding the national interest, where time is of the essence. A severe compromise may be caused if the individual is very likely to escape while approval of the LIW and the collection of the location information are pending, making it very difficult or impossible to locate the individual or identify the individual. A severe impediment may be caused if the location information collected after the LIW is issued may not be useful or relevant any longer. A severe compromise is also one that is unable to be remedied after the LIW has been collected.

Despite the above exceptions, the issuing authority must in any event be informed of the following, at all relevant times, when access to location information is required, and be given copies of records within a reasonable time, after issuing an authorisation and notification to the Telco to collect the location information:

b. The justification, based on reasonable grounds and in good faith, for seeking to avoid having to apply for the LIW. The reasons may include that applying for the LIW may cause unreasonable delays that may severely compromise the investigation, the inquiry or the enforcement of the criminal law.
c. A copy of the authorisation and notification, the TAR, TCN and TAN issued to the Telco and the SMP, stating specifically that the officer considered the facts at hand; outline the facts; how he or she applied the Privacy Tests and the Reasonably Necessary or Directly Related Tests to the facts; the reasons for and against issuing the authorisation; and why the authorisation was approved to be issued and why it should not be denied.
d. The location information collected from the Telco and SMP.
e. The records kept that relate to the authorisation and notification. The records should include written and oral requests made over electronic and telephonic means.

8.5.4 The Role of the Issuing Authority

The issuing authority may study the authorisation and retrospectively validate the authorisation, and impose any restrictions, prior to the collection of the location information. If the location information was already collected the issuing authority may direct how privacy risks identified may be minimised going forward.

The Agencies, the Telco and SMP must keep the approving authority updated about how the location information was used, how BD analytics software was used, how useful it was or not, how privacy risks were minimised, and if the authorisation needs to be renewed, the reasons for such renewal.

8.5.5 The Procedure to Request Location Information

The existing procedures used for warrants, investigations, the *CAC Determination 2018* and the AG's Guidelines would be strengthened by implementing the following recommendations:

a. In the event the Agencies, the Telco or SMP applies for a LIW, the Agencies may inform the Telco and SMP and they may in turn inform the Agencies of the application to the issuing authority. The other party can be informed of the details of the LIW intended to be disclosed, and the reasons, based on reasonable grounds and in good faith. The notice can request the other party to take any preparatory action while the application is being processed. In this manner any time delays may be minimised. The preparatory action would relate to any action the other party would be approved to take under the LIW. The Telco and SMP may start the initial process of gathering the location information, so as to be able to disclose the location information once the LIW is approved and issued;

b. The LIW warrant may be applied for on an *ex parte* basis;

c. The issuing authority of the LIW must assess and be satisfied that the Agencies only collected location information that was reasonably necessary, on reasonable grounds, in good faith, and that the disclosure or use was justifiable and proportionate, based on the gravity of the offence and related matters, and that the location information was relevant and useful;

d. The applying party should specify the facts, the allegations under investigation or matter being inquired into, the law enforcement and security activities of the Agencies, on suspicion of a past, present or future offence, based on reasonable grounds;

e. The applying party should clearly set out reasons to the issuing authority, based on the relevant circumstances, why the person should not be informed of the collection and the use of the location information. There may be circumstances that justifies that the person is informed. For example, it may be in the interest of national security if a person is being recruited by a foreign government, to warn the person of such efforts, so as not to cooperate. If informing the person would prejudice security and compromise law enforcement investigations, not informing the person may be justified;

f. The applying party should clearly set out reasons to the issuing authority, based on the relevant circumstances, why the person should not be given copies of the authorisation and notification issued under the *CAC Determination 2018*, the TAR, TCN or TAN to collect and use the location information and should not be allowed to challenge the collection and use of the location information;

g. The reasons for the application of the authorisation and reasons why it should not be denied, based on reasonable suspicion and belief, under oath or affirmation;

h. The likely relevance and usefulness of the location information to the investigation, inquiry and the law enforcement and security activities directly or indirectly related to the functions and purposes of the Agencies;

i. The issuing authority may request further information;

j. The issuing authority may grant or refuse to grant the application for the LIW in full, or partially grant or partially refuse the application for the LIW;

k. A reasoned statement by the issuing authority, based on the supporting documents submitted, outlining the reasons for the decision;

l. The reasons for the decision should state the privacy risks identified and how those risks were mitigated; and

m. The decision by the issuing authority should state relevant restrictions regarding the collection and use of the location information.

8.5.6 The Types of Location Information Requested to Be Disclosed

Under the LIW, the following types of location information may be requested and be approved to be disclosed by the independent authority:

a. The location information used to deliver the Short Message Service (SMS) or voice communication to the mobile device (*TIA Act 1979* s 187AA (1) item 6);

b. The location information not used to deliver the SMS or voice communication to the mobile device, in other words, the neighbouring or Enhanced cell-ID (E-CID) (Revised Explanatory Memorandum 2015: 44 [246]);

c. The location information generated prior to, during, at the end of and after a voice or SMS communication;

d. The location information generated when the individual is not using the device, also referred to as pings and regular connections that mobile devices make to cell towers (Revised Explanatory Memorandum 2015: 44 [246]);

e. The location information stored by the Telco for any period, for commercial and for purposes to maintain the telecommunications network, if the Telco has the location information in its possession (*TA 1997* s 275A, 276, 280, 313(3), 313(4), 313(7); *TIA Act 1979* ss 175–184); and

f. The IMSI and (International Mobile Equipment Identity) IMEI of the mobile device, and similar device-type identifiers that may be in use.

8.5.7   The Standards to Safeguard Privacy

The standards discussed below are proposed to be incorporated into the LIW to strengthen privacy protection. Section 180H of the *TIA Act 1979* may need to be re-worded accordingly.

8.5.7.1   Transferring Privacy Protections to the LIW

Firstly, it is recommended that the existing privacy protections included in the AG's Guidelines be transferred to the LIW, so that it has the force and effect of a legislative instrument and minimises the discretionary powers of ASIO (AG's Guidelines ss 10.4, 13). The AG's Guidelines should be updated to address how ASIO must address situations where sensitive information such as political affiliations and ideologies, such as climate change and projects that impact the environment and conflict with national economic interests, including how they are to be resolved and how ASIO must prevent political influence from the executive branch of the government and staff members in the various government departments, to operate at arm's length.

8.5.7.2   Transferring the Privacy Standards from Section 180F of the TIA Act 1979 to the LIW

The privacy protections under section 180F of the *TIA Act 1979* should be applied to ASIO under the LIW. The Administrative Appeals Tribunal (AAT) member, the Judge or magistrate should be satisfied that the 'Privacy Tests' justifies the collection and use of the location information.

8.5.7.3   Guidelines for Methods Considered Intrusive and Methods Considered Less Intrusive

The LIW should require the Agencies to '. . . clearly document whether less intrusive methods have been considered and explain if they are not likely to be effective in a particular case' (IGIS, 2015: 2425). ASIO is required to use less intrusive techniques if feasible (AG's Guidelines s 10.4(b)). To access and use location information, clear guidelines should be developed distinguishing between what is considered less intrusive in accessing and using historical location information versus the level of intrusion from using prospective location information. In the interest of public trust and transparency, these guidelines should be made public.

8.5.7.4   Guidelines for Activities That May Be of Interest to National Security

The United States has guidelines on racketeering and domestic terrorism offences. These are the 'Attorney General's Guidelines On General Crimes, Racketeering Enterprise And Domestic Security/Terrorism Investigations' for the Federal Bureau of Investigations (FBI) and they are public (DoJ 2017). Australia should have similar guidelines. The AGs' Guidelines and the AFPs' Ministerial Guidelines should be amended, to clear distinguish between activities that would qualify as threats to the national security and economic interests, vis-à-vis political activities that are acceptable in a democratic society. Overlaps should be addressed, and the criteria should clearly state how the one overrules the other, the reasons for it and how such a decision can be challenged. The AG's Guidelines should clearly outline how these types of sensitive activities will be referred by any member of the Executive to ASIO and the AFP, for an inquiry, investigation, law enforcement or national security assessment, and how such matters should be handled. The guidelines should be contained in a legislative instrument. The independent issuing authority should be granted powers to inquire into the operational activities and those affected should be allowed access to the evidence that will be used against them to challenge the collection and use of metadata and when presenting charges in court.

8.5.7.5   Review of the LIW

Currently, the individual is not able to see the location information collected about them. The individual should be allowed to access the LIW. The individual should be allowed to challenge the disclosure of the location information, under the LIW, by means of judicial, quasi-judicial review (administrative review) and freedom of information disclosure procedures. Any objections to a request should be subject to an administrative challenge and review by the courts.

8.5.7.6   The Oversight Roles of IGIS and the Commonwealth Ombudsman

If the privacy standards cannot be met by the Agencies, the oversight bodies should report on the extent to which it was met or not, and the reasons and specific recommendations in each case. The oversight bodies should make specific recommendations of changes to be made to the laws and the legislative instruments, as part of their annual reporting.

8.5.7.7 Creating a Positive Feedback Loop

The full report of IGIS and the Commonwealth Ombudsman, with classified details, should be submitted to the Judge or magistrate with a security clearance that issued the LIW. The issuing authority must consider the report and issue a separate report to the Agencies, the Commonwealth Ombudsman, IGIS, the AG, the Prime Minister and the Parliamentary Joint Committee on Intelligence and Security (PJCIS), with recommendations. In this manner there is a full feedback loop that all relevant and interested authorities have insight into the exercise of the powers and the information is shared, transparently and are less reliant on boilerplate non-specific formal statements, and in this manner, privacy is better protected, and risks of excessive intrusion are minimised.

8.5.7.8 The Journalist Information Warrant

The Agencies are not clear on when to apply for a Journalist Information Warrant (JIW). The JIW should be included as a sub-category under the LIW. The sub-category should clarify that whenever any matter where the location information of a journalist, the employer of the journalist, or the source of the journalist is to be collected for an inquiry, investigation, to enforce the criminal law, to perform an activity related to the functions and purposes, or an activity related to performing their functions and purposes, the LIW should be applied for.

8.5.7.9 Reporting Statistics

In the interest of transparency, the statistics should specifically indicate the disclosure of location information whether disclosed under an authorisation or voluntarily by the Telco or SMP, in respect of both Agencies, and any other body that may be obtaining access.

8.5.7.10 Amendments to the TIA Act 1979 and the TA 1997

The necessary amendments need to be made to the *TIA Act 1979,* the *Privacy Act 1988,* the *TA 1997,* the *CAC Determination 2018*, the AG's Guidelines and the Ministerial Guidelines to cater for the above changes.

8.6 Conclusion

The court decisions in the UK, EU and the USA all affirm a fundamental premise of democracy—checks and balances. The judiciary must remain a key check on the exercise of executive power in a modern society where advances in communications technology are ever invasive to the privacy of the citizen and resident. The advances in technology cannot be allowed to give the executive an advantage that tips the scales in its favour and acts to exclude the oversight role of the courts. The courts should not be let to conveniently go-dark, be ostracized and be disabled to scrutinize the administrative exercise of power. The court has a role to play in continuing to shine a light on the executive exercise of power. Such power must be exercised openly. As such, the judiciary must be let in the door. The citizen and resident must have the practical ability to seek redress in front of the court, in a manner that is practical and not simply theoretical. This is what is required in a country of laws, and not of men or women.

The LIW process is based on the recognition of the much-needed broad powers of the Agencies to effectively detect, prevent and disrupt dynamic criminal and security threats. There is no logical sense in restricting the established powers of the Agencies, especially given the generally good track record of a compliance and rule-based culture. Lately however, this relatively new regime has had the Agencies under pressure. The established principles such as the directly related, reasonably necessary and in connection with principles as demonstrated by the court cases, coupled with the discretionary ambit of the executive to continue to decide the national security parameters are to be maintained. What is however crucial to balance is this: the advantage that technological developments grant the Agencies and the executive arm of government that in exercising their roles, gives in accessing unprecedented levels of personal and sensitive information, with the unprecedented help of global information and communication technology companies. Governments and the Agencies continue to invest in innovative technologies to better combat crimes and to safeguard the national interest. The Telco is given funding to ensure it implements the regime and is refunded for the cost of compliance. Through it all, the citizen and resident is the central figure. It is therefore necessary that clear and open guidelines, that will ensure that investigations and inquiries are conducted effectively are enabled, but simultaneously that there are independent checks and balances to ensure potential misuse is minimised, but that moreover, public trust and confidence is maintained—the people will continue to trust that the executive and the Agencies will continue to do the right thing—because they too, much like the ordinary citizen, also has nothing to hide.

References

Attorney-General's Department (AGD) (2014) Confidential industry consultation paper. Telecommunications data retention—Statement of requirements. http://www.rogerclarke.com/DV/Data_retention_consultation_1.pdf. Accessed 29 Aug 2019

Attorney-General's Department (AGD) (2015) Submission No 27 to the Parliamentary Joint Committee on Intelligence and Security, Parliament of Australia, Inquiry into the Telecommunications (Interception and Access) Amendment (Data Retention) Bill 2014, January 2015

Attorney-General's Department (AGD) (2016) Attorney-General's Guidelines in relation to the performance by the Australian Security Intelligence Organisation of its function of obtaining, correlating, evaluating and communicating intelligence relevant to security (including politically motivated violence) (Attorney-General's [AG's] Guidelines)

Australia & New Zealand Bank v Ryan (1968) 88 WN (Pt l) (NSW) 368

Australia Federal Police (AFP) (2015) Processing of prospective data authorisations. https://assets.documentcloud.org/documents/3119594/AFP-Disclosure-Log.pdf. Accessed 29 Aug 2019

Australia Federal Police Act 1979 (Cth) (*AFP Act 1979*)

Australia Security Intelligence Act (Cth) 1979 (*ASIO Act 1979*)

Australian Privacy Commissioner (APC) (2015) Submission No 92 to the Parliamentary Joint Committee on Intelligence and Security, Parliament of Australia, Inquiry into the Telecommunications (Interception and Access) Amendment (Data Retention) Bill 2014, January 2015

Barclays Bank v Taylor [1989] 1 WLR 1066

Carpenter v. United States (Supreme Court of the United States of America, No. 16-402, 22 June 2018) IV 18. https://www.supremecourt.gov/opinions/17pdf/16-402_h315.pdf. Accessed 3 Sept 2019 (the *Carpenter court case*)

Charter of Fundamental Rights of the European Union [2000] OJ C (364/012000/C)

Christoj v Barclays Bank [2000] 1 WLR 937

Convention for the Protection of Human Rights and Fundamental Freedoms, opened for signature 4 November 1950, 213 UNTS 221 (entered into force 3 September 1953)

Crown (2019) OCDA. https://www.gov.uk/government/organisations/office-for-communications-data-authorisations/about. Accessed 23 Sept 2019

Data Retention Act 2015 (Cth) (*DRA 2015*)

Data Retention and Acquisition Regulations 2018 (UK). https://www.legislation.gov.uk/uksi/2018/1123/contents/made. Accessed 23 Sept 2019

Data Retention and Investigatory Powers Act 2014 (UK) c X (*DRIPA Act*)

Department of Justice (DoJ) (2017) Attorney General's Guidelines On General Crimes, Racketeering Enterprise and Domestic Security/Terrorism Investigations (2 March 2017). https://www.justice.gov/archives/ag/attorney-generals-guidelines-general-crimes-racketeering-enterprise-and-domestic. Accessed 29 Aug 2019

Digital Rights Ireland Ltd (C-293/12) v Minister for Communications, Marine and Natural Resources C-293/12 and C-594/12 (8 April 2014) (the D*igital Rights court case)*

Directive 2006/24/EC of the European Parliament and of the Council of 15 March 2006

European Telecommunications Standards Institute (ETSI) (2017) LTE; Evolved Universal Terrestrial Radio Access Network (E-UTRAN); Stage 2 functional specification of User Equipment (UE) positioning in E-UTRAN (3GPP TS 36.305 version 14.2.0 Release 14)

Evidence to Parliamentary Joint Committee on Intelligence and Security, Parliament of Australia, Canberra, 29 January 2015, 41 (Vivienne Thom, Inspector-General of Intelligence and Security, Office of the Inspector-General of Intelligence and Security)

Evidence to Parliamentary Joint Committee on Intelligence and Security, Parliament of Australia, Canberra, 30 January 2015, 31 (Peter Leonard Guildford, Chairperson of the Media and Communications Committee, Business Law Section of the Law Council of Australia)

Federal Commissioner of Taxation v Australia & New Zealand Banking Group (1979) 143 CLR 499

Gant v Commissioner Australian Federal Police [2006] FCA 1475 (the *Gant court case*)

George v Rockett (1990) 170 CLR 104 20 June 1904 (the *George court case*)

Home Office (2018) Communications Data Code of Practice. https://assets.publishing.service.gov. uk/government/uploads/system/uploads/attachment_data/file/757850/Communications_Data_ Code_of_Practice.pdf. Accessed 23 Sept 2019

Inspector-General of Intelligence and Security (IGIS) (2015) Annual Report 2014–2015

Inspector-General of Intelligence and Security Act 1986 (Cth) (*IGIS Act 1986*)

International Convention on Civil and Political Rights (ICCPR), opened for signature 19 December 1966, 2200A (XXI) (entered into force 23 March 1976)

Keenan M (12 May 2014) Ministerial Direction Australian Federal Police. https://www.afp.gov.au/ about-us/governance-and-accountability/ministerial-direction. Accessed 28 Aug 2019

Laster (1989) Breaches of confidence and of privacy by misuse of confidential information. Otago Law Rev 7, 31:424

Loyd v Freshjeld (1826) 2 Car & P 325; 172 ER 147

Minister for Justice (Cth) (2016) Investing in innovation for our law enforcement elite. (Media Release, 15 June 2016)

Office of the Australian Information Commissioner (OAIC) (2014) Guidelines on Data Matching in Australian Government Administration (June 2014). https://www.oaic.gov.au/privacy/guid ance-and-advice/guidelines-on-data-matching-in-australian-government-administration/. Accessed 29 Aug 2019

Parliamentary Joint Committee on Human Rights (PJCHR) (2016) Parliament of Australia, Human rights scrutiny report Thirty-fifth report of the 44th Parliament (25 February 2016)

Privacy Act 1988 (Cth)

Privacy Commissioner v Telstra Corporation Limited [2017] FCAFC 4 15 (the *Privacy Commissioner court case*)

Regulation of Investigatory Powers Act 2000 (UK) cX

Revised Explanatory Memorandum, Telecommunications (Interception and Access) Amendment (Data Retention) Bill 2015 (Cth)

Robertson v Canadian Imperial Bank of Commerce [1994] 1 WLR 1493

Samsonidis v Commissioner, Australian Federal Police [2007] FCAFC 159 (5 October 2007) (the *Samsonidis court case*)

Secretary of State for The Home Department and Tom Watson MP and others [2018] EWCA Civ 70 *(SSHD v Watson & Others,* (the *Watson court case*)

Selvadurai N (2017) The retention of telecommunications metadata: a necessary national security initiative or a disproportionate interference with personal privacy? Comput Telecommun Law Rev 23(2):36

Taylor G (2000) Why is there no common law right of privacy? Monash Univ Law Rev 26:240–241

Technology Companies, 'Brief for Technology Companies as Amici Curiae in Support of Neither Party', Timothy Ivory Carpenter v. United States (Supreme Court of the United States of America, No. 16-402, 28 September 2016) (August 2017). https://www.scotusblog.com/wp-content/uploads/2017/08/16-402-ac-technology-companies.pdf. Accessed 29 Aug 2019

Technology Experts, 'Brief of Technology Experts as Amici Curiae in Support of Petitioner', Timothy Ivory Carpenter v. United States (Supreme Court of the United States of America, No. 16-402, 28 September 2016) (14 August 2017). https://papers.ssrn.com/sol3/papers.cfm? abstract_id=3019294. Accessed 29 Aug 2019

Telecommunications (Interception and Access) (Requirements for Authorisations, Notifications and Revocations) Determination 2015 (Cth) (at 9 October 2015) (CAC Determination 2015)

Telecommunications (Interception and Access) Act 1979 (Cth) (*TIA Act 1979*)

Telecommunications (Interception and Access) Amendment (Data Retention) Act *2015 (Cth) (DRA 2015)*

Telecommunications (Interceptions and Access) (Requirements for Authorisations, Notifications and Revocations) Determination 2018 (Cth) (at 20 November 2018) (*CAC Determination 2018*)

Telecommunications Act 1997 (Cth) (*TA 1997*)

Telstra (2019) Submission 35 to the PJCIS, Review of the mandatory data retention regime, July 2019

Timothy Ivory Carpenter v United States (Supreme Court of the United States of America, 16-402, 26 September 2016). https://www.supremecourt.gov/search.aspx?filename=/docket/docketfiles/html/public/16-402.html. Accessed 29 Aug 2019. (the *Carpenter court case 2016*)

Tournier v National Provincial & Union Bank of England [1924] 1 KB 461

Vodafone Hutchinson Australia (2019) Privacy. https://www.vodafone.com.au/about/legal/privacy. Accessed 29 Aug 2019

Winterton Constructions v Hambros (1992) 39 FCR 97, 114-15

Chapter 9
Conclusion: Restoring the Balance of Power

9.1 Restoring the Balance of Power

Chapter 1 discussed the generation of near-precision 4G, 5G and social media location information estimates. As illustrated in Chaps. 1, 2 and 6, the 4G and 5G mobile networks allow for more precise location estimates about the person from identifiers used by the mobile device such as the serial number, the IMEI (ETSI 2017, 13 [4.3]).[1] This makes it personally identifiable information. Chapters 2 and 3 critically analysed the legal scheme for mobile telecommunications companies, internet service providers and social media platforms to retain and disclose location information to the Agencies. Chapter 3 demonstrated how content is protected better than location information. The traditional distinction in protection, based on content versus non-content, is therefore increasingly incompatible with how location information is generated, exchanged, and stored in the modern Internet-Protocol (IP)-mediated 4G and 5G networks; and with how easily the location information can be analysed using easily available Big Data algorithmic analytics software, using machine learning. A standardised and harmonized framework is required for the law to be aligned to how modern communications technology operates and can reveal personal and sensitive information from the analysed location information. The same standards must be applied to all types of personal information. The Australian Privacy Principles (APPs) are equally applicable to location information, voice and SMS communication to the extent that this reveal location information, as demonstrated in Chap. 6. However, the Agencies are not allowed to use a 'self-certification' process to collect and use the contents of a voice or SMS communication, or to collect the contents of a voice call or SMS without suspicion of an offence based on reasonable grounds (Leonard 2015: 7), as shown in Chap. 3. It is only in respect of location information that the Agencies can use a self-certification process to collect and use historical location information without the need for suspicion

---

[1]International Mobile Station Equipment Identity.

© Springer Nature Switzerland AG 2020
S. Shanapinda, *Advance Metadata Fair*, Law, Governance and Technology Series 44, https://doi.org/10.1007/978-3-030-50255-3_9

based on reasonable grounds for minor offences, as was critically analysed in Chaps. 4 and 5. The problem with this is that the Agencies alone decide what is reasonable and justifiable, and do so at the time they are collecting the location information. The continued treatment of location information as metadata entrenches the existing power structure that has tipped in favour of the Agencies to allow less stringent access to location information, because the Agencies rely heavily on metadata for their investigations and inquiries. As such, the Agencies are empowered to access location information by using a 'self-certification' process, without prior external and independent oversight, as described in Chap. 3. The labelling of location information as metadata, as described in Chaps. 2 and 3, allows for the disclosure of location information without a judicial warrant, and without a domestic preservation notice to the Agencies (*TA 1997* ss 276, 280, 313(7)(d)(e)). As such, the Telco, the ISP and the SMP can store and disclose location information to the Agencies under less stringent requirements than applies to the contents of a communication, as demonstrated in Chaps. 4 and 5. This demonstrates the impact of labelling location information as metadata, on the powers of the Agencies. The labelling leads to greater power, greater discretion, less stringent requirements and less oversight over the Agencies, as illustrated in Chaps. 4, 5, 6 and 7 (*CAC Determination 2018* ss 8-12; *TA 1997* ss 275A, 276, 280, 313(3), 313(4), 313(7)). This treatment of location information is unfair to individuals that have legitimate expectations of personal privacy, location privacy, information privacy, privacy over their personal information and privacy over their communications. It results in less privacy protection for location information than for the contents or the substance of a communication. There is no justifiable reason for this distinction. This distinction between how location information, voice and SMS communication is treated is not fair, given that location information can have personal and sensitive information dimensions, just as much as the contents of an SMS or a voice communication, based on near-precise locations that are disclosed that are reliable from which inferences are drawn, as opposed to words that may be misleading and less reliable, as shown in Chap. 6. The contents of a communication are personal and sensitive and therefore require a warrant to be issued. Similarly, location information is communication and equally personal in nature. It is based on these arguments, amongst others, that the warrant process is proposed to collect and use location information.

The Agencies have the broad discretion to specify and demand any type and volume of location information to be disclosed to them (*CAC Determination 2018* ss 8-12), as critically discussed in Chap. 4. It is however in the public interest that administrative power in this very intrusive domain is granted fairly, based on evidence, and exercised with suitable checks and balances, as was proposed in Chap. 8.

As described in Chap. 2, the metadata retention regime was passed into law in 2015 and became operational in April 2017. Since then, the Telco and the ISP must store location information, for a minimum period of 2 years. These companies may however retain location information for any indefinite period of time, for their own commercial purposes. Social media platforms are not required to retain location information for any period of time but are required to assist the Agencies by disclosing what is referred to as 'technical information'. Technical information is not defined, and there is nothing in the law that prevents the Agencies from requesting access to location information as 'technical information' (*AAA* 2018 ss 317C Items 4, 6, 317D). This is especially so given that that under the mandatory data retention scheme location information is treated technically as metadata—data about data. Both sets of companies may retain location information for cybersecurity and maintenance purposes. They may retain location information to research new products and services, and to see how existing services perform, in terms of quality and value addition, as described in Chap. 2. As a result, both sets of companies possess a treasure trove of location information that is of considerable value to law enforcement, national security and to third party advertisers in the digital economy. As revealed by Snowden, unlike the STELLARWIND or PRISM mass surveillance or bulk data collection programs America's National Security Agency (NSA) itself kept, and could search for relevant crime data about any American, the combined effect of the Australian mandatory metadata retention and disclosure scheme imposed on the Telco, the ISP; and the assistance scheme that is imposed on social media platforms (the SMP), to disclose technical information in 2018, creates the perfect alternative—it's a type of outsourcing. The companies retain the location information for legal purposes and for commercial purposes, for any period of time, which information the Agencies may search and collect at will. The location records are not required to be deleted after a 2-year period by none of the parties stated above. The Agencies do not need to run the costs of managing the original storing databases but can also built their own databases with the information collected from the Telco, the ISP and the SMP, to complement their operations. The information request need not be targeted because they are used to help draft affidavits to apply for targeted interception warrants from the judiciary. The content can be overlayed with the metadata, which metadata is more accurate and reliable then the content of communications, where people may lie, or use languages that may not be well understood, or where the context is misplaced. So, metadata is more valuable, but is treated as if it is not, and this value is publicly underplayed or denied, by making statements to the effect that it is only the gross data that is requested and not precise location data. And so, the illusion of the lesser value and importance of metadata must be maintained. The telecommunications companies at the same time are seeking to monetise data in the age of artificial intelligence (AI) and Big Data analytics, and so it's perfect timing that all this comes together like this—it's a symbiotic relationship. The Agencies and companies have therefore found a mutually beneficial arrangement—an incentive to retain and disclose location information with the Agencies, and simultaneously to monetise location information for commercial advertising and other business purposes.

This mutually beneficial arrangement, whether deliberate or otherwise, is structured and operates in such a manner that it divests the consumer of any agency over their location information. Australian law enforcement and security Agencies may collect and use location information about a mobile telecommunications device to perform their functions, but without requiring a judicial warrant to do so. Mobile telecommunications companies and social media platforms may collect the location information, for these law enforcement collection purposes and simultaneously for their commercial purposes, all without the prior informed consent of the individual to monetise the data under data sharing arrangements with advertisers and other third parties in what is termed the digital economy. The only benefit the individual is said to enjoy is improved services and public safety—the information is retained to keep them safe, and their consent is not needed. In fact, they are not even supposed to be informed that their data has been collected by the Agencies. At the same time, they are not informed when their data is collected by third parties under data sharing arrangements.

Given that the digital economy refers to data as the 'new oil', valorised and commodified, to grow economies, not only is the exploitation of the data, legalised, but so is the labour of the individual causing such data to be generated. The individual uses social media messenger services, checks into locations on Facebook, uses Google maps to search for their favourite restaurant, carries their phone everywhere all the time. This technically accounts to the tracking of the individual. At the same time the individual's location information is stored by the companies and may be requested by the Agencies at any given time, with no real and tangible restrictions as to the volume that may be collected. The storage of the data is not required to be reasonable or merit the type of crime committed, but the collection by the Agencies must be. The problem with this is that the Agencies may collect the data for minor offenses, and even if the individual is not suspected of having committed an offence, as described in Chaps. 4 and 5. The location information may be collected to even if the individual is not reasonably suspected of having committed a crime. In such instances, how does the requirement that the location information must be collected be reasonable, squared against the broad powers of the Agencies that the person need not be a suspect in the first place? A person that is supposed to be presumed as innocent, their location information may be collected without judicial involvement, and in a modern-day democracy. Given how precise 5G location information is, because it is using a dense network of antenna's and is powered by satellites, similar to tracking devices, how is it reasonable to allow such access to historical and near real-time location information, which may be stored by the Agencies indefinitely? The location information may be processed using artificial intelligence, and be merge with other data, to reveal a sensitive profile of the individual, as described in Chap. 6. When this type of data aggregation and analytics is performed, even anonymised data reveals the identity of the individual, their habits, their traits, their activities, their hidden secrets, all without any reasonable suspicion of having committed or being in the process of committing a crime. Reasonable suspicion and the presumption of innocence were introduced to prevent witch hunts—this state of legal affairs, may allow such misuse but it will be defended as being legal, and within the limits of the Agencies simply doing their jobs.

Chapter 4 described the broad powers of the Agencies to collect and use location information, and Chap. 5 demonstrated how the limits placed on the powers of the Agencies by the 'Privacy Tests' in 2015 are ineffective. This was contrasted against how location information is unfairly treated, compared to the contents of a communication in Chaps. 3 and 6. Chapter 5 showed that the various 'Privacy Tests', which include the 'Reasonably Necessary or Directly Related Tests', did strengthen privacy in 2015 but there is still room for improvement (AFP 2015, 7, 57; *CAC Determination 2018* ss 8-9). The inadequate current state of privacy protection is demonstrated by factors such as the lack of a standard which requires suspicion of an offence that is based on reasonable grounds; the lack of a 'good faith' standard to minimise biases; and the rule that the collection and use of location information only needs to be directly related to or be reasonably necessary for a relatively open-ended range of security and law enforcement activities of the Agencies (*TIA Act* 1979 ss 6A, 6B, 178(2); *CAC Determination 2018* ss 8-12). The inherent conflict between the powers of the Agencies and privacy does not allow for privacy to be treated fairly under the existing location information collection and use framework, even after the 2015 changes. As illustrated in Chaps. 2, 5, 6 and 7, the privacy of the individual is at the mercy of the commercial (which includes third party data sharing arrangements), cybersecurity, law enforcement and technical operational interests of the Agencies and the Telco, pursued with minimal or no independent judicial or quasi-judicial participation (*TIA Act* 1979 ss 6A, 6B, 175(3), 177; *the Gant court case 2006*, 12 [42]; *Re Nanaimo court case 1944*, 638, 639; Evidence to PJCIS 2015: 31 (Leonard); the Jaffarie court case 2014, 19 [48]). Based on their interests, the Agencies, the Telco, the ISP and the SMP can in effect choose how much location information to retain and disclose above a statutory baseline and decide what operations and activities the location information can be used for (*TIA Act* 1979 ss 177(1), 178 (3)). The discretion granted to the Agencies, the Telco, the ISP and the SMP, are too broad, and not properly restricted in the publicly available oversight tools studied. The Telco, the ISP and the SMP are not required to apply privacy safeguards such as the 'Privacy Tests' when deciding to voluntarily disclose location information to the Agencies (*TIA Act* 1979 ss 177(1), 178(3)). The location information can be used for numerous other investigations and inquiries, including to try to assess whether a person is likely to commit a crime in future (predictive policing), without being suspected of an offence in the first place (*TIA Act* 1979 ss 5(1), (definition of 'offence'), 6A, 6B; *the R v Zhi Qiang Han case* 2011, [1], [21]). Chapters 5 and 6 showed that the primary use of location information in some cases does require privacy safeguards to be applied, but the secondary use of the same location information, perhaps in respect of another person and based on other facts, can allow for the privacy safeguards to be bypassed (*the R v Zhi Qiang Han case* 2011, [1], [21]; *CAC Determination 2018*), and this with the blessing of the courts.

   Chapter 6 continued to demonstrate how accessing location information can equally be personal and equally intrusive as accessing the contents of a voice or SMS communication. The amount of location information required to be stored for a minimum 2-year period easily reveals personal information with the use of Big Data analytics software. This analytics software is already easily available to the Agencies. The Agencies announced plans to use Big Data algorithmic software powered by artificial intelligence. The Agencies are also developing similar bespoke capabilities. Even if the location information is 'de-identified', the person, the habits of the person, and the political and religious views of a person can be profiled. Location information is mostly 'about the individual', as demonstrated by the activities and commercial operations of the Agencies and of the companies, as discussed in Chaps. 2 and 6.

The Agencies yield great power over the personal information of individual persons, but as illustrated in Chap. 7, the oversight mechanisms do not sufficiently recognise this. This is evident from the fact that the oversight is only carried out by public bodies that are part of the executive branch of government, such as the Commonwealth Ombudsman and OIGIS,[2] without the prior involvement of the third branch of government—the judiciary (Hardy and Williams 2014, 2016). The oversight is conducted only after the location information has already been collected and used, and privacy has already been impacted. This impact on privacy is not analysed and addressed by independent external oversight bodies, nor before the location information is collected. The ideal time for oversight is prior to or at the time the location information is collected from the Telco, the ISP and the SMP. This so given that Big Data analytics can reveal more personal and sensitive information of a person presumed innocent, than may be necessary or reasonable, for the exercise of the law enforcement and security functions.

The oversight role and the power to exercise security and law enforcement functions are concentrated, directly and indirectly, in the hands of the Attorney-General's Department (AGD 2016) and the Department of Home Affairs and the public oversight bodies that are part of the executive arm of government. Chapters 5, 6 and 7 demonstrated the judiciary does not play a major review role in the collection of the location information, and this is partly attributed to the pre-approval process (*CAC Determination 2018*). The non-transparent nature of the location information collection and use process leads to the judiciary being largely omitted. Ironically, as demonstrated in Chap. 5, in those rare instances where courts intervened, the courts made decisions that favoured the broad law enforcement and national security powers of the Agencies, by enforcing principles such as the 'in connection with' principle and the 'Connection Test' (*the Caratti court case* 2017 1 [2]; *the Day court case* 2000 5 [15]; *the George court case* 1990 4 [8]; *the Farrell case* 2017, 16 [49]). As long as the collection and use of location information is linked to the functions of the Agencies, the Agencies are legally allowed to collect and use the location information. The goodwill of the Agencies is not tested. The courts gave weight to the broad activities of the Agencies and did not impose greater restrictions when interpreting the 'in connection with' principle and the 'Connection Test'. Added to this, the avenues for judicial oversight barely exist, given the confidential nature of the location information collection and use process, a demonstrated in Chap. 7. The person is not able to lodge a complaint to the oversight bodies for misuse of their location information. Given this low oversight threshold supported by the 'Connection Test', it is also not clear under what instances the information may be misused, that could give rise to an actionable complaint.

---

[2]Office of the Inspector-General of Intelligence and Security.

The Agencies are generally compliant with existing oversight rules, as shown in Chap. 7, but this is in effect because of quite a low compliance bar as these rules are flexible and not sufficiently rigid, being instead too permissive. The oversight process described in Chap. 7 is not properly aligned to how privacy is impacted, and how it is most effectively protected—in advance, rather than after the fact. Asking the Agencies, the Telco, the ISPs and MSPs to guard privacy is like asking the cat to look after the gold fish. The judicially issued location information warrant is therefore proposed in Chap. 8, as a proper safeguard to protect privacy when it matters the most—at the time of collection from the Telco. As shown in Chap. 6 with the location information of Mr. Ockenden, the use of location information after it has been collected takes on a life of its own by helping to reveal all sorts of personal information and becomes ever harder to supervise in order to protect privacy. The IP-mediated 4G and 5G network, interlinked with satellite and location tracking social media applications, poses challenges to the *TIA Act 1979* and the *TA 1997* when it comes to the proper characterisation of location information, as described in Chaps. 2 and 6. The law should not appear to be unfairly discriminatory towards one form of data or another but should instead be applied fairly to all types of communications, especially if voice calls and location information reveal significant personal information about the individual, as they can increasingly do in the hands of capable analysts motivated by law enforcement interests, but may harbour political, racial or religious biases. The algorithms used may themselves be developed with pre-conceived biases against certain groups of society.

As critically described in Chap. 7, the individual is not supposed to know their location information was collected, or that they were considered persons of interest to the Agencies, and without a reasonable suspicion being required under the law. Granting the individual, the right to complain about the use of their location information under this legal environment makes a mockery of the oversight process. It's like saying a blind person has every right to enter a public building, provided they find their own way around the building, and not installing the building with lifts and augmented hearing. How can any self-respecting oversight body certify under such circumstances that the Agencies did not misuse their powers, if the person is practically barred from knowing and then lodging any complaints, if their oversight role is based on the lodging of complaints? How can the public trust the oversight role, as meaningful and effective, and not distrust the Agencies. If the Agencies have nothing to hide about misuse, why is it that they do not allow themselves to be held accountable in a manner that is meaningful? The compliance threshold is to only perform their functions and with such a low threshold, there is no meaningful oversight, of course the Agencies are supposed to do their work and only their work, what else?

Given that Australia's position is different to its Western counterparts in the Five Eyes Alliance, Chap. 8 proposed the judicial location information warrant, to better protect privacy. This is because independent judicial participation is the best privacy protection mechanism. The location information warrant framework proposed includes measures for improved openness to allow for greater judicial and quasi-judicial participation. There are ways in which the process can be more transparent and not unreasonably impede security and police operations—a better balance is struck between the functions of the Agencies and the privacy of the individual. Exceptions are proposed where time may be of the essence, but feedback loops are provided for, to ensure constant and effective independent oversight. The Agencies can therefore still continue their operations and functions without major compromises that would defeat their functions and purposes Shanapinda (2018).

As the last word, giving credit where its due, Australia made changes to its privacy protection framework in April 2015—the access and use must be justifiable and proportionate to the offence. The book steered the debate towards dissecting these privacy changes, where privacy is used as a tool to limit the powers of the Agencies. At the same time, privacy is also a target of the exercise of the powers of the Agencies. Creating a conflicting situation, where privacy must be safeguarded by the Agencies, but the same Agencies are the ones having the last say as to what counts as a reasonable interference of privacy—playing a judge and jury at the same time. This situation is allowed by the Ministerial guidelines that empower the Agencies to pursue personal information, to invade the private space of the private citizen and resident, but does not outline clear demonstrable rules, as to how the Agencies can balance their discretionary powers, given the latest technological developments that are very revealing and aid the powers of the Agencies, having the effect of increasing their powers. This is not compatible with values of competent accountability, especially given the latest technological developments in artificial intelligence. The Agencies have the power to use algorithmic software to visualise and identify individuals that may pose future security and criminal risks. However, the Agencies are not always required to act on the basis that the individual is suspected of an offence, with suspicion based on reasonable grounds. The Agencies are only required to act in connection with their functions. Their activities only need to be directly related to their broad law enforcement activities and purposes. I must therefore conclude that the privacy safeguards that were revised in 2015 improved the privacy protection standards in some respects, but what fundamentally remains the same and undermines the privacy protections is this: the protection of privacy is subject to the sole discretion of the Agencies, the telecommunications, ISPs and social media companies, and their combined broad third party data sharing commercial, network maintenance, law enforcement and national security interests. The Agencies are permitted to self-certify the collection and use of the location information and apply the privacy tests, as was done in times past, without prior external independent oversight. Under the proposed location information warrant system, an independent judicial body would conduct privacy impact analyses in advance. The location information would then only be collected, used, stored, re-used and shared based on the suspicion of an offence, thereby minimising speculative location data-matching. Such speculative data-matching is primarily discriminatory towards minority groups that may be overpoliced, young people that a tach-savvy and use social media to live their life's but also to organise climate change and animal rights protests. The policy of the government seems to be that protesting coal mine projects poses a threat to national security, given the economic and job creation value of coal mining. The government is allowed by the courts to take such a policy decision because national security is not limited to wartime situations. This theoretically allows for a protestor's location information to be collected, and stored for any period of time, without the court's involvement, even if their protests are peaceful. No guidelines exist to prevent such collection. Lastly, the combined effect is that the metadata retention and disclosure framework, coupled with the assistance scheme for social media platforms, entrenches the powers of the Agencies, and the new privacy protections do very little to make any inroads into ensuring, in an effective manner, the responsible use of location information. The framework is designed in the following manner, that creates an imbalance between the powers of the Agencies, privacy and technological advancements: the investigative powers are broad; the limits are more enabling than restrictive; the collection procedures are not transparent; the standards are high and based on the 'reasonable man' test but at the same time are subject to the sole discretion of the Agencies, with no avenue to challenge whether the test was complied with objectively; and the Telco is not required to follow the privacy standards of reasonable, necessary, justifiable and proportional when disclosing the location information voluntarily to the Agencies, whereas the Agencies are required to do so when requesting the location information (AG's Guidelines 2016; *CAC Determination* 2018; *TIA Act* 1979 ss 107H, 108(1), 175-184; *TA 1997* ss 275A, 276, 313(3), 313(4), 3131(7)). The result is that the collection of the metadata of journalists without warrants was excused as human error and poor training, and no individual was held responsible, as described in Chap. 3.

In the end, the individual is left exposed to the powerful forces of the authorities, and there is very little the individual can do to take on the authorities. The discretion of the Agencies and the Telco to retain location information for any length of time and which jointly outweigh the privacy interests of the individual in an unfair manner that leads to poor privacy protection. Australia's legal framework, when taken as a whole in the context of location information collection and use, leads to inadequate protection of privacy, and leaves privacy vulnerable as a check on the powers of the Agencies. The balance must be restored, and location information should only be collected with a judicial warrant approved by the judiciary, and in advance. In doing so metadata would be advanced fairly.

Future research can map the Privacy Tests and the Connection Tests onto other types of metadata, such as website addresses or Uniform Resource Locators (URLs) and Internet Protocol (IP) addresses, to assess the contextual impact on privacy.

References

AGD (2016) Attorney-General's Guidelines in relation to the performance by the Australian Security Intelligence Organisation of its function of obtaining, correlating, evaluating and communicating intelligence relevant to security (including politically motivated violence) (Attorney-General's [AG's] Guidelines)

Australia Federal Police (AFP) (2015) Processing of prospective data authorisations. https://assets. documentcloud.org/documents/3119594/AFP-Disclosure-Log.pdf. Accessed 29 Aug 2019

Caratti v Commissioner of the Australian Federal Police [2017] FCAFC 177 (10 November 2017) 1 [2]

Day v Commissioner, Australian Federal Police [2000] FCA 1272 (11 September 2000) 5 [15]

ETSI, 'LTE; Evolved Universal Terrestrial Radio Access Network (E-UTRAN); Stage 2 functional specification of User Equipment (UE) positioning in E-UTRAN', 2017, (3GPP TS 36.305 version 14.2.0 Release 14)

Evidence to Parliamentary Joint Committee on Intelligence and Security, Parliament of Australia, Canberra, 30 January 2015, 31 (Peter Leonard Guildford, Chairperson of the Media and Communications Committee, Business Law Section of the Law Council of Australia)

Farrell; Secretary, Department of Immigration and Border Protection (Freedom of information) [2017] AATA 409 (31 March 2017) 16 [49]

George v Rockett (1990) 170 CLR 104 20 June 19904 [8]

Gant v Commissioner Australian Federal Police [2006] FCA 1475, 12 [42]

Hardy K, Williams G (2014) National security reforms stage one: intelligence gathering and secrecy. Law Soc NSW J 6(November):68. https://search.informit.com.au/fullText; dn=20151952;res=AGISPT. Accessed 28 Aug 2019

Hardy K, Williams G (2016) Executive oversight of intelligence agencies in Australia (June 7, 2016). In: Goldman ZK, Rascoff SJ (eds) Global intelligence oversight: governing security in the twenty-first century (2016); UNSW Law Research Paper No. 2016-35. https://ssrn.com/abstract=2804835. Accessed 3 Sept 2019

Jaffarie v Director General of Security [2014] FCAFC 102 (18 August 2014) 19 [48]

Leonard P (2015) 'Mandatory internet data retention in Australia – looking the horse in the mouth after it has bolted', 2015, 7 https://www.gtlaw.com.au/sites/default/files/Mandatory-Internet-Data-Retentionin-Australia_0.pdf. Accessed 26 Aug 2019

Re Nanaimo Community Hotel Ltd [1944] 4 DLR 638, 639

R v Zhi Qiang Han [2011] NSWCCA 120 [1], [21]

Shanapinda S (2018) Advance metadata fair: the retention and disclosure of location information as metadata for law enforcement and national security, and the impact on privacy—an Australian story. Dissertation, UNSW Sydney

Telecommunications, (Interception and Access) (Requirements for Authorisations, Notifications and Revocations) Determination 2015 (Cth) (at 9 October 2015) (CAC Determination 2015)

Telecommunications (Interceptions and Access) (Requirements for Authorisations, Notifications and Revocations) Determination 2018 (Cth) (at 20 November 2018) (*CAC Determination 2018*)

Telecommunications (Interception and Access) Act 1979 (Cth) (*TIA Act 1979*)

Telecommunications (Interception and Access) Amendment (Data Retention) Act 2015 (Cth) (*DRA 2015*)

Telecommunications Act 1997 (Cth) (TA 1997)

Telecommunications and Other Legislation Amendment (Assistance and Access) Act 2018 (*AAA 2018*)

Index

CPSIA information can be obtained
at www.ICGtesting.com
Printed in the USA
LVHW022155070920
665255LV00015B/587

9 783030 502546